This well orchestrated volume provides a very welcome addition to postcolonial debates in Europe, avoiding colonial aphasia and making connection to contemporary issues of austerity, global processes of precarization and new landscapes of migration and racism. It gives a refreshing and original perspective on how colonial memories impact on current patterns of austerity and fiscal inequalities and vice versa on how new economic and political regimes are imbricated in processes of memorialization, commemoration and monumentalization of the past.

It is in this multidisciplinary, comparative and historiographic effort that Europe emerges as a new arena where current economic and political crises affect not just our present but also our past.

Sandra Ponzanesi, *Professor of Gender and Postcolonial Studies,*
Utrecht University, the Netherlands

Austere Histories in European Societies

In recent years European states have turned toward more austere political regimes, entailing budget cuts, deregulation of labour markets, restrictions of welfare systems, securitization of borders and new regimes of migration and citizenship. In the wake of such changes, new forms of social inclusion and exclusion appear that are justified through a reactivation of differences of race, class and gender.

Against this backdrop, this collection investigates contemporary understandings of history and cultural memory. In doing so, the reader will join the leading European contributors of this title in examining how crisis and decline in contemporary Europe trigger a selective forgetting and remodelling of the past. Indeed, *Austere Histories in European Societies* breaks new paths in scholarship by synthesizing and connecting current European debates on migration, racism and multiculturalism. In addition to this, the authors present debates on cultural memory and the place of the colonial legacy within an extensive comparative framework and across the boundaries of the humanities and social sciences.

This book will appeal to scholars and students across the social sciences and humanities, particularly in European studies, memory studies, sociology, postcolonial studies, migration studies, European history, cultural policy, cultural heritage, economics and political theory.

Stefan Jonsson is Professor of Ethnic Studies at Linköping University, Sweden.

Julia Willén is a doctoral candidate at Linköping University, Sweden

Routledge Advances in Sociology

For a full list of titles in this series, please visit www.routledge.com/series/SE0511

186 **Popular Music and Retro Culture in the Digital Era**
Jean Hogarty

187 **Muslim Americans**
Debating the notions of American and un-American
Nahid Kabir

188 **Human Sciences and Human Interests**
Integrating the social, economic, and evolutionary sciences
Mikael Klintman

189 **Algorithmic Cultures**
Essays on meaning, performance and new technologies
Edited by Robert Seyfert and Jonathan Roberge

190 **Becoming Anorexic**
A sociological study
Muriel Darmon

191 **European Social Integration and the Roma**
Questioning neoliberal governmentality
Cerasela Voiculescu

192 **How to Do Politics With Art**
Edited by Violaine Roussel and Anurima Banerji

193 **Urban Music and Entrepreneurship**
Beats, rhymes and young people's enterprise
Joy White

194 **Multigenerational Family Living**
Evidence and policy implications from Australia
Edited by Edgar Liu and Hazel Easthope

195 **Sociology of Crisis**
Myrto Tsilimpounidi

196 **Praxeological Political Analysis**
Edited by Michael Jonas and Beate Littig

197 **Austere Histories in European Societies**
Social exclusion and the contest of colonial memories
Edited by Stefan Jonsson and Julia Willén

Austere Histories in European Societies

Social exclusion and the contest of colonial memories

**Edited by Stefan Jonsson and
Julia Willén**

LONDON AND NEW YORK

First published 2017
by Routledge
2 Park Square, Milton Park, Abingdon, Oxon OX14 4RN

and by Routledge
711 Third Avenue, New York, NY 10017

Routledge is an imprint of the Taylor & Francis Group, an informa business

British Library Cataloguing in Publication Data
A catalogue record for this book is available from the British Library

Library of Congress Cataloging in Publication Data
Names: Jonsson, Stefan, 1961– editor. | Willâen, Julia, editor.
Title: Austere histories in European societies : social exclusion and the
contest of colonial memories / Stefan Jonsson and Julia Willâen.
Description: Abingdon, Oxon ; New York, NY : Routledge, 2017. |
Includes bibliographical references and index.
Identifiers: LCCN 2016022887 | ISBN 9781138909380 (hardback)
Subjects: LCSH: Marginality, Social–Europe. | Social stratification–Europe. |
Immigrants–Europe. | Minorities–Europe. | Citizenship–Europe. |
Postcolonialism–Europe. | Europe–Cultural policy. | Europe–Social
policy. | Europe–Economic policy. | Europe–History.
Classification: LCC HN380.Z9 M26185 2017 | DDC 306.094–dc23
LC record available at https://lccn.loc.gov/2016022887

ISBN: 978-1-138-90938-0 (hbk)
ISBN: 978-1-315-69399-6 (ebk)

Typeset in Times New Roman
by Wearset Ltd, Boldon, Tyne and Wear

MIX
Paper from
responsible sources
FSC
www.fsc.org   FSC® C013056

Printed and bound in Great Britain by
TJ International Ltd, Padstow, Cornwall

Contents

Notes on contributors   ix
Preface   xii

1 **Introducing austere histories**   1
STEFAN JONSSON AND JULIA WILLÉN

PART I
Cases   19

2 **'Our island story': the dangerous politics of belonging in austere times**   21
GURMINDER K. BHAMBRA

3 **The politics of colonial remembrance in France (1980–2012)**   38
NICOLAS BANCEL AND PASCAL BLANCHARD

4 **The selective forgetting and remodelling of the past: postcolonial legacies in the Netherlands**   59
ESTHER CAPTAIN

5 **From austerity to postcolonial nostalgia: crisis and national identity in Portugal and Denmark**   74
ELSA PERALTA AND LARS JENSEN

6 **Austere curricula: multicultural education and black students**   92
ROBBIE SHILLIAM

PART II
Conjunctures 113

7 **Exclusion through citizenship and the geopolitics of austerity** 115
MANUELA BOATCĂ

8 **Refugee Keynesianism? EU migration crises in times of fiscal austerity** 135
PEO HANSEN

9 **Restrained equality: a sexualized and gendered colour line** 161
NACIRA GUÉNIF-SOUILAMAS

10 **Writing history for an uncertain future: concluding remarks** 182
JULIA WILLÉN AND STEFAN JONSSON

Index 195

Contributors

Editors

Stefan Jonsson is Professor of Ethnic Studies at the Institute for Research on Migration, Ethnicity and Society (REMESO), Linköping University. His recent books include *Eurafrica: The Untold History of European Integration and Colonialism* (2014; co-authored with Peo Hansen), *Crowds and Democracy: The Idea and Image of the Masses from Revolution to Fascism* (2013) and *Stories from Scoresbysund: Photographs: Colonisation and Mapping* (2010; co-authored with Pia Arke).

Julia Willén is a doctoral candidate at the Institute for Research on Migration, Ethnicity and Society (REMESO), Linköping University. Her research is framed by postcolonial and decolonial historiography, heritage and memory studies, and critical race and whiteness studies. She is completing a dissertation on the idea of white Africanity, dissident whites and decolonization in the context of Apartheid South Africa and the Pan-African movement.

Authors

Nicolas Bancel is historian, professor at the University of Lausanne, and the director of the university's Institute of Sport Sciences, ISSUL. He is also co-director of the research group Achac. A specialist on colonial and postcolonial issues, questions of cultural memory and the history of sport, he is co-editor of the seminal volumes *La Fracture coloniale* (La Découverte, 2005), *Ruptures postcoloniales* (La Découverte, 2010), and *The Invention of Race* (Routledge, 2014).

Gurminder K. Bhambra is Professor of Sociology at the University of Warwick and Guest Professor of Sociology and History at the Centre for Concurrences in Colonial and Postcolonial Studies at Linnaeus University, Sweden. She is author of *Connected Sociologies* (Bloomsbury, 2014) and *Rethinking Modernity: Postcolonialism and the Sociological Imagination* (Palgrave, 2007), which won the 2008 Philip Abrams Memorial Prize for best first book in sociology.

Pascal Blanchard is historian, researcher at the Laboratory for Research in Communication and Politics at the University of Paris-Dauphine, co-director of the research group Achac and documentarist. A specialist in the areas of colonial legacy and immigration in contemporary France, he has published several works on the colonial legacy in France, including *La Fracture coloniale. La société française au prisme de l'héritage colonial* (La Découverte, 2005), *Les années 30 sont de retour* (Flammarion, 2014) and *Le Grand repli* (La Découverte, 2015).

Manuela Boatcă is Professor of Sociology and Head of School of the Global Studies Programme at the Albert-Ludwigs-University Freiburg, Germany. She was Visiting Professor at IUPERJ, Rio de Janeiro in 2007/08 and Professor of Sociology of Global Inequalities at the Latin American Institute of the Freie Universität Berlin from 2012 to 2015. She is author of *Global Inequalities beyond Occidentalism* (Ashgate, 2015) and co-editor (with E. Gutiérrez Rodríguez and S. Costa) of *Decolonizing European Sociology. Transdisciplinary Approaches* (Ashgate, 2010) and of *Dynamics of Inequalities in a Global Perspective* (2016).

Esther Captain is Head of the Centre for Applied Research in Education at Amsterdam University of Applied Sciences and associated researcher at the Institute for War, Holocaust and Genocide Studies. She has been postdoctoral researcher at Utrecht University and the University of Amsterdam and visiting fellow at the Rutgers Center for Historical Analysis, Rutgers University. She has published on the legacy of WWII, memory and heritage studies and postcolonial history, including *Oorlogserfgoed overzee. De erfenis van de Tweede Wereldoorlog in Aruba, Curaçao, Indonesië en Suriname [Heritage of the War Overseas. The Legacy of WWII in Aruba, Curaçao, Indonesia and Surinam]* (Bert Bakker, 2010) and *Traces of Slavery in Utrecht* (Utrecht University, 2012).

Nacira Guénif-Souilamas is Professor of Sociology at Université de Paris VIII–Vincennes-Saint-Denis, and former research fellow at Wellesley College, Columbia University and the Institute of French Studies of NYU. Her PhD dissertation was awarded 'Le prix le Monde de la recherche universitaire' and published as *Des Beurettes aux descendants d'immigrants nord-africains* (2000). She has co-authored with Éric Macé *Les féministes et le garçon arabe* (2004) and edited *La république mise à nu par son immigration* (2006). She is a collaborator and fellow in several research projects on civil society, feminism, religion, Orientalism and diversity. Her most recent publication in English is: 'Straight Migrants Queering European Man', in *What's Queer about Europe?* edited by Mireille Rosello and Sudeep Dasgupta (Fordham University Press, 2014).

Peo Hansen is Professor of Political Science at the Institute for Research on Migration, Ethnicity and Society, Linköping University. His research focuses on European integration, EU migration policy, theories of citizenship and nationalism, postwar European geopolitics, and the history of colonialism and decolonization. His most recent publications include *The Politics of European Citizenship* (co-authored with Sandy B. Hager, Berghahn Books, 2012); and *Eurafrica: The Untold History of European Integration and Colonialism* (co-authored with Stefan Jonsson, Bloomsbury 2014).

Lars Jensen is Associate Professor at Cultural Encounters, University of Roskilde, Denmark. He is co-editor of *The Historical Companion to Postcolonial Literatures: Continental Europe and its Empires* (EUP, 2008), co-editor with Kristín Loftsdóttir of *Whiteness and Postcolonialism in the Nordic Region* (Ashgate, 2012), and *Crisis in the Nordic Countries and Beyond: At the Intersection of Environment, Finance and Multiculturalism* (Ashgate, 2014). His latest monograph is *Beyond Britain: Stuart Hall and the Postcolonializing of Anglophone Cultural Studies* (Rowman & Littlefield, 2014).

Elsa Peralta (PhD in Anthropology, University of Lisbon, 2006) is a research fellow at the Centre for Comparative Studies (CEC), University of Lisbon. Her work draws on perspectives from anthropology, memory studies and postcolonial studies and focuses on private and public modes of recall of past events, in particular of the colonial past. She coordinates the project 'Legacies of Empire and Colonialism in Comparative Perspective' and is working on the research project 'Narratives of Loss, War and Trauma: Portuguese Cultural Memory and the End of Empire'. She was the curator of the exhibition 'Return – Traces of Memory', produced by the City Council of Lisbon.

Robbie Shilliam is Reader in International Relations at Queen Mary University of London. He is author of *German Thought and International Relations: The Rise and Fall of a Liberal Project* (2009) and *The Black Pacific: Anti-Colonial Struggles and Oceanic Connections* (Bloomsbury Academic Press, 2015) and he is co-convener of the Colonial/Postcolonial/Decolonial working group of the British International Studies Association.

Preface

This book is an investigation into how current economic and political crises affect not just our present but also our past. At the heart of the investigation are two questions. How do new regimes of historiography and memory culture relate to emerging and established patterns of integration, discrimination, and social fragmentation in European societies? How do present policies of austerity and the ensuing social exclusion of migrants and minorities influence our perceptions of the position of minorities, migrants and colonized peoples in European history? In asking such questions, the book intervenes into a trans-European discussion on multiculturalism, diversity, integration and migration, and it offers a new approach to disputes about the legacy of imperial and colonial systems that shaped Europe's position in the world. A distinctive feature of the book is its combination of perspectives from the social sciences and the humanities; this is a multidisciplinary book.

Our premise is that European societies have recently turned toward more austere political regimes. Proposed and executed budget cuts, changes on the labour market, restrictions of welfare systems and new regimes of migration and citizenship are examples of this tendency. In the wake of such changes, new forms of social inclusion and exclusion appear that are justified through a reactivation of differences of race, class and gender, all this serving, in its turn, to justify new forms of labour extraction and the formation of a new subaltern underclass or 'precariat'. Another consequence is that democracy itself has become precarious. While the agents and adherents of austerity programmes promote themselves as democracy's saviours, practitioners of democracy often find themselves pushed toward the extra-parliamentary margins.

It is against this backdrop that the book investigates contemporary understandings of history and cultural memory. Can we speak of an austere historiography, an enforcement of conformity on Europe past and present? Are we witnessing a turn toward austerity in theories and practices of historiography, in the same way as we speak about economic, social and political austerity programmes as a dominant way of wielding power in contemporary Europe and the West?

The impetus of the book was the symposium 'Austere Histories: Social Exclusion and the Erasure of Colonial Memory in Contemporary European

Societies', organized by the Institute for Research on Migration, Ethnicity and Society (REMESO) at Linköping University in November 2013, where contributions to this volume were presented in preliminary form. As editors, we wish to thank the authors gathered in this book and other participants at the symposium. The collective commitment to intellectual inquiry and criticism expressed by all involved has sustained our conviction that the problems raised in this book are both important and urgent. We also want to acknowledge our many colleagues at REMESO, a research community and intellectual collective whose members have developed path-breaking research on policies of austerity, global processes of precarization and new landscapes of migration and racism in Europe, all of which have enriched the conceptualization of this book. We also want to express our gratitude to the Swedish Research Council (Vetenskapsrådet) and FORTE: the Swedish Research Council for Health, Working Life and Welfare, which helped finance the symposium. A grant from the Sven och Dagmar Saléns stiftelse helped fund the edition and publication of this volume. We acknowledge this support with gratitude. Thanks are also due to Gila Walker for translation of one chapter and to Emily Briggs and her colleagues at Routledge for patience, friendly encouragement, experience and expertise. Finally, and especially important for a collection that addresses a political and cultural landscape in rapid transformation, we should like to point out that contributions to this book were completed between August 2015 and February 2016.

This book is dedicated to the victims of austerity, living and dead, in the open seas of the Mediterranean, on the islands of the Aegean, in the jungle of Calais, the streets of Barcelona, the hostels of Norrköping and elsewhere, everywhere.

S.J. and J.W. Norrköping, March 2016

1   Introducing austere histories

Stefan Jonsson and Julia Willén

Teaching conformity

Austere histories? 'People will just have to pull their socks up. And tighten their belts. And figuratively rearrange other parts of their apparel until the mess is sorted out,' writes Richard Seymour (2014: 29), decoding the overtones in the discourse of austerity that for some years has been disseminated from economic and political power centres of the West. Austerity indicates a withdrawal of entitlements, a condition of severity, or a situation of scarcity; it discharges people to look for work and scavenge for food to put on the table, as they must struggle to make ends meet. Austerity is also associated with commands, authoritarian or authoritative superiors whose calls to order and discipline, be they intended to mobilize against external threats or close ranks in times of internal troubles, necessitate prohibitions. Thus, a policy of austerity apparently institutes a more frugal order of life – some would say more safe and orderly, others more gloomy and dangerous – than what preceded it. The near past no longer appears as an era of stability and comfort, but as one of undeserved affluence and irresponsible excess. After days of butter and cream, come the lean years of bark and rye. This is how the strange rhetoric of austerity, as political economist Mark Blyth (2013a: 13) has it, turns economic concerns into 'a morality play' about Western civilization.

The new morality play of the West

Austere Histories is a book that analyses this drama: how austerity turns economic concerns into moral and cultural ones; how it remodels historical consciousness and conceptions of Europe's colonial past; how it changes the relationships between classes, ethnic minorities, majorities and migrants; and how all this affects the very definition and self-image of contemporary *European Societies*.

If translated into Freudian language, the idea of austerity would mean that desire has to be curbed and sublimated. It would compel us to renounce enjoyment and obey the command of the super-ego, the agent of austerity *par excellence*. Put differently, we would find ourselves in a social world teaching us to bow to Identity – the social, cultural, racial, sexual or gendered identity ascribed to us by society, the symbolic order, or what Lacan used to call 'the Name of the Father' (Lacan, 1966/1997: 67). As identity here becomes a disciplinary force, 'normal' social processes in which relationships of self and other are incessantly reshaped, would be inhibited, giving way to an antagonistic relation between the two, the paranoid I being besieged by its countless projections of otherness. On a psychological and existential level, then, austerity implies a regime that consolidates identities. Austerity captures the psyche much in the same way as it trims the welfare state. In both, redistribution is replaced by repression.

Interestingly, analyses focusing on the economy are likely to match the psychoanalytic view. True, if one takes a superficial view of the matter, today's neoliberal austerity policies demand not firm identities but flexible ones. However, the called-for flexibility is regimented. It demands exceptional self-restraint. It trains the employee to postpone wish-fulfilment and renounce pleasure altogether (Southwood, 2011). This is because work life and labour markets are increasingly offering the opposite of what most people desire: to have a modest but stable income and lead orderly, predictable lives within their family circle and community, and to enjoy free time and leisure. As such, work life in its austere fitting precludes most forms of social bonding except one: loyalty to the employer. If you want to have a job and earn a living, you must be prepared to prioritize your employer; if in addition to that you want to make a career, you must also renounce family, children, home, health, holidays, education, dreams and expectations of the future.

Social and cultural theorists define this new relation between worker and employer, labour and capital, as 'precarization' (Bourdieu and Accardo, 1993; Schierup *et al.*, 2015). Some argue that it entails a new class formation: a 'precariat' or global underclass created by processes of competition, downsizing, deregulation and exclusion (Standing, 2011). What are the people who are suffering this exclusion to do? If we take the case nearest to us, the political transformation of Sweden, we find that solutions recently on offer include career planning, job coaching, cognitive behaviour therapy, shopping around for the right schools, apprenticeships, and accepting lower wages.

Poverty, unemployment, social exclusion and ethnic discrimination are supposed, in this programme, to get fixed through cutbacks and intensified adaptation and competition, in which the excluded ones are expected to outdo one another in refashioning their personas and making themselves employable (Means, 2013). And if they fail? Austerity pundits will say that they are not trying hard enough; that they are unsuitable, by nature or nurture lazy, ruined by welfare benefits or have inadequate cultural values (Candieas, 2008). Those who fail to adapt to new job-market realities are often harassed and called white trash, unless they are called brown trash, or Muslim trash, or NEETs (not in education, employment or training), a dumped lot of outsiders, members of an underclass that, in addition (and whether white, brown or black), are often blamed for the rise of everything from populism and racism to urban riots and terrorism. In short, they are thrown outside the system and their misery is explained by shortcomings inherent in their identity, if not in their genes. While these processes affect the lower classes the most, and undocumented migrants in particular, it also erodes the social security taken for granted by the middle classes, the members of which run the risk of similar degradation if they are fired, become ill or are hit by family crises. This has been graphically illustrated in recent years by numerous novels, theatre plays and TV series catering to the anxious middle classes, but also by anthropological work like Marc Augé's ethnofiction *No Fixed Abode* (2013).

Such are, in terms all too sweeping and general, some of the major ways in which the politics of austerity is transforming present-day European societies. It does not matter whether we view the world through a psychoanalytic or economic lens; in either case evocations of austerity elicit interpretations of society and human life as subjected to a regime that selects, sorts and separates human beings on criteria of identity. What we see emerging, it seems, is a social and political landscape starkly different from a regime founded in notions of equal rights and democratic citizenship. This landscape is the first point of departure for this book.

Austere histories for an austere present

Our second point of departure has to do with the past. *Austere Histories* is the result of a shared investigation of the ways in which the politics of austerity translates into specific modalities of historical consciousness, modalities that would then also be marked by a consolidation of identity, and hence of antagonism and exclusion. Can we speak of an 'austere historiography', an enforcement of conformity on Europe past and present? As several authors in this collection exemplify, strong interests are today working to purge the histories of specific European nations, but also those of Europe and the West, from cultural plurality. Heroic and homogeneous stories about the past of nations, regions and religions are being retold and reinvented.

Is this a new tendency? Has not historiography, as Paul Veyne (1988: 77) once argued, always been complicit in issuing identity certificates for this or that community? Was this not, as Nietzsche (1874) observed, one of the essential functions of history writing?

To be sure, yes. But it is also true that, until recently, many of the historical narratives in light of which nations, regions, continents and civilizations understood themselves were in the process of multiplying. To use an expression by Michael Rothberg (2009), Europe's collective memory has since the 1960s become 'multidirectional', increasingly complex and heterogeneous, opening itself for long-occluded memories of the working classes, women, subalterns, defeated protest movements, persecuted minorities, migrants, colonized peoples, queer lives and experiences. Especially from the 1980s and onward, inaugurated by postcolonial critiques of Eurocentric narratives, historiography has become less concerned with drawing boundaries around communities and more interested in tracing relations, subterranean connections, suppressed voices, and marginalized memories, all of which then, supposedly, provided new points of entry to the past.

Twenty years ago, Edward Said summed up this state of affairs in *Culture and Imperialism*: 'We are, so to speak, *of* the connections, not outside and beyond them' (Said, 1993: 55). After the inaugurating moment of Said and postcolonial theory, there has been a great deal of work that has employed postcolonial perspectives in a variety of historical and geographical contexts. There are by now few states and regions, few major institutions and international organisations, few modern traditions and canonised cultural figures that have not been subjected to intelligent and often revealing scrutiny from a postcolonial point of view. Yet today, this project of historical unlocking, multiplication and contestation appears to be challenged. Multiculturalism, postcolonial memories and minority discourses are being marginalized, and this at the very moment when it was reasonable to expect that they would be confirmed and inscribed as central concerns in any overview of European history and European society. An increasing number of historians and intellectuals are again turning a blind eye toward less gratifying parts of European history. Their ignorance is often politically sanctioned.

To what extent is this narrowing of the historical imagination related to the present moment of austerity politics in the contemporary West? Combining the two observations outlined above – that is, austerity as a general description of everyday life, work and media discourse in the present and austerity as a narrowing of historical consciousness and obsessions with group identity – we reach a third, synthetic problem, which is the one, precisely, that we confront in this book. If 'austerity' is an idea that informs economic, political and social policy in contemporary Europe, to what extent does it also influence the ways in which historians and intellectuals represent European history and the history of Europe's nation-states? Or, if we turn the question around: to what extent and in which ways do present-day historical debate and practice of history writing support and legitimize the idea of 'austerity' and its social and political consequences, in the areas of citizenship and migration, for instance?

More specifically, the chapters that follow make up a shared endeavour and collective thinking that address two critical questions:

1 How do present policies of austerity and the ensuing social exclusion of migrants and minorities influence the perceptions and interpretations of the place of minorities, migrants and colonized peoples in European history?
2 How do new regimes of historiography and memory culture relate to emerging and established patterns of discrimination and social segmentation in today's European societies?

The contributors to this collection have for a long time in their own national, local and regional contexts and debates dealt with colonial legacies in contemporary Europe. They recognise and emphasise that the respective histories of Europe's nation-states are *imperial* histories more than national ones, and that this fact must be accounted for in intellectual inquiry and reflected in public life and discourse. Whereas the history of imperialism and colonialism has so far been addressed mostly by separate national discussions, this collection treats it as a shared European concern. In this sense, the book contributes to an emerging trans-European conversation involving several intellectual milieus, projects and publishing ventures.[1] The almost simultaneous emergence of several such efforts shows that a rethinking of Europe's past from its migrant and postcolonial margins is both long overdue and urgent. For, as mentioned, it stands in radical opposition to present-day austere histories and their emphasis on national, continental or ethnic identity.

Austere Histories differs from these related publications in its emphasis on the relation of economy and culture. It also puts greater stress on mechanisms of social and historical exclusion. We keep a persistent focus on how austerity, in prompting an adaptation or revision of the past, also consolidates its grip on Europe's present and future. As a book, and as a concept, *Austere Histories* thus situates itself at the intersection of at least three contemporary issues, cultural contexts and academic discussions: first, discussions on Europe's cultural memory and the precarious place of the colonial legacy in it; second, controversies on multiculturalism, racism, xenophobia and Europe's migration crises; third and finally, the debate on austerity as policy and as ideology.

In the rest of this introduction we will sketch the context and relevance of these perspectives, first by fleshing out the connections between austerity policy and what we call *austere histories*, by which we mean, as should be clear by now, the increased role of historical scholarship and popular history in processes of social, cultural and historical exclusion. Second, and as a way of introducing the contributions to this collection, we will assess the real stakes involved in such exclusions especially as concerns groups designated as minorities, migrants and (former) colonial subjects in Europe past and present, colonial and postcolonial. Finally, we discuss what may lie ahead as alternatives to those histories and sociological cases of austerity that are analysed in both breadth and detail and from a variety of different angles in the following chapters.

Social exclusion and the contest of colonial memories

While there is much to support the general intuition that the current politics of austerity corresponds to a historiography of austerity, it is not easy to define what the latter actually is. A historiography of austerity? But which, then, are the criteria according to which a piece of history writing can be classified as being austere or marked by austerity? As we shall see, one's perspective on matters of definition will depend upon one's perception of exclusion, and hence also on the role of identity – the identity of communities, peoples, countries, states, ethnic groups, or the like – in the realm of historiography.

We should also observe that although it is easy to confirm, again, the intuition of some correlation between the exclusion generated by relentless austerity policies, on the one hand, and a narrowing and homogenizing scope of historical imagination, on the other hand, it is not at all clear how that relation should be interpreted. These two processes are usually not related to one another as a cause to its effects. Were we to establish such a causal explanation, it would immediately be challenged by long-standing critiques against interpretations that treat cultural and intellectual tendencies as super-structural manifestations of transformations in the socioeconomic base. This is to say that austere history is not a mere expression of a global political economy organized according to the neoliberal principles of fiscal restraint and budgetary discipline. That such economic policies have caused the slashing of welfare is possible to prove (Farnsworth and Irving, 2015; Krugman, 2015). But it is far more difficult to demonstrate how economic austerity policy affects the presentation of history in, say, museums or textbooks in contemporary France, Germany, the United Kingdom or Sweden.

An interpretation of this latter relationship therefore requires consideration of the mediations at work within and between different levels and sectors of contemporary society. This is why we propose, as an indispensable methodological perspective, that attempts to engage with the relation of exclusionary processes in today's European societies to the redefinition of collective identities and boundaries in historical accounts of the past must start out with a serious reflection on the concept of historical mediation as such. Rather than connecting neoliberal austerity policy to austere historiography by looking for causal relations, we thus suggest that both *mediate* one another, in the sense that they, in combination, show something that neither is able to reveal when considered separately or in sequence. The juxtaposition evoked by the subtitle of this book – 'social exclusion and the contest of colonial memories' – is thus less a causal relation than a dialectical one: by relating the two, we become capable of apprehending a more general shift that is under way. The coupling of policies of austerity to austere historiography would serve its purpose if it helps us identify, interpret and conceptualize an emerging social and cultural order, which may be that of a generalized or 'perennial' austerity, an apparatus of exclusion and inclusion whose true scope and range we may still be unable to fathom, but of which several of the following chapters offer a glimpse.

The ideology of austerity

Let us start charting this process of mediation by considering first the economic notion austerity, sometimes referred to as fiscal conservatism. In this sense, which is the most common one, austerity has become a catch-all term for economic adjustments in times of real or expected deflation. These adjustments aim to restore market competitiveness by reducing, for instance, wages, prices and public spending, and they are most efficiently executed by simply cutting the state's budget, debts and deficits. As Mark Blyth (2013a: 2) explains, this strategy supposedly restores optimal conditions for investments and growth, 'since the government will neither be "crowding-out" the market for investment by sucking up all the available capital through the issuance of debt, nor adding to the nation's already "too big" debt'.

It is by now well established that this recipe for economic recovery has been unsuccessful in most places where it has been tried, not only because it has generated enormous social polarisation, creating massive poverty at one end and unprecedented wealth for the few at the top, but also because it has no consistent record of creating the economic growth it pledges to deliver (IMF, 2012; Kuttner, 2013; Schafer and Streeck, 2013; Blyth, 2013a: 178–226; Sommers and Woolfson, 2014).

Yet, austerity persists, which indicates that austerity is not only a policy of fiscal conservatism, or a matter of economics in the strict sense. 'Because there is such extensive opposition to the idea that economic "austerity" is the right approach', Rebecca Bramall (2013: 2) states, 'it is a rare commentator who does not recognize that the policy of austerity also has an ideological dimension'. Several economists and social scientists have thus inferred that the reason why austerity remains the guiding principle of European and Western politics and policy recommendations – despite the doctrine's internal shortcomings and the social disintegration and human suffering it has caused – is less to do with the economy per se than with extra-economic factors and forces (Blyth, 2013b; Jabko, 2013; Thompson, 2013; Streeck, 2013; Peck, 2013). They tend to explain austerity's persistence by the fact that political power has become too dependent on big banks and financial investors – a sector of the economy that over the past decades has supplied wealthy people with an almost infinite source of additional wealth. Austerity may thus be seen as an ideology that serves to protect such forms of wealth-procurement. Jeff Madrick (2012) puts it squarely: 'Austerity is essentially about smaller government, and a small-government ideology means lower taxes and fewer regulations – a boon to big business, especially the finance industry, and the rich.'

Ideological power typically operates by persuasion, propaganda and media dissemination, for the purpose of implementing policy. This implies, importantly, that it operates through a range of emotional and affective appeals to people's sense of identity, belonging and community. Even as austerity may be under way of being discarded as economic doctrine, it therefore retains traction as a 'truth' about welfare, class structure, human relations, society and the meaning of politics itself. It is precisely at this point that we can grasp 'austerity' as a form of mediation by which particular economic interests are transformed into a set of ideas – or an ideology – that appears to serve some general interest. This is also where we see, with Rebecca Bramall, that it 'is vital to recognize that austerity is both an economic policy *and* a complex ideological phenomenon, to explore austerity's cultural politics as well as its financial politics and to grasp the interpenetration of culture and economy' (2013: 3). Mark Blyth employs stronger language to capture this 'interpenetration', or what should perhaps more properly be called austerity's ideological mediation of economy and culture:

> In sum, when those at the bottom are expected to pay disproportionately for a problem created by those at the top, and when those at the top actively

eschew any responsibility for that problem by blaming the state for their mistakes, not only will squeezing the bottom not produce enough revenue to fix things, it will produce an even more polarized and politicized society in which the conditions for a sustainable politics dealing with more debt and less growth are undermined. Populism, nationalism, and calls for the return of 'God and gold' in equal doses are what unequal austerity generates [...].

(Blyth, 2013a: 15)

In this light, austerity appears less as economic doctrine and more as what Foucault would have called a disposition of power, a way of governing and organizing society in a situation where the effects of fiscal conservatism in tandem with neoliberal deregulation and privatization of welfare have led to growing social polarization and inequality within the polity, as well as to disempowerment, exclusion and exploitation of its most vulnerable members.

What are the features of such forms of austere governance? Robbie Shilliam provides one answer in his chapter below: 'Austerity is not just an economic project but a broader sensibility that structures exclusions and inequalities across the many dimensions of social life.' Richard Seymour, for his part, emphasizes two general traits: 'The reorganisation of the state as a less welfarist and more penal and coercive institution', and 'the dissemination of cultures which value hierarchy, competitiveness and casual sadism toward the weak' (Seymour, 2014: 4).

The chapters

Cases

As the ideology of austerity mediates economic concerns into political, cultural and historiographical ones, its most conspicuous effect seems to be multiple forms of *exclusion*. Just as economic austerity policies generate social polarization, depriving increasing numbers of people of employment, social security and health care, so also do we witness related processes in popular history and institutions mandated to maintain, display, relate and discuss Europe's historical and cultural heritage. The reader will find that the following chapters engage this problematic in different ways.

First, the chapters may be read as a set of extended case studies, showing how austerity operates as an ideological configuration within which attitudes to the past and historiographical practices are renegotiated in a struggle of memories. These contests generate versions of history and models of knowledge that often justify the exclusion of the memories of minority groups and colonized peoples, to the benefit of more nation-centred and Eurocentric narratives. The chapters in Part I, 'Cases', thus indicate how institutions of historical knowledge, education, cultural heritage and social life are strapped to identity-building agendas of various kinds. In this context our book provides a preliminary inventory of phenomena that are currently influenced by austere conceptions of history. They include museums, academic historiography and curricula, popular history, monuments and archives, particularly those that engage with histories of colonialism, migration and ethnic minorities. Gurminder Bhambra, Robbie Shilliam and Esther Captain, as well as co-authors Nicolas Bancel and Pascal Blanchard and co-authors Elsa Peralta and Lars Jensen all show how such phenomena have become sites of symbolic struggles over the past.

As Captain discusses in her chapter on the Netherlands, cutbacks in the funding of museums, archives and heritage institutions have had immediate exclusionary effects in that they diminish access to historical knowledge and cultural memory for the two million Dutch citizens who have migrant or colonial backgrounds. This serves to further facilitate the erasure or the colonial past, and the active forgetting of this past, especially in the light of Captain's first case in her text, where she makes a critical inquiry into the Dutch commemorations of the tercentenary of the Treaty of Utrecht, the 150-year anniversary of the Dutch abolition of slavery as well as the 400th anniversary of the *Dutch East India Company*. Captain discusses how these all worked to stage a narrow narrative of the Dutch past, without taking into account the heterogeneity of histories and heritages that these commemorations could have entailed. Such histories of the Dutch colonial legacy 'is not an optional extra', Captain concludes, but fundamental building blocks for Europe in the twenty-first century.

Bancel and Blanchard, for their part, show how ideologies of austerity have exacerbated a situation in which French republican identity and history is explicitly defended in open antagonism to certain representatives of internal otherness, who thereby find their citizenship devalued because of their religion (Islam), skin colour (non-white), or background (African, Asian or Caribbean). The 'official' silence of the French government on the colonial past deprives second- and third-generation children of colonial and postcolonial immigration of their past. This is a form of discrimination in its own right, argue Bancel and Blanchard, and it comes on top of more concrete forms of racism and discrimination. Resulting from this is 'the construction of worlds separated from and rejected by the society at large'. As they conclude, the refusal to address colonial history in combination with explicit forms of racial exclusion offer explanations of the radicalisation of minority youth and hence also of the extreme violence that France experienced first in January 2015 as Islamist terrorists attacked the magazine *Charlie Hebdo*, and again with the Paris mass killings on 13 November 2015.

Gurminder Bhambra discusses how contemporary politics in times of austerity entails a sharp dividing line between the British Empire and its colonies on the one hand, and the United Kingdom as a nation-state on the other. Bhambra exposes how the shunning away from this correlation enables current politics to sustain the historical exclusion of immigrants (including those who were once citizens of the Empire) and to secure the image of British imperialism as a benevolent and progressive system. There is a different approach to this 'island story' that is rarely applied, Bhambra argues, because it would expose how the Empire affected and transformed the United Kingdom *in* the United Kingdom.

Stressing that these historical conjunctures should be seen as 'connected histories', Bhambra thus reconsiders the hegemonic story and demonstrates the ways in which this story has disrupted the historical linkages between the imperial subjects in the past and their transformation, through decolonisation, into 'immigrants' in the UK of today. Another occluded connection is of course the current wealth of Britain, which 'in no small part [is due] to its imperial activities', but also the very process by which the Empire moved from staging itself as multicultural to portraying itself as an austere nationalist 'island' that, despite obvious historical connections, excludes immigrants from any narrative of belonging.

Peralta and Jensen, in their chapter, discuss Denmark and Portugal's responses to austerity measures following the financial crisis beginning in the fall of 2007. Both Portugal and Denmark have a history as largely forgotten empires, and both countries have orchestrated imperial narratives of exceptionalism and benevolence. As Peralta and Jensen show, austerity has prompted the two countries to reinvent their relations with the now ex-colonial world as a safety measure against the uncertain future of the EU's pan-European project. Above all, the moment of austerity has inaugurated specific forms of imperial nostalgia. This nostalgia has highlighted selected elements of the colonial past while suppressing others. It has also been disturbed by the fact that ex-colonial peoples no longer submit to the political needs or comply with the cultural imageries projected upon them by the former imperial metropoles. The most profound aspect of this reality, as Peralta and Jensen argue, is the difficulty presented by the arrival of migrants from the ex-colonial world, a process that inevitably transforms Europe's contemporary history and with which contemporary history has not yet come to terms. However, the case of Portugal may offer an interesting path out of the containment marking most austere histories of contemporary Europe. In Portugal, as Peralta and Jensen show, the movement of people and market opportunities is also directed towards the former colonies, and the global financial crisis has thus 'reinvigorated the attention on the ex-colonial world' as a way of meeting the challenges imposed by Europe's current austerity climate.

Robbie Shilliam takes his point of departure in the 'deficit model' of the 1950s, which served to explain black students' lower attainment in terms of 'lacks' and 'deficits' in comparison with white peers who were constructed as the norm. This contested model was largely abandoned in the 1980s, yet Shilliam exposes how it lingers and is constitutive to what he calls an 'austere curriculum' in present-day UK. In the austere curriculum, black students' heritage and cultural assets are considered either as a 'lack' in relation to mono-cultural curricula, or as an 'excess' that needs to be paired down. Shilliam proves this by showing how the drop in attainment among black students in higher education can be linked to the long-term exposure of the 'deficit model' experienced by settled diaspora African-Caribbeans. He also shows how the aspirations and upward mobility for 'immigrant' African-continental students are being countered by racialized structures, racial immobility and curbed career expectations.

Yet, black is black is black, and Shilliam argues that this attainment drop is a consequence of the austere mono-cultural curriculum in the tertiary level that forces black students to unencumber themselves from their own background. Austere curricula thus not only reproduce social inequalities according to the old deficit model, they also create new racialized inequalities. As Shilliam shows – in an argument that can easily be extended to national contexts outside the UK – 'the heritage' is today more than ever becoming 'a privilege that constitutes the apparently impartial, detached and universal conventions of the curriculum' for the white student. He argues, by way of conclusion, that multicultural curricula on all educational levels would counter both white supremacy in general and the austere curricula characterizing contemporary schools and universities in particular.

In different ways, then, these chapters disclose Europe's recognition or disavowal of itself as multicultural territory and postcolonial space. They show that postcolonial memories, minority discourses and migrant experiences have been marginalized in many national contexts, as the majority has been rallied up to support patriotic and patronymic narratives of the national community.

It deserves mention here that this applies equally to a number of national and historical contexts not covered in this volume. One example that we find important, because it otherwise goes unmentioned in the chapters of this book, is provided by the austere approaches by Swedish scholars and authorities to the country's past. For while it is true that Sweden has successfully staged itself as a neutral player in international affairs, having enjoyed '200 years of peace' and maintaining, not without an air of moral superiority, a strong programme for international development and aid as well as high levels of social and gender equality and social cohesion, it is not equally well known that Sweden, too, is entangled in a number of colonial histories. The image of Sweden as a case of Nordic benevolence and exceptionalism is built on an almost full denial of all the ways in which Sweden throughout modernity participated in and profited from the colonial system (Jonsson, 2009). Above all, this applies to Sweden's role in the slave trade (see Wilson, 2015) and in the scramble for Africa and exploitation of its peoples (Granqvist, 2001), to the massive participation of Sweden's industry and business as furnishers and commissioners in colonial ventures (Nilsson, 2013), to the keen interest from Swedish scientists and scholars in colonial expansion, eugenics and racial biology (Broberg and Roll-Hansen, 2005), and, perhaps above all, to the colonization of and mineral extraction in Sápmi, at the cost of the indigenous population (Axelsson and Sköld, 2006). The Swedish government has yet to account – let alone make reparations – for Swedish colonial involvement, which frequently was both blind and brutal. Many of the phenomena just mentioned are still not integrated in historical scholarship and education, much less in history textbooks. In the present period of austerity, the collective memory of these colonial processes and institutions has become ever more contested, and the question as to whether or not they are part of Sweden's national narrative is unsettled, which contributes to the social and cultural exclusion of contemporary minorities who are the immediate inheritors of such memories of oppression and dispossession.

Conjunctures

The chapters that make up Part II of the book, 'Conjunctures', indicate that the 'European project', if such can be said to exist, seems to be in the process of establishing an 'austere community' ruled by restricted, majoritarian and particularistic notions of the European identity. These chapters discuss institutions, regulations, practices and discourses that circumscribe identities of nations, minorities and communities in new ways and in some cases also to differentiate the distribution of rights and entitlements to individuals according to identity, religion, background, profession, income and other criteria.

Manuela Boatcă and Peo Hansen, respectively, thus analyse the ways in which austerity programmes transform the definition and implementation of foundational political instruments such as citizenship and human rights. Under austerity, paths to citizenship and rights of residency that used to be distributed according to principles of equality have in effect become tools of segregation and demographic selection.

Boatcă demonstrates that the unwillingness or inability of Europe to address the global inequalities caused by the colonial system has led to a situation where citizenship – and the rights to residence, mobility and welfare linked to it – has today become a commodity. As Boatcă shows, citizenship, which is seen in the West as an instrument for the creation of *internal* equality, is at the very same time the world's most powerful instrument for a racially determined distribution of life opportunities and human rights. In this sense, global inequality is today upheld by citizenship. The regime of austerity makes this more evident than ever, Boatcă argues. It has established a system where

> wealthy investors from certain non-Western regions are actively encouraged to purchase European citizenship rights in an unprecedented wave of commodification [...], while financially strained states and non-Western labour migrants face mounting criminalisation, sanctions, and austerity measures when attempting to access the same rights.

Peo Hansen's chapter addresses one of the areas in which policies of austerity are impacting reality most directly. Analysing the European Union's migration policy in relation to the EU's responses to the 2015 'refugee crisis', Hansen shows how both are shaped by the current EU orthodoxy of financial austerity. On the one hand, it is the objective of the EU to restrict as far as possible the numbers of asylum-seekers in Europe. 'Less migration' has become the mantra of the refugee crisis. On the other hand, no European politician or EU policy-maker of any stature denies that the member states, within the coming years and decades, need millions of migrants to avert a population decrease that would erode the basis of Europe's long-term economic sustainability, including its welfare systems and retirement schedules. 'More migration' is thus the mantra of the EU's demographic crisis and its efforts to attract external labour migration. Why, asks Hansen, do Brussels and member states not greet the refugees as a first, albeit modest, step towards amending the EU's demographic crisis? As he contends, the answer has to do with a combination of racial austerity and financial austerity that reject, exclude and exploit non-white migrants, many of whom arrive from areas previously ruled by Europe's imperial powers. The ideology of austerity that currently rules Europe's economic policymaking and informs its cultural self-understanding thus effectively thwarts the type of expansive public investment and citizenship regime that would be required to allow the EU's demographic deficit to be perceived as congruent with the global refugee surplus, Hansen argues.

With no such solution in sight, the politics of austerity in combination with austere history is likely to produce what Nacira Guénif-Souliamas in her chapter describes as a 'regime of restrained equality'. Guénif-Souilamas's chapter powerfully argues that a new concept – perhaps even a new episteme – must be produced in order to see how European societies have been transformed over the last decades, and at accelerating speed since the beginning of the 'war on terror'. This new concept is precisely 'restrained equality'. In the semantic sense an oxymoron, restrained equality is nonetheless a precise designation of a system where – under the dominance of late financial capitalism and its austerity policies – equality has become a scarcity and, hence, a privilege for select ones. Whereas this system obviously contradicts any authentic notion of democracy and human rights, it can operate as the hidden agenda in contemporary Western implementations of democracy and equality. The regime of restrained equality, as Guénif-Souilamas contends, supports itself, first, on austerity policies that compel entire population to see equality and egalitarianism as a scarcity that can only apply to parts of the population and, second, on austere histories, which seize every imaginable difference, and above all differences inherited from Orientalist ideology, racial supremacy and sexism, to naturalize uneven access to equality. Dwelling on a number of revealing instances and illustrations of 'austere histories' – in which she includes the ideological figure of Islam and the Muslim, the sexualized notion of the 'Arab Boy', the images of Roma, ethnic minorities and migrants, the omnipresence of 'terrorism' as a source of panic, the prevalence of so-called 'search-and-rescue narratives' that victimize migrants, in combination with 'stop-and-search operations' that vilify the same migrants – Guénif-Souilamas evokes a sinister landscape where, as she states, 'Euro-America' undergoes reunification along colour lines in order to protect its powers and privileges. The regime of restrained equality, supported by austere varieties of European and colonial history from which minorities and migrants are evicted, thus serves a 'biopolitical objective', which is to define the complexion of Europe's present and future population: 'The racialization and sexualization entrenched in the restrained equality regime derives from its task to perpetuate structural inequalities by drawing a colour line that justifies why certain rights are denied to certain groups or individuals.' As Guénif-Souilamas concludes, it 'all boils down to the assumption that equality is scarce; hence the need for a regime that confines equality within a gendered and racial colour line.'

The return of the civilizing mission

We mentioned above that our notion of austere histories is partly conceived to capture the strong interests that are currently working to summon the history of Europe and its nation-states in the struggle of majority 'identities' against intruders and enemies within. In this predicament, it is also important to investigate to what extent history (including public debate on history and history education) is again becoming 'nationalistic' or 'cosmopolitan' – and to what extent this cosmopolitan turn tends to celebrate the achievements of Europe and posit the West as a model of universality, humanism and perhaps also of the human as such.

While we cannot enter here into the vast literature on Europe as a model of a cosmopolitan future, we do recognize that the austere histories discussed in this book tend to reduce the very complexity and contradictoriness of Europe and the West, i.e. the very features that would have to serve as a base of any 'cosmopolitan' project of any credibility (for this discussion, see Hansen, 2009; Narayan and Bahmbra, 2016). Under the paradigm of austerity, colonial and postcolonial memories are evicted from their recently claimed habitats in the European past, and again seen as being external to Europe. This development raises not just intellectual concerns, but political and ethical ones as well, for it cuts off Europe's access to the very sources of its auto-critique. Europe's colonial and postcolonial memories have only recently been recognized and inscribed in the 'official' annals of European culture. Now, as is seen in the contributions to this book, an increasing number of historians and intellectuals are again becoming blind to such less gratifying parts of Europe's history.

It is perhaps still too early to speak of a historical *revisionism* in the strict sense. As some of the chapters show, there are also important counter-tendencies in parts of the academic community and postcolonial and migrant communities and organizations. Still, a transformation, corresponding to a new politics of austerity that seems impatient with both democracy and the complexities of past, is set in motion. Should this transformation continue, we risk losing one of the main accomplishments of European historiography in recent decades: the establishment of Europe's history and enlightenment as a dialectical phenomenon and process. If this dialectical nature is suppressed, it becomes all the easier to dismiss the constitutive relationship of colonialism to the European project, or of coloniality and modernity in general. The European project and enlightenment will then again become what it was before the revelatory moments of Auschwitz and anti-colonial struggles: a naïve belief in and backing of the colonizer's civilizing mission.

What is at stake here is thus more than the place of colonialism in narratives of Europe's past. What is at stake is also the symbolic right of residency and cultural citizenship for the millions of Europeans whose backgrounds and collective memory are shaped by Europe's imperial history. And what is at stake for non-white and minority Europeans is their actual civil rights and equality, which they must already today ferociously defend against structural discrimination, institutional racism, police surveillance and violence. Evidently, these issues concern the very identity of Europe, which was fatefully construed in opposition to societies and peoples with whom Europeans, through imperial dominance and colonial exploitation, once established those enduring, ineradicable and unequal connections that the advocates of austere history now teach us to ignore.

Note

1 Closest to the issues addressed in this book are works such as *Echoes of Empire* (Nicolaïdïs *et al.*, 2015) and *Postcolonial Transitions in Europe* (Ponzanesi and Colpani, 2015). For more country-specific studies and overviews, see *Colonial Switzerland: Rethinking Colonialism From the Margins* (Purtschert and Fischer-Tiné, 2015; for the more substantial original in German, see Purtschert *et al.*, 2012), *Postcolonial Italy: Challenging National Homogeneity* (Lombardi-Diop and Romeo, 2012), *Postcolonial Netherlands: Sixty-five Years of Forgetting, Commemorating, Silencing* (Oostindie, 2011), *Culture coloniale en France: De la Révolution française à nos jours* (Blanchard *et al.*, 2008) as well as *La fracture coloniale* (Bancel *et al.*, 2005), *Kolonialismus und Erinnerungskultur. Die Kolonialvergangenheit im kollektiven Gedächtnis der deutschen und niederländischen Einwanderungsgesellschaft* (Lutz and Gawarecki, 2005), *Globalisation and the Nation in Imperial Germany* (Conrad, 2014), *Danmark: Rigsfællesskab, tropekolonier og den postkoloniale arv* (Jensen, 2012), *Kein Platz an der Sonne: Erinnerungsorte der deutschen Kolonialgeschichte* (Zimmerer, 2013), *Whiteness and Postcolonialism in the Nordic Region: Exceptionalism, Migrant Others and National Identities* (Loftsdóttir and Jensen, 2012). For theoretical interventions concerning Europe as a whole, see *Rethinking Modernity* (Bhambra, 2011) and *Connected Sociologies* (Bhambra, 2014), as well as *Decolonizing European Sociology* (Boatcă, 2012), *Eurafrica: The Untold History of European Integration* (Hansen and Jonsson, 2014) and *Global Inequalities Beyond Occidentalism* (Boatcă, 2015).

Bibliography

Augé, M. (2013) *No Fixed Abode*. Trans. by C. Turner. Calcutta and London: Seagull Press.

Axelsson, P. and Sköld, P. (2006) 'Indigenous Populations and Vulnerability. Characterizing Vulnerability in a Sami Context', *Annales de démographie historique*, 1 (no. 111), pp. 115–32.

Bancel, N., Blanchard, P. and Lemaire, S. (eds) (2005) *La fracture coloniale: La société française au prisme de l'héritage colonial*. Paris: La Découverte.

Bhambra, G. (2011) *Rethinking Modernity: Postcolonialism and the Sociological Imagination*. London and New York: Palgrave Macmillan.

Bhambra, G. (2014) *Connected Sociologies*. London: Bloomsbury.

Bhambra, G. and Narayan, J. (2016) *European Cosmopolitanism: Colonial Histories and Postcolonial Societies*. London: Routledge.

Blanchard, P., Lemaire, S. and Bancel, N. (eds) (2008) *Culture coloniale en France: De la Révolution française à nos jours*. Paris: CNRS Éditions.

Blyth, M. (2013a) *Austerity: The History of a Dangerous Idea*. Oxford: Oxford University Press.

Blyth, M. (2013b) 'Austerity as Ideology: A Reply to My Critics', *Comparative European Politics*, 11 (6), pp. 737–51.

Boatcă, M. (ed.) (2012) *Decolonizing European Sociology: Transdisciplinary Approaches*. Farnham, Surrey: Ashgate.

Boatcă, M. (2015) *Global Inequalities Beyond Occidentalism*. Farnham, Surrey: Ashgate.

Bourdieu, P. and Accardo, A. (1993) *La misère du monde*. Paris: Editions de Seuil.

Bramall, R. (2013) *The Cultural Politics of Austerity: Past and Present in Austere Times*. London: Palgrave Macmillan.

Broberg, G. and Roll-Hansen, N. (2005) *Eugenics and the Welfare State: Sterilization Policy in Denmark, Sweden, Norway, and Finland*. Ann Arbor: University of Michigan Press.

Candieas, M. (2008) 'Genealogie des Prekariats'. In: Altehhain, C. (ed.), *Von 'Neuer Untersicht' und Prekariat: Gesellschaftliche Verhältnisse und Kategorien im Umbruch*. Bielefeld: Transcript Verlag.

Conrad, S. (2014) *Globalisation and the Nation in Imperial Germany*. Cambridge: Cambridge University Press.

Farnsworth, K. and Irving, Z. (2015) *Social Policy in Times of Austerity: Global Crisis and the New Politics of Welfare*. Bristol: Policy Press.

Granqvist, R. (2001) ' "Virvlande svarta lemmar" och "goda svenskar" i Kongo i hundra år: om svensk rasism i vardande'. In: McEachrane, M. and Faye, L. (eds), *Sverige och de Andra*. Stockholm: Natur och kultur.

Hansen, P. (2009) 'Post-National Europe – Without Cosmopolitan Guarantees', *Race and Class*, 50 (4), pp. 20–37.

Hansen, P. and Jonsson, S. (2014) *Eurafrica: The Untold History of European Integration*. London: Bloomsbury.

IMF (2012) World Economic and Financial Surveys. World Economic Outlook, 'Coping with High Debt and Sluggish Growth'. International Monetary Fund, October 2012. Available at: www.imf.org/external/pubs/ft/weo/2012/02/ [accessed 7 March 2016].

Jabko, N. (2013) 'The Political Appeal of Austerity', *Comparative European Politics*, 11 (6), pp. 705–12.

Jensen, L. (2012) *Danmark: Rigsfællesskab, tropekolonier og den postkoloniale arv*. Copenhagen: Hans Reitzels forlag.

Jonsson, S. (2009) 'The First Man: On the North, Literature and Colonialism', *Eurozine*, 1 July. Available at: www.eurozine.com/articles/2009-07-01-jonsson-en.html [accessed 20 March 2016].

Krugman, P. (2015) 'The austerity delusion: The case for cuts was a lie. Why does Britain still believe it?', *Guardian*, 29 April. Available at: www.theguardian.com/business/ng-interactive/2015/apr/29/the-austerity-delusion [accessed 8 March 2016].

Kuttner, R. (2013) *Debtor's Prison: The Politics of Austerity versus Possibility*. New York: Knopf.

Lacan, J. (1966/1997) *Écrits: A Selection*. Trans. A. Sheridan. London: Routledge.

Loftsdóttir, K. and Jensen, L. (eds) (2012) *Whiteness and Postcolonialism in the Nordic Region: Exceptionalism, Migrant Others and National Identities*. Farnham, Surrey: Ashgate.

Lombardi-Diop, C. and Romeo, C. (eds) (2012) *Postcolonial Italy: Challenging National Homogeneity*. Berkeley and Los Angeles: University of California Press.

Lutz, H. and Gawarecki, K. (eds) (2005) *Kolonialismus und Erinnerungskultur. Die Kolonialvergangenheit im kollektiven Gedächtnis der deutschen und niederländischen Einwanderungsgesellschaft*. Waxmann Verlag: Münster.

Madrick, J. (2012) 'The Austerity Myth', *Harper's Magazine*, October. Available at: http://harpers.org/archive/2012/10/the-anti-economist/ [accessed 8 March 2016].

Means, A.J. (2013) *Schooling in the Age of Austerity: Urban Education and the Struggle for Deocratic Life*. New York: Palgrave Macmillan.

Nicolaidïs, K., Sebe, B. and Maas, G. (eds) (2015) *Echoes of Empire: Memory, Identity and Colonial Legacies*. London: I.B. Tauris.

Nietzsche, F. (1874) *Unzeitgemässe Betrachtungen. Zweites Stück: Vom Nutzen und Nachtheil der Historie für das Leben*. Leipzig: E.W. Fritzsch.

Nilsson, D. (2013) *Sweden–Norway at the Berlin Conference 1884–85: History, National Identity-making and Sweden's Relations with Africa*, Current African Issues 53, Nordic Africa Institute.

Oostindie, Gert. (2011). *Postcolonial Netherlands: Sixty-five Years of Forgetting, Commemorating, Silencing*. Amsterdam: Amsterdam University Press.

Peck, J. (2013) 'Austere Reason and the Eschatology of Neoliberalism's End Times', *Comparative European Politics*, 11 (6), pp. 713–21.

Ponzanesi, S. and Colpani, G. (eds) (2015) *Postcolonial Transitions in Europe: Contexts, Practices and Politics*. London: Rowman and Littlefield.

Purtschert, P. and Fischer-Tiné, H. (eds) (2015) *Colonial Switzerland: Rethinking Colonialism from the Margins*. New York: Palgrave Macmillan.

Purtschert, P., Lüthi, B. and Falk, F. (eds) (2012) *Postkoloniale Schweiz: Formen und Folgen eines Kolonialismus ohne Kolonien*. Bielefeld: Transcript Verlag.

Rothberg, M. (2009) *Multidirectional Memory: Remembering the Holocaust in the Age of Decolonization*. Stanford: Stanford University Press.

Said, E. (1993) *Culture and Imperialism*. New York: Alfred A. Knopf.

Schafer, A. and Streeck, W. (2013) *Politics in the Age of Austerity*. London: Polity Press.

Schierup, C.-U., Munck, R., Likić-Brborić, B. and Neergaard, A. (eds) (2015) *Migration, Precarity, and Global Governance: Challenges and Opportunities for Labour*. Oxford: Oxford University Press.

Seymour, R. (2014) *Against Austerity: How We Can Fix the Crisis They Made*. London: Pluto Press.

Sommers, J. and Woolfson, C. (2014) *The Contradictions of Austerity: The Socio-Economic Costs of the Neoliberal Baltic Model*. London: Routledge.

Southwood, I. (2011) *Non-Stop Inertia*. Washington: Zero Books.

Standing, G. (2011) *The Precariat: The New Dangerous Class.* London: Bloomsbury Academic.

Streeck, W. (2013) 'Will Expansion Work? On Mark Blyth, Austerity: The History of a Dangerous Idea', *Comparative European Politics*, 11 (6), pp. 722–8.

Thompson, H. (2013) 'Austerity as Ideology: The Bait and Switch of the Banking Crisis', *Comparative European Politics*, 11 (6), pp. 729–36.

Veyne, P. (1988) *Did the Greeks Believe in Their Myths? An Essay on the Constitutive Imagination*. Trans. P. Wissing. Chicago: University of Chicago Press.

Wilson, V. (2015) *Commerce in Disguise: War and Trade in the Caribbean Free Port of Gustavia, 1793–1815*. Åbo: Åbo Akademi University Press.

Zimmerer, J. (ed.) (2013) *Kein Platz an der Sonne: Erinnerungsorte der deutschen Kolonialgeschichte*. Frankfurt am Main: Campus Verlag.

Part I

Cases

2 'Our island story'

The dangerous politics of belonging in austere times

Gurminder K. Bhambra

The politics of austerity being played out across Europe in the early decades of the twenty-first century is accompanied by populist and far-right rhetoric scapegoating migrants and minorities (especially in Northern Europe and former communist states).[1] In the context of financial collapse and economic recession since 2008, questions of belonging are once again becoming increasingly pertinent to political debate. One of the common features of this debate is the presentation of the history of European states – and Europe more generally – as culturally and ethnically pure, or culturally homogeneous, only to be disrupted by the subsequent arrival of a diversity of peoples from elsewhere. In this chapter, I use the example of the United Kingdom to examine attempts to purify national history. I will call into question the very idea of autonomous national histories existing separately and separated from their locations within broader complexes of empire and colonialism. I then address contemporary political discussions on belonging, citizenship and rights to suggest that basing political arguments for citizenship and rights in exclusionary histories of belonging and citizenship is, at best, politically naive and, at worst, a precursor to authoritarian populism.

I

The politics of austerity, since 2008, has been marked by a growing mobilization of authoritarian and far-right political activity across Europe, both on the streets and at the ballot box. Together with the aftermath of 9/11, it has led to a general rightward shift – Syriza and Podemos notwithstanding – both in the formation of new parties of the right and within many of the mainstream parties in European Union countries. Speeches by the German Chancellor Angela Merkel, the British Prime Minister David Cameron, and the then President of France Nicolas Sarkozy, for example, have publicly disavowed the project of multiculturalism in their own countries and, by implication, in Europe more generally. Angela Merkel, in 2010, declared the death of multiculturalism in Germany (see Connolly, 2010). She argued that it had always been an illusion to think that the 'guest-workers' invited to Germany during the labour shortages of the 1960s would simply do the required work and then leave; the reality was that they had stayed, or rather, she implied, they had overstayed. While initially, Merkel suggested, there had been a belief that Germans and foreign workers could 'live happily side by side', this has not happened. Her conclusion was that multiculturalism, as a concept and a practice, had 'failed, and failed utterly' in Germany.

David Cameron followed Merkel's lead by declaring, in 2011, that the doctrine of what he called 'state-multiculturalism' had failed. He argued that the idea that different cultural groups could simply live separately alongside each other had allowed Islamic extremism to flourish and that what was now needed was a new 'muscular liberalism' and a greater advocacy of 'liberal values' (Cameron, 2011), or what he has later 'nationalized' as 'British values'. Nicolas Sarkozy, for his part, argued along similar lines that multiculturalism, understood as the practice of diverse communities living side by side, had been 'a failure' and that for too long, 'in all our democracies we have been too preoccupied with the identity of those who arrived and not enough with the identity of the country that welcomed them' (cited in Hollinger, 2011). The association of multiculturalism with post-war migration to Europe has entrenched a very particular understanding of it within public discourse.

Multiculturalism, and the presence of minorities more generally, was put forward in these speeches as something that happened *to* Europe and against the wishes of wider European populations, possibly at the instigation of political elites, but now repudiated by their latest incarnations. More importantly, there was no acknowledgement of the long-standing histories of connections between populations, the earlier migratory patterns of Europeans as part of colonialism and empire, or that many migrants came not as migrants, but as citizens, or at least subjects, of the broader polities within which they were based – namely empires. The British Nationality Act of 1948, for example, gave all Commonwealth citizens (those who had previously been subjects of the Empire) the right to migrate to the UK and to all social, economic, and political rights in the UK. While this had not necessarily been the intention of the Act, according to Hansen (2000), it nonetheless formalized what had been past customary practice, that is, the free movement of subjects of the British Empire throughout its domain. Similarly, in France, the movement of people from Algeria to the French mainland was not understood to be problematic given that Algeria was seen to be 'an integral part of France' (Hansen, 2003: 27).

Within the UK, the erasure of these *connected histories* was formalized in proposals put forward by the then Minister of Education, Michael Gove, when he launched a review of the National Curriculum for primary and secondary education in England in 2011. This review covered most subjects within the curriculum, including a consideration both of the way in which the subject of history was taught and what the content of the history curriculum ought to be. The first draft of the proposed programme of study for history was published by the Department of Education (2013) in early February 2013 to general disquiet from primary and secondary school teachers (see Riley, 2013), academic historians (see Husbands, 2013, Sheldon, 2013, Priestland *et al.*, 2013), the Historical Association (2013), as well as scholars involved with initiatives such as the Black and Asian Studies Association (see Gregory, 2013). The only prominent voice in favour of the proposals was celebrity historian Niall Ferguson (2013), who, writing in the *Guardian*, called the draft 'a major improvement' on the current curriculum.

One issue that many commentators picked up on in the proposed changes was the reduction of history to a version of the *Our Island Story* narrative: a history book for children written by Henrietta Marshall (2005 [1905]) in 1905, where British history was understood only in terms of the events that took place within the territorial bounds of the nation. What *Our Island Story* misses, however, is that, in the first instance, the UK consists of *two* islands and that second, at the height of the British Empire in the early twentieth century, the UK governed over at least one quarter of the Earth's land territory and over one-fifth of its total population. As Alexander *et al.* argue in their discussion of the proposed changes to the national curriculum, ' "Our Island Story" is necessarily a globalized one, and has always been' (2012: 8). The idea that this broader context is irrelevant is to present a parochial, distorted vision of our collective past. How we represent the past is central to the politics of the present. It should be no surprise, then, that with the promotion of such a narrow and exclusive history came narrow-minded policies in its wake.

In summer 2013, the UK government launched its 'returns' pilot policy as part of its broader agenda for immigration reform that included 'creating a hostile environment for irregular immigrants' (Home Affairs Committee, 2013). The 'returns' pilot was ostensibly aimed at making it easier for those who were in the country 'illegally' to 'go home'. For some commentators, however, it seemed to be more about reclaiming votes that the Conservative leadership believed had been lost to the UK Independence Party in recent elections as a consequence of their stance on immigration (see Syal, 2013).[2] The pilot involved two vans with the slogans 'In the UK illegally?' 'Go home or face arrest' and a phone number for people to call for advice about repatriation. These vans were driven around areas of London with settled immigrant populations (although not around the areas largely inhabited by Australian, New Zealand and US immigrants who often overstay their visas) and the language options when calling the telephone 'helpline' were Hindi, Punjabi and Urdu, hardly a comprehensive selection of the languages of immigrants in London. This was accompanied by a number of raids by the UK Border Agency at underground stations seeking to ascertain the citizenship status of commuters. From eyewitness reports, the majority of people stopped were black and ethnic minority commuters, raising concerns of racial profiling by the border police (see Wright and Withnall, 2013). The slogan 'Go home' – the language of racist abuse in the 1960s and 1970s – has also been used on posters in asylum reporting centres in Glasgow (Adams, 2013).

While these specific measures can be seen to be related to the rise in public support for the UK Independence Party, the general scapegoating of 'multicultural migrants' as responsible for exacerbating the effects of austerity upon 'native' populations is not new. Indeed, such scapegoating goes at least as far back as Enoch Powell's infamous 'rivers of blood' speech in 1968. Within the current period of austerity, however, the following statement was made by

Liberal Democrat candidate Jackie Pearcey, standing in Bolton West in the run-up to the general election in Britain in 2010: 'We're in danger of a lost generation – parents and grandparents worry about a future where their children can't repay student loans, can't find a decent job and don't have a sniff of a chance at getting on the housing ladder. Their concern about the knock-on effects of immigration is genuine and it isn't racist' (cited in Jack, 2010).

What is significant here is the association of immigration with specific concerns such as their children's education, finding a job and getting on the housing ladder. The suggestion, albeit implicitly, is that immigration is the *cause* of these problems and that the effects of these problems upon migrants or minorities themselves is of no concern. What is not addressed in this narrative is that it was a British government that brought in tuition fees and undercut access to higher education; it was a British government that undermined the unions and deregulated the labour market; and it was a British government that sold off council houses, didn't build any more and thus allowed the pool of social housing to contract. All of this in response to an electoral politics of the majority population – who voted for these measures – now mobilized to undermine the claims to equality and inclusion made by migrants and minorities.

Both the recent Coalition and the Conservative governments, together with the Labour opposition, have mobilized arguments for denying benefits to migrants in order also to cut spending on (non-immigrant) UK citizens. The proposals made by David Cameron as part of the UK's negotiations prior to its referendum to leave or remain in the EU have placed a residency limit on EU 'migrants' before they can access in-work benefits. As such, it breaches EU principles of solidarity and workers' rights and represents the basis for other countries making similar arguments. In addition, it creates a welfare discourse of 'earning' benefits which is used to limit benefits for national citizens, especially young people yet to enter the labour market (Buchanan, 2015). The attacks on multiculturalism are also used to sow division among, usually poorer, citizens, which then leads to a worsening of conditions for all citizens. So, whereas a multicultural society had initially been blamed for the deteriorating conditions of 'native' citizens, the wish to deny benefits to 'migrant' citizens is now being used to worsen the conditions of all citizens – 'native' and 'migrant'. In this way, the attacks on our multicultural present can be seen to be the thin end of the wedge that will also ultimately undermine the cosmopolitan liberal order that is otherwise celebrated.[3] Such mobilization is occurring not only by politicians, however; key British intellectuals are also promoting this line.

In comment pieces for the *Guardian* and BBC Radio 4's *A Point of View*, for example, Roger Scruton (2013a, 2013b) has addressed issues of democracy, political freedom and national identity. He has questioned whether democracy isn't, after all, over-rated and criticized the abstractions of human rights foisted upon us against the common-law freedoms of England. For him, these abstractions represent a loss of national sovereignty which, apparently, we can now begin to see when 'wave after wave of immigrants seek the benefit of our hard-won assets and freedoms' (2013b). It is clear from his wider discussion that these immigrants are not included in the 'we' of the political community under discussion. Despite their apparent appreciation of *common* freedoms, their traditions are represented as different and as a threat. Equally significantly, he fails to address the origins of 'our collective assets'. In representing the political community as an 'island home', he neglects the broader histories of British capitalism and its colonial and imperial past when 'our assets' were once the (potential) assets of others. Scruton cites Edmund Burke's appreciation of the 'small platoons' that make up society, but neglects entirely the latter's critique of the gunboats of international commerce and empire. For Burke (2009 [1791]), the problem of abstractions was not restricted to 'human rights', but also included the 'market' and 'empire'. It was pursuit of market and empire that would, for him, corrupt the nation. In failing to address the constitution of national assets by the coerced imposition of markets and the plunder of empire, Scruton seeks an idealized England (he elides Britain and England, precisely because the United Kingdom is bound to that imperial history).

II

There is, of course, a need for any political community to express itself collectively as a 'we'. How that 'we' gets defined, however, is central to the politics undertaken in its name. The boundaries of the political community and the rights of citizenship are usually imagined to be congruent with the territorial boundaries of the state as understood in national terms. The idea of the political community as a *national* political order has been central to European self-understanding. Yet most European states were imperial states as much as they were national states – and often prior to or alongside becoming national states – and so the political community of the state was much wider and more stratified than is usually now acknowledged. The standard histories of the British nation-state, for example, usually starts with the Act of Union in 1707 – which brought together the kingdoms of England and Scotland – and its political development is predominantly seen in terms of events and processes that took place within the territorial bounds of the new nation. However, both England and Scotland had acquired colonies prior to union, and continued their colonial conquests after union, and so they were already imperial states prior to becoming a conjoined nation-state – and alongside this process (Colley, 1992, 2002). Refusing to take into account this broader history has many implications, including misidentifying the emergence of the multicultural state as a post-1960s phenomenon rather than seeing empire itself as the beginnings of multiculturalism. As Adam Elliott-Cooper (2015) asks: 'When did we come to Britain? You must be mistaken, Britain came to us.'

Where empire is discussed, it is often presented in benign form – for example, as *Pax Britannica* or in terms of how Britain 'made the modern world' – as the popular histories recently published by commentators such as Niall Ferguson (2003) and Jeremy Paxman (2011) illustrate. *Pax Britannica* refers to the period of the long nineteenth century, which is simultaneously regarded by historians as a period of peace *and* as the period when the British Empire became globally hegemonic. Given that the construction of empire is rarely a peaceable project, to present it as such is to present 'empire' as a quasi-natural phenomenon with little discussion of how it came into being, what measures were necessary for its maintenance, and the consequences of its eventual dismantling through the decolonizing efforts of those who had been colonized. As Richard Drayton argues, 'post-colonial Imperial and world history is still written mainly for the pleasure of the reading classes of past and present imperial powers' (2011: 680). As such, the violence through which empire was constituted and maintained is elided to other concerns such as 'values' and 'progress'. Indeed, Drayton (2011) suggests that, apart from the exceptional work of scholars such as David Anderson (2005) and Caroline Elkins (2005), few British historians of empire have addressed violence as a constitutive aspect of it. Further, and as mentioned, the impact of empire is generally seen in terms of how Britain 'made the world', and there is relatively little focus on the impact of empire on Britain itself. In the following section, I focus on Paxman's *Empire* as illustrative of particular *ideas* of empire and how these feed into public understandings of what it is to be British today. Part of the reason for focusing on Paxman's book is his stated wish to understand the impact of empire on Britain.

Paxman starts his book with the statement, 'We think we know what the British Empire did to the world' and then asks a follow-up question, which is presented as the motivating question of the book, 'But what did it do to us?' (2011: 3). He goes on to suggest that while most 'thoughtful' Indians would acknowledge the shaping influence of the Empire on contemporary India, there has been little serious analysis of its corresponding effect on Britain. 'Can we seriously pretend', he asks, 'that a project which dominated the way that Britain regarded the world for so many hundreds of years has had no lasting influence on the colonizers, too? Without understanding how we looked at the rest of the world,' he continues, 'we cannot really understand ourselves' (2011: 3). He ends this paragraph by stating that, 'In a strange way, the one place which has yet properly to decolonize itself is Britain' (2011: 3). While Paxman claims, then, to address the consequences of Britain's imperial endeavours on Britain itself, I suggest that these consequences are nonetheless significantly neglected aspects of his story. Indeed, the narrative arc is predicated on a rather standard story of empire told in terms of episodes and anecdotes with little by way of either a systematic historical accounting for empire or a discussion of the consequences of empire for Britain. That is, to put it more plainly, an empire that in the late nineteenth century covered one-fifth of 'the habitable globe' and governed over one in every five people on the planet is not an outcome of how one *regards* the world or how one may *look* at it. It is a consequence of military endeavour, of the dispossession of native inhabitants, of the appropriation of land, of the exploitation of resources, of the enslavement of Africans and Indians, of theft, genocide, colonialism and imperialism … themes which are oddly absent from a book titled *Empire*.

Paxman's account is one in which Britain acquires empire in a fit of absent-mindedness and then, manfully, shoulders the burden of leading the world out of a period of tutelage to full adulthood. He details a number of episodes within British imperial history – usually occurring on territories beyond the island – but does not add together the implications and consequences of these episodes to present an argument for how empire had an impact upon Britain. The lack of an explicit grand narrative, I suggest, is part of the process of evading the very imperialism upon which and through which empire was built. However, discussing empires without any mention of imperialism is part of a long tradition within Anglo-American scholarship, as Jeanne Morefield (2014) has pointed out in her book, *Empires without Imperialism*. Such narratives are, she suggests,

> rife with not merely claims about the *good* intentions of imperialists, but with stories that stress a profound *lack* of imperial intention on the part of states and individuals, as though somehow much of the world's population ended up under British control … by accident.
>
> (2014: 24)

This is certainly the narrative that Paxman presents – of empire-builders as missionaries, whose heart was in the right place and who were committed to the highest of ideals and who, even when they did wrong, were doing it for the rightest of ideas – democracy, liberty, development and free trade. At one point in the book, for example, Paxman recounts the 'genuine affection for Africa and Africans' that he believes was discernible among many of the missionaries (colonists?) who went to those countries. 'Often', he writes, 'this concern for indigenous peoples expressed itself in a conviction that Africans were "childlike". The term is repugnant to modern ears', he continues, 'but it was not intentionally malicious, for many of the missionaries saw their role as protecting indigenous people' (2011: 126). Protecting them from what? Or whom? Perhaps from those very people who arrived in their lands? As Paxman notes later in the book, but unconnected to this statement about their protection, 'We have simply no idea how many indigenous peoples in the British Empire were killed either directly or indirectly by the settlers arriving from Britain to make real [their] dreams and schemes' (2011: 164). In world visions, such as Paxman's, 'the imperial state', as Morefield argues, 'is compelled to act imperially to save the world from illiberalism, and yet is never responsible for having created the conditions that require it to [be] save[d] in the first place' (2014: 3).[4]

Similarly, on slavery – another constitutive aspect of the British Empire – Paxman starts by acknowledging that Britain's involvement in the enslavement and trade in human beings was responsible for much of its 'earlier' wealth and 'corrupted just about everything' (2011: 66) within Britain. But, instead of discussing the ways in which this 'corruption' might be understood and examining the impact of having enslaved and traded in other human beings upon British society and politics, Paxman instead deflects attention away from slavery to discussing abolition. Parliament, he suggests, 'was eventually jolted out of its complacency [towards slavery]' – complacency, note, not complicity – by the power of the abolitionist campaigns and this, he goes on to claim, is indicative of its 'innate commitment to decency' (2011: 67). The enslavement and trade in other human beings just happened, Parliament was wrong in being complacent about this happening, it was eventually forced to recognize this wrong, and its recognition of this wrong is indicative of its inherent goodness. Indeed, as Paxman writes, 'The abolition of slavery could attest to an idea of the British as champions of freedom' (2011: 68).

No comment on the fact that the slave trade was itself instituted and supported for over two centuries by Parliament and British traders, or that the abolition of the trade in human beings from Africa was simply replaced by the trade in human beings from India in another form of unfree labour, that of indenture. Further, there is no discussion of the fact that abolition was more likely a consequence of the financial compensation to be paid to those who owned human beings, rather than any newly found morality consequent to the abolitionist campaigns. As Catherine Hall and Nick Draper have documented through their Legacies of British Slave Ownership project, the British government paid out £20 million in compensation – 'in relation to the size of the economy … [this] would be equivalent to around £65 billion' in 2007 (Draper, 2007: 79) – this money was paid to those people who owned other human beings as recompense for the loss of their property; for 'property' is how these human beings were defined. It is not clear where the moral compass is pointing when what is paid is compensation to those who enslaved other human beings, rather than, what would have been the decent thing to do, that is, paying reparations to those human beings (or their descendants) who had been enslaved.

The process by way of which Paxman addresses empire is to acknowledge its historical existence as an institutional form, but to evade all discussion of its substance and the meaning of the substance of empire (that is, imperialism) to understanding our present. While there is much to criticize in Paxman's *Empire*, I would argue that the errors are not his alone, but part of a more systematic accounting for empire through a forgetting of imperialism and a forgetting of those who were subject to its dictates. As Walter Rodney wrote in his book, *How Europe Underdeveloped Africa*, 'to be colonized is to be removed from history, except in the most passive sense' (1972: 246). Paxman presents 'empire' as the territory out there within which events occurred that could be understood as the history of the British Empire. Those events are rarely seen to have an impact either on the nation-state of Britain or the idea of Britain as 'innately decent'. But what is also erroneous in such a presentation is maintaining the distinction between empire and nation. As I suggested earlier, the failure to account for the systematic processes by way of which empire is produced, and empire and nation presented as separate entities, is not an individual error. It is the commonsense understanding that motivates more scholarly research, such as that by Fernand Braudel and Immanuel Wallerstein, as well.

The renowned historian Fernand Braudel, for example, in discussing the relations between Europe and the rest of the world, suggests that 'we still do not really know how this position of superiority was established and above all maintained' (1985: 533–4). Throughout his text, however, there are occasional references to the explanation of Europe's dominance resting in her involvement in the enslavement of Africans and the genocide of the indigenous populations of the Americas, the appropriation of natural resources from other parts of the world, the destruction of foreign markets to enable the better distribution of her own commodities, the exploitation of technological advances and discoveries made elsewhere, the subjugation of other peoples and so on. These references, however, are fragmentary and are not brought together as a systematic explanation. Instead, the dynamics of European history are regarded as explainable only in terms of internal forces and the rest of the world is simply the space into which European activities spill out.

To give another example: the world-systems theorist, Immanuel Wallerstein, in explaining the dominance of Europe, writes that 'the discovery of America was to give Europe a richer source of gold than the Sudan and especially a far richer source of silver than central Europe' (1974: 41; see also Quijano, 2000). There is little mention, however, of the processes of colonialism, dispossession or appropriation (or, more simply, theft) that enabled Europe to have access to those precious metals and to use them for her development alone and, in the process, create the conditions for the underdevelopment of others. To the extent that he does mention these processes, Wallerstein writes,

> the Europeans first seized Inca gold, then mined Potosi and Mexican silver.... They sent settlers to control the area of the Americas politically and to supervise the economic operations, and they imported labor as well. In short, they incorporated the Americas into their world-economy.
>
> (1980: 109)

This rather glosses over the violence and force necessary in seizing Inca gold, the coerced and enslaved labour required to mine the silver, the forced transportation of human beings from one part of the world to work for Europeans in another part of the world. While Wallerstein may at various points address the violence that was necessary for 'incorporation', that violence is never made central to or constitutive of the subsequent world system or the 'nation-states' that are seen to be its building blocks, as opposed, that is, to empires (for discussion, see Bhambra, 2014: 50–7).

III

Even when historians acknowledge that such narratives present history simply from the point of view of the winners, they often, as William McNeill does, then go on to suggest that we must nonetheless 'admire those who pioneered the enterprise and treat the human adventure on earth as an amazing success story, despite all the suffering entailed' (1990: 3). Questions of who this 'we' consists of, and whether 'we' must celebrate the successes (of some) despite the suffering (of others) entailed by a purportedly inclusive human adventure, forms the nub of postcolonial, and other, criticisms. Postcolonial and decolonial arguments have been explicit in their challenge to the insularity of historical narratives and historiographical traditions emanating from Europe, arguing instead for the necessity of taking into account the broader histories of colonialism, empire and enslavement. Drawing on such perspectives, I have argued for the need to rethink how we do sociology (and the social sciences more generally) through a new lens, that of 'connected sociologies' (Bhambra, 2014). It is inspired by the call, by historian Sanjay Subrahmanyam, for 'connected histories' (1997).

While knowledge can never be total, the selections we make have consequences for its ordering. That ordering is always open to challenge in the light of different selections and re-orderings. In standard accounts, the consequence of such challenges is often to argue for a plurality of positions and interpretations – that is, we can have many histories of the British Empire, for example. 'Connected sociologies', however, recognizes a plurality of possible interpretations and selections of historical accounts, not as a 'description', but as an opportunity for reconsidering what we previously thought we had known. So, to go back to the themes of this chapter, how can a different understanding of imperial connections and recognition of the forms of domination and appropriation those connections entailed help us to understand issues of citizenship and political community differently?

Empire, as I have argued, has rarely been deemed to be significant for understanding the history or contemporary society of the nation-state. For example, while the social and political community of the British Empire was a multicultural community historically, this understanding rarely enters contemporary political discourse where the boundaries of political community are imagined as congruent with the territorial boundaries of the state as understood in national terms. This has particular exclusionary consequences. The colonial and imperial state expressed a formal system of domination whereby the colonized were second-class subjects of the Empire. Political decisions were made at the centre, which affected the lives of people elsewhere, but there was no accountability to the people for these decisions. These others were also rarely allowed to engage with politics back at the centre. With decolonization, and the migration of the formerly colonized to Europe, the colonial system of domination has been translated domestically into one organized on racial and, latterly, religious grounds. It is one which has maintained the de facto second-class status of these citizens.

For example, one of the processes of post-war reconstructions of citizenship is to transform those who were once subjects of empire (albeit delimited in rights) to citizens of new states with no claims upon previous political authorities to which they had been subject and, in many cases, with problematic status in those new states. From being subjects with claims to a wider (imperial) polity, they became immigrants within the lands in which they had resided or refugees from them. Indian subjects of the British Empire residing in East Africa during the period of decolonization, for example, were effectively left stateless when Britain refused to allow them entry to the UK and instead argued for them to be classed as refugees – this despite the fact that the majority of them had gone to

East Africa as British subjects, holding British passports, to work for the British Empire in its variety of outposts (see Hansen and King, 2000). Similarly, British subjects in the West Indies who answered the call for workers and labourers in the post-war reconstruction of Britain were treated as immigrants and not as subject-citizens upon arrival in the UK. This, despite the fact that they came on the basis both of being invited and having the right to live and work in the UK (see Hansen, 2000).

The maintenance of a conceptual and political distinction between national citizens and subjects of empire is problematic and erroneous. The key issue at stake here is how the social and political community is defined historically and the impact this has on contemporary understandings of citizenship and who is included and excluded as a consequence.

What is striking is that if present historians and commentators have no current understanding of the continuity of empire and nation-state, this was not something that was lost on contemporaries of the Empire. For example, in 1884, Richard Temple, President of the Economic Science and Statistics section of the Royal Statistical Society, gave an address on 'The General Statistics of the British Empire'. In the course of a quite astonishing speech detailing a whole list of facts and figures relating to the British Empire, was this gem: 'there are in the empire about 100,000 square miles of forests which are being formally and professionally preserved, to become a mighty source of national wealth' (1884: 470). This was followed by a statement on 'the annual revenue and receipts collected in the British empire for the general government or administration' of the state, which amounted to £203 million sterling of which £89 million pertains to the UK, £74 million pertains to India and £40 million to other colonies and dependencies. That is, over half of the annual revenue of the British national government came from the labour and resources of those within its empire beyond the national state (there was an additional tax levied on imperial populations for local purposes) (1884: 472). The population of the Empire was stated as being '305, to perhaps 315, millions of souls' (1884: 482) who were all regarded as British subjects. By adding together earnings and other sources of wealth from across the populations of the Empire, that is from British subjects and those subject to British rule, Temple was able confidently to state 'that this empire is the richest State on the face of the earth' (1884: 477).

Could there be a clearer statement that the British Empire and the British state are one and that the populations of empire contributed significantly to the wealth that was then appropriated for 'national' ends? Obviously, Richard Temple is expressing his political arithmetic to an elite audience who would have understood that unity. Now, however, the situation is rather different. The complex historical processes that I have discussed, albeit briefly, are frequently neutralized in academic discourse and journalistic commentary.

IV

The failure to acknowledge the multicultural histories of colonialism and empire as pertinent to our understandings of the contemporary political state can have serious political repercussions as the debates on immigration, which disfigure most national elections, demonstrate. A recent documentary on Channel 4, *Britain's Racist Election*, examined the events in 1964 in Smethwick in the West Midlands. It was here that the infamous slogan 'if you want a coloured for your neighbour, vote Labour' was used to great effect to peel the working-class vote away from Labour. Of course, a different word to 'coloured' was used in the graffiti and the unofficial pamphlets of the Conservative Party. The general claim was about 'them' coming here and taking away 'our' jobs and 'our' homes. In a similar vein, the UK Independence Party today talks about 'them' paying into the system before 'they' can have access to 'our' benefits and so on. This distinction between 'them' and 'us' is only sustainable to the extent that we fail to acknowledge the histories that bring us together. The earlier claim that 'we are here because you were there' continues to be a necessary assertion in contemporary struggles for social and political equality.

The current wealth and prosperity of Britain is due in no small part to its imperial activities as expressed through enslavement, dispossession, extraction and the domination of populations, understood as British subjects, within empire. These earlier relations of formal domination are seen to be dissolved at the point of independence and decolonization. The arrival in Britain of those who were formerly subjects of empire is seen to be a problem by those already living in Britain. They are framed as immigrants without legitimate claim on the resources of the British state and, indeed, the state through its political representatives seeks to exclude them and to deny their claims to be treated as equals. While elections are about the negotiation of *present* conditions, they occur in the context of particular *historical* narratives of belonging. Immigrants, by definition, are excluded from the history of the state understood in national terms and thus from the history of belonging to the political community. In this way, contemporary narratives on migration (even sympathetic ones) which elide the historical connections of empire and seek to maintain a distinction between a national state and imperial colonies – and between citizens and immigrants – underpin and, however unwittingly, give false succour to anti-immigration and racist parties and policies.

Britain, properly understood, would be a country which understood that its historical constitution in colonialism cannot be rendered to the past by denial of that past. In a similar manner, it is necessary to recognize that the origins of the European Union are themselves to be found in its shared colonial past. As Hansen and Jonsson have demonstrated, the emergence of the European Economic Community in the post-war period was predicated on the very idea of 'bringing Africa as a "dowry" to Europe'; that is, Africa's natural resources – land, labour and markets – were seen to be available for the European project under colonial conditions (2011: 455). Not only were Europe's African colonies unquestioningly put at the service of the incipient European project, but there was a stronger statement 'that Europe's unification could succeed only if it also was fashioned as a joint colonization of Africa' (Hansen and Jonsson, 2013: 11). This shared history of exploitation and appropriation is part of the context in which Africans seek now to migrate to a Europe which threatens them with military action to prevent the movement of people rather than of capital.

While the speeches by European leaders discussed at the start of this chapter included rhetorical attacks upon migrants and minorities within their countries, the refugee 'crisis' in Europe has led to increasing attacks on such people and the centres and shelters set up to house them (Quine, 2016; Hill, 2016). Further, the scale of the current crisis has severely challenged European Union ideas of free internal movement as borders are beginning to be re-erected within the EU (Traynor, 2016). These borders operate as a zero-sum game to contain refugees in the countries where they first land with little practical realization of pledges to provide assistance to those countries. In this way, the European Union's claim to be a birthplace of universal human rights looks hollow in the face of its denial of those rights when sought by refugees and migrants.

If we want a different Europe in the present and the future, we need to narrate the colonial past of its constituent countries and the implications of the colonial past in the very project of Europe itself. We need to acknowledge the imperial past as the very condition of possibility of Europe and European countries today – with all the rights, duties and obligations to reparatory justice that that entails.

Notes

1 This chapter was written before the UK referendum on continued membership of the European Union which produced a vote to 'leave'. For further discussion of these themes in relation to 'Brexit', please see Bhambra 2016. Earlier versions or parts of this chapter have been presented at the Austere Histories of Europe Symposium, Linköping University, and at the Marshall Lecture at Southampton University at the invitation of Susan Halford. I would like to thank Susan and colleagues at Southampton for their constructive questions and comments. Thanks are also due to John Holmwood and Alice Mah for their comments.

2 There was no outright winner in the 2010 general election in the UK and so the Conservative Party formed the government by going into coalition with the Liberal Democrats.

3 As is increasingly apparent in the UK context, one of the pillars of cosmopolitanism – a commitment to human rights demonstrated through participation in the European Court of Human Rights and being signatory to the Human Rights Act – is being undermined by key members of the government (both the earlier Coalition government, 2010–15, and the Conservative government since 2015). The Justice Secretary, Chris Grayling, and the Home Secretary, Theresa May, have lobbied strongly for the UK to pull out of the Court and the Convention (see Bowcott, 2013) and the Prime Minister, David Cameron, in June 2015, refused to rule out leaving the European Convention on Human Rights (see Dathan, 2015). These moves are opposed, even by other Conservative MPs, such as Dominic Grieve, and senior figures from the party,

such as the former Justice Secretary Ken Clarke (see Bowcott, 2015). They suggest that this move would lead to the unravelling of fundamental liberties that are at the heart of the very idea of European, and British, civilization. Roger Scruton, however, concurs with May and Grayling, criticizing European courts for their lack of care for our 'unique social fabric'. He forgets, or refuses to address, how that social fabric has already been rent by inequality and poverty. One in four children currently live in relative poverty, and this is predicted to rise with the impact of austerity policies (Brewer *et al.*, 2011; Doward and Burke, 2013); over half a million people are reliant on emergency food parcels from charitable associations (Cooper, 2013); and a recent OECD (2015) report predicts levels of inequality to continue to rise as a consequence of austerity cuts, with the UK already one of the most unequal countries in the world.

4 For a more thorough accounting of Europe's relationship with Africa, see the recent book, *Eurafrica*, by Hansen and Jonsson (2014).

Bibliography

Adams, L. (2013) 'Outrage as UKBA tells asylum-seekers: let us help you go home', *Herald Scotland*, 30 August. Available at: www.heraldscotland.com/news/home-news/offensive-immigrant-campaign-under-fire.22009436 [accessed 1 July 2015].

Alexander, C., Chatterji, J. and Weekes-Bernard, D. (2012) *Making British Histories: Diversity and the National Curriculum.* Runnymede Perspectives. London: Runnymede.

Anderson, D. (2005) *Histories of the Hanged: The Dirty War in Kenya and the End of Empire.* London: Weidenfeld & Nicolson.

Bhambra, G.K. (2014) *Connected Sociologies.* London: Bloomsbury Academic.

Bhambra, G. K. (2016) 'Viewpoint: Brexit, Class and British 'National' Identity' Discover Society #34 July http://discoversociety.org/2016/07/05/viewpoint-brexit-class-and-british-national-identity. Accessed 1 August 2016

Bowcott, O. (2013) 'Conservatives divided over human rights legislation', *Guardian*, 3 March. Available at: www.theguardian.com/law/2013/mar/03/conservatives-human-rights [accessed 1 July 2015].

Bowcott, O. (2015) 'Tory plans will destroy human rights across Europe, warns Dominic Grieve', *Guardian*, 11 June. Available at: www.theguardian.com/law/2015/jun/11/tory-plans-human-rights-europe-strasbourg-dominic-grieve [accessed 8 July 2015].

Braudel, F. (1985) *The Perspective of the World. Civilization and Capitalism, 15th–18th Century: Volume 3.* Trans. S. Reynolds. London: Fontana Press.

Brewer, M., Browne, J. and Joyce, R. (2011) 'Child and Working-Age Poverty from 2010 to 2020', *Institute for Fiscal Studies.* Available at: www.ifs.org.uk/comms/comm121.pdf [accessed 1 July 2015].

Buchanan, M. (2015) 'EU migrant benefit plan "could hit thousands of young Britons"', *BBC News*, 11 August. Available at: www.bbc.co.uk/news/uk-33850247 [accessed 6 December 2015].

Burke, E. (2009 [1791]) *Reflections on the Revolution in France.* Oxford: Oxford University Press.

Cameron, D. (2011) 'PM's Speech at Munich Strategy Conference'. Available at: www.gov.uk/government/speeches/pms-speech-at-munich-security-conference [accessed 3 March 2014].

Colley, L. (1992) *Britons: Forging the Nation 1707–1837.* New Haven, CT: Yale University Press.

Colley, L. (2002) *Captives: Britain, Empire and the World 1600–1850.* New York: Pantheon Books.

Connolly, K. (2010). 'Angela Merkel declares death of German multiculturalism', *Guardian*, 17 October. Available at: www.theguardian.com/world/2010/oct/17/angela-merkel-germany-multiculturalism-failures [accessed 8 July 2015].

Cooper, N. (2013) 'Walking the breadline: tackling the scandal of food poverty in Britain', *Oxfam Policy and Practice blog*, 30 May. Available at: policy-practice.oxfam.org.uk/blog/2013/05/the-scandal-of-food-poverty-in-britain [accessed 1 July 2015].

Dathan, M. (2015) 'David Cameron refuses to rule out quitting the European Convention on Human Rights', *Independent*, 3 June. Available at: www.independent.co.uk/news/uk/politics/david-cameron-refuses-to-rule-out-quitting-the-european-convention-on-human-rights-10294385.html [accessed 8 July 2015].

Department of Education (2013) *The National Curriculum in England Framework document for consultation.* Available at: media.education.gov.uk/assets/files/pdf/n/national%20curriculum%20consultation%20-%20framework%20document.pdf [accessed 1 July 2015].

Doward, J. and Burke, T. (2013) 'Britain 2013: children of poor families are still left behind', *Guardian*, 24 August. Available at: www.theguardian.com/society/2013/aug/24/child-poverty-britain-40-years-failure [accessed 1 July 2015].

Draper, N. (2007) '"Possessing Slaves": Ownership, Compensation and Metropolitan Society in Britain at the time of Emancipation 1834–40', *History Workshop Journal*, 64 (Autumn), pp. 74–102.

Drayton, R. (2011) 'Where Does the World Historian Write From? Objectivity, Moral Conscience and the Past and Present of Imperialism', *Journal of Contemporary History*, 46 (3), pp. 671–85.

Elkins, C. (2005) *Imperial Reckoning: The Untold Story of Britain's Gulag in Kenya.* New York: Henry Holt.

Elliott-Cooper, A. (2015) 'When did we come to Britain? You must be mistaken, Britain came to us', *Verso Blogs*, 20 October. Available at: www.versobooks.com/blogs/2294-when-did-we-come-to-britain-you-must-be-mistaken-britain-came-to-us [accessed 6 December 2015].

Ferguson, N. (2003) *Empire: How Britain Made the Modern World.* London: Allen Lane.

Ferguson, N. (2013) 'On the teaching of history, Michael Gove is right', *Guardian*, 15 February. Available at: www.theguardian.com/commentisfree/2013/feb/15/history-teaching-curriculum-gove-right [accessed 1 July 2015].

Gregory, P. (2013) 'Black British History Must Feature throughout the School Curriculum', *The Black Presence in Britain*, 18 February. Available at: www.blackpresence.co.uk/black-british-history-must-feature-throughout-the-school-curriculum/ [accessed 1 July 2015].

Hansen, R. (2000) *Citizenship and Immigration in Post-War Britain.* Oxford: Oxford University Press.

Hansen, R. (2003) 'Migration to Europe since 1945: Its History and Its Lessons', *Political Quarterly*, 74 (1), pp. 25–38.

Hansen, P. and Jonsson, S. (2011) 'Bringing Africa as a "Dowry" to Europe', *Interventions*, 13 (3), pp. 443–63.

Hansen, P. and Jonsson, S. (2013) 'A Statue to Nasser? Eurafrica, the Colonial Roots of European Integration, and the 2012 Nobel Peace Prize', *Mediterranean Quarterly*, 24 (4), pp. 5–18.

Hansen, P. and Jonsson, S. (2014) *Eurafrica: The Untold History of European Integration and Colonialism.* London: Bloomsbury Academic.

Hansen, R. and King, D. (2000) 'Illiberalism and the New Politics of Asylum: Liberalism's Dark Side', *Political Quarterly*, 71 (4), pp. 396–403.

Hill, J. (2016) 'Migrant attacks reveal dark side of Germany', *BBC*, 22 February. Available at: www.bbc.co.uk/news/world-europe-35633318 [accessed 1 March 2016].

The Historical Association (2013) 'The New National Curriculum Draft'. Available at: www.history.org.uk/news/index.php?id=1714 [accessed 1 July 2015].

Hollinger, P. (2011) 'Sarkozy joins multiculturalism attack', *Financial Times*, 10 February. Available at: www.ft.com/cms/s/0/05baf22e-356c-11e0-aa6c-00144feabdc0.html#axzz3fTPR0tJT [accessed 10 July 2015].

Home Affairs Committee (House of Commons) (2013) 'The work of the UK Border Agency (January–March 2013), Eighth Report of Session 2013–14', 29 October. Available at: www.publications.parliament.uk/pa/cm201314/cmselect/cmhaff/616/616.pdf [accessed 1 July 2015].

Husbands, C. (2013) 'The end of History? Let's make sure it's not', Institute of Education London, Blog, 11 February. Available at: https://ioelondonblog.wordpress.com/2013/02/11/the-end-of-history-lets-make-sure-its-not/ [accessed 1 July 2015].

Jack, I. (2010) 'Battleground Bolton – "We're more real about life up here"', *Guardian*, 30 April. Available at: www.guardian.co.uk/politics/2010/apr/30/ian-jack-bolton-bigotgate-effect [accessed 4 April 2013].

McNeill, W.H. (1990) '*The Rise of the West* after Twenty-Five Years', *Journal of World History*, 1 (1), pp. 1–21.

Marshall, H. (2005 [1905]) *Our Island Story: A History of Britain for Boys and Girls from the Romans to Queen Victoria*. London: Civitas.

Morefield, J. (2014) *Empires without Imperialism: Anglo-American Decline and the Politics of Deflection*. New York: Oxford University Press.

OECD (2015) 'Income inequality data update and policies impacting income distribution: United Kingdom'. February. Available at: www.oecd.org/unitedkingdom/OECD-Income-Inequality-UK.pdf [accessed 1 July 2015].

Paxman, J. (2011) *Empire: What Ruling the World Did to the British*. London: Viking, Penguin Group.

Priestland, D., Reynolds, M., Wentworth, R., Parker, M., Baker, Y., Hamnett, C. and Byrne, N. (2013) 'Michael Gove's new curriculum: what the experts say', *Guardian*, 12 February. Available at: www.theguardian.com/commentisfree/2013/feb/12/round-table-draft-national-curriculum [accessed 1 July 2015].

Quijano, A. (2000) 'Coloniality of Power, Eurocentrism, and Latin America', *Nepantla: Views from South*, 1 (3), pp. 533–80.

Quine, O. (2016) 'Calais Jungle refugees targeted by armed far-right militia in brutal campaign of violence', *Independent*, 12 February. Available at: www.independent.co.uk/news/world/europe/calais-jungle-refugees-targeted-by-armed-far-right-militia-in-brutal-campaign-of-violence-a6870816.html [accessed 1 March 2016]

Riley, M. (2013) 'The unthinking history curriculum', Schools History Project, blog, 11 February. Available at: www.schoolshistoryproject.org.uk/blog/2013/02/the-unthinking-history-curriculum/ [accessed 1 July 2015].

Rodney, W. (1972) *How Europe Underdeveloped Africa*. London: Bogle-L'Ouverture Publication, and Dar-es-Salaam: Tanzania Publishing House.

Scruton, R. (2013a) 'Identity, family, marriage: our core conservative values have been betrayed', *Guardian*, 11 May. Available at: www.theguardian.com/commentisfree/2013/may/11/identity-family-marriage-conservative-values-betrayed [accessed 1 July 2015].

Scruton, R. (2013b) 'Of the People, By the People', *A Point of View*, BBC Radio 4, 11 August. Available at: www.bbc.co.uk/programmes/b037vb15 [accessed 1 July 2015].

Sheldon, N. (2013) 'Back to the past for the school history curriculum?', History and Policy, blog, 20 February. Available at: www.historyandpolicy.org/opinion-articles/articles/back-to-the-past-for-the-school-history-curriculum [accessed 1 July 2015].

Subrahmanyam, S. (1997) 'Connected Histories: Notes towards a Reconfiguration of Early Modern Eurasia', *Modern Asian Studies*, 31 (3), pp. 735–62.

Sveinsson, K. Páll (ed.) (2009) *Who Cares about the White Working Class?* Runnymede Perspectives. Available at: www.runnymedetrust.org/uploads/publications/pdfs/Who CaresAboutTheWhiteWorkingClass-2009.pdf [accessed 1 July 2015].

Syal, R. (2013) 'Anger at "Go home" message to illegal migrants', *Guardian*, 25 July. Available at: www.theguardian.com/uk-news/2013/jul/25/coalition-row-adverts-illegal-immigrants [accessed 8 July 2015].

Temple, R. (1884) ' "The General Statistics of the British Empire." The Address of the President of Section F, "Economic Science and Statistics," of the British Association at the Fifty-Fourth Meeting, held at Montreal, in August, 1884'. *Journal of the Statistical Society of London*, 47 (3), pp. 468–84.

Traynor, I. (2016) 'Is the Schengen dream of Europe without borders becoming a thing of the past?', *Guardian*, 5 January. Available at: www.theguardian.com/world/2016/jan/05/is-the-schengen-dream-of-europe-without-borders-becoming-a-thing-of-the-past [accessed 1 March 2016].

Wallerstein, I. (1974) *The Modern World-System I: Capitalist Agriculture and the Origins of the European World-Economy in the Sixteenth Century.* New York: Academic Press.

Wallerstein, I. (1980) *The Modern World-System II: Mercantilism and the Consolidation of the European World-Economy, 1600–1750.* New York: Academic Press.

Wright, O. and Withnall, A. (2013) 'Exclusive: Doreen Lawrence pledges to condemn "racial profiling" spot checks in the House of Lords', *Independent*, 2 August. Available at: www.independent.co.uk/news/uk/politics/exclusive-doreen-lawrence-pledges-to-condemn-racial-profiling-spot-checks-in-the-house-of-lords-8742754.html [accessed 1 July 2015].

3 The politics of colonial remembrance in France (1980–2012)

Nicolas Bancel and Pascal Blanchard

Competing memories

Museum practices are a good indicator of the crosscurrents of colonial memory in France, their conflictual dimensions as well as the importance of memory in the formation of a collective identity and in marking a political territory.[1] For decades after the end of the Algerian War in 1962, colonial history remained the forgotten continent of French history. For a nation that cultivates the myth of its grandeur and that regards teaching history to children as central to the transmission of this mythology, the collapse of the French Empire had no place in the 'national narrative'. Practically inexistent in textbooks until the late 1980s and confined as it was to a few specialists in the academic world, colonial history did not seem to represent a major issue.

But collective memories cannot be abolished by decree. Inevitably they resurface, and they do so from unexpected directions. At the origin of this memory trend, three social groups can be identified, all of them 'heirs to colonization' and all of which directly or laterally partook in the history of the Empire. The first group is constituted of the 800,000 French and European Algerians repatriated to France after the French defeat, the majority of whom live in the south of France. The second group consists of the immigrant workers from Algeria, but also from Morocco and Tunisia, and then those from former French Africa. Finally, there are the *Harkis* – the Muslim Algerians who served as Auxiliaries in the French army – who were repatriated to France or massacred in Algeria after March 1962. The potential conflict between these diverging memories, suppressed until the early 1990s, was soon to return to the surface, delineating the contours of a *guerre de memoires*, or a 'war of memories'. Until then, following the example of General de Gaulle's 'will to forget', the French government chose not to encourage initiatives that could put colonial history on the agenda of public debates.

Yet in the 1990s, a new process began that pushed colonial history to the centre of controversy. The process was the result of a new culture of commemoration that came in the wake of the French government's belated acknowledgment of its involvement in the deportation of the Jews of France during the Second World War. The pioneering research on the Shoah by Raoul Hilberg

(1961), published in France in the 1970s, Robert Paxton's book on Vichy France (1973), Serge Klarsfeld's (1978) efforts to keep alive the memory of the Jewish victims of Occupied France, and finally the opening in 1979 of the Institute of Present Day History (Institut d'histoire du temps présent, IHTP), devoted in part to France during the Second World War – all these worked together to break through the wall of apathy to the scale of what happened during the 'dark years' and of French compromises with Germany.

So a shift took place in the 1980s from commemorating those 'who died for France' to commemorating also and at the same time those 'who died because of France' (Barcellini, 2008).[2] This expansion of the historical narrative came with a multiplication of commemorations, tributes, inaugurations, projects and monuments preserving the memory of the Shoah and the deportation of the Jews of France.[3] It wasn't until 1995 and then-President Chirac's declaration on the participation of France in the deportation of the Jews, that the French government recognized its responsibility in these historic events, having placed the blame until then on the 'illegitimate Vichy regime' alone. Nonetheless the memory of the deportation and the growing body of historical knowledge documenting the participation of entire sectors of the administration and of civil society at large –greatly exceeding the 'small group of collaborators' designated until then – opened the door to a less binary understanding of this tragic period. This state of affairs is fundamental for the understanding of the context in which, between 1990 and 1995, the French public rediscovered the Algerian War and the torture committed at the time, and began questioning the colonial past and examining the history of slavery and its abolitions.

The new memorial spaces dedicated to preserving the memory of the deportation amplify this major shift of the post-war period (Gilzmer, 2009), thus heralding the memorial spaces commemorating the deportation of homosexuals and Romas (the one in Berlin on a European scale and the one in Saliers near Arles), but also focusing on the Armenian genocide of 1915–16 (in Lyon and Marseille[4]) or paying homage to the *Harkis* (museum project in Rivesaltes and ceremony in Perpignan in 2007), or commemorating the victims of the slave trade and the abolition of slavery (notably on the docks of Nantes with *Les Anneaux* – The Rings; in the 17th arrondissement of Paris with 'Les Fers' in tribute to General Dumas and in remembrance of slavery; or through the dedicated rooms in Nantes' historical museum Château des Ducs de Bretagne as well as the Musée d'Aquitaine in Bordeaux).

Whereas debates focused on the colonial period emerged as part of this great post-Communist memorial movement, dominated by tributes to the 'victims of history', museums still disregarded the colonial period, except – as we shall see in a moment – from a 'nostalgic' standpoint.

An official monument, as Serge Barcellini (2008) has observed, is at once a memorial tool for those who use it and a reflection of the ideological intentions of the institution that puts it up. When it comes to colonialism, the initial silence of public authorities gradually gave way to an uncritical (and sometimes even nostalgic) attitude. The issues around the colonial past are weighty. On the one hand, the heirs of this period are divided, as we have seen, and the views they hold are incompatible (although no group can be said to be internally homogeneous, of course). Whereas groups of repatriates tend to have a rosy, nostalgic view of the colonial period (in Algeria, in particular), immigrants from the colonial and postcolonial periods and their descendants have a much more critical view. All of the groups suffer from the lack of recognition of colonial history as an integral component of French history, for this alone can impart meaning to the narratives they carry.

Colonial memory has thus become a dividing line in French society, one that systematically, albeit unconsciously, raises the (loaded) question of *national identity* and, by collateral effect, of the presence of colonial and postcolonial immigrants.

To understand this situation, let us look at an article entitled '*Pieds-noirs*, a French wound' that appeared in the conservative weekly *Valeurs actuelles* in October 2009; it summarizes the symbolic stakes around the colonial past (Folch, 2009). The article criticizes Rachid Bouchareb's film *Outside the Law* (*Hors-la-loi*), sequel to his 2006 success *Days of Glory* (*Indigènes*), which it describes as a biased 'official version' of the Algerian War that refuses to show the 'truth' about the *pieds-noirs* and even 'demonizes' them. The logical conclusion of the film, according to the article, is that the 'victims' are not so much the colonized as the 'repatriates' (and *Harkis*). The president of the *pieds-noirs* organization Cercle algérianiste is quoted as saying: 'Twice we were victims: first when we became orphans of Algeria and then when we were not adopted by France' (Folch, 2009).

The article ends with a review of the state of affairs in the 'memory war'. On the one hand, there are several reasons for satisfaction: the bill adopted by the French Assembly in February 2005 encouraging textbooks to include the 'positive aspects' of colonialism (an act that was partially repealed, as we will see); the historian Jacques Marseille's demonstration that the colonies cost more than they profited France; the many books and films paying tribute to the 'true history' of colonialism;[5] as well as memorials erected in Southern France (notably the one in Perpignan to which the magazine elsewhere devoted two pages).

But in spite of these 'positive signs' there is an impending storm. Not only did the state finance 15 per cent of Rachid Bouchareb's film, but Nicolas Sarkozy all too quickly forgot his speech in Toulon in 2007, in which he praised the colonial enterprise and reasserted his refusal to 'repent', and maintained diplomatic ties with Bouteflika's Algeria.[6] In this newly mapped perspective, the role of 'victim' is reversed: speaking 'ill' of the past or speaking of repentance amounts to 'falsifying' history and betraying France.[7]

It is on this context that we will be focusing in this chapter in an attempt to highlight the issues revolving around colonial memory with which the country has been grappling over the past two decades (Coquery-Vidrovitch, 2009).

Conflictual socializations of colonial memories

Fifty years after the independence of sub-Saharan Africa (1960–2010), the multiplication of competing memory claims regarding the colonial period no doubt contributed to upending 'colonial aphasia' (Stoler, 2010). But at the same time the polemics on the subject stood in the way of building places of learning and institutionalizing commemorations for all – political signs that the colonial chapter would have been integrated into the 'national master narrative'. Instead distinct social groups bear distinct memories of the colonial period that have become mere instruments of recognition in the social arena, with each side sticking doggedly to its positions: on the one hand, projects aiming at 'rehabilitating' colonial history and the activities of France in the colonies are supported by groups of repatriates and, in a smaller proportion, of *Harkis*; on the other, projects seeking an acknowledgment of colonial violence and the contemporary consequences thereof are mainly driven by postcolonial diaspora minorities (as evidenced by the CRAN – Representative Council of Black Associations – and the Indigènes de la République). The way in which the controversy was instrumentalized – first during the 2002 presidential campaign, when Jean-Marie Le Pen made it into the second round, and then during the 2007 campaign, when the 'repentance' theme became ubiquitous – contributed to further entrenching the camps in their respective positions. This is a profoundly conflictual memorial configuration.

The conflictual political socialization of colonial history raises the question of the state insofar as it has played a capital role since the end of the nineteenth century in heritagizing history and overseeing commemorations. The institutionalization by the state of commemorations of Vichy, the deportation or the Resistance was a long, complex process,[8] which ultimately led to integrating these memories in the state's representation of national history. By giving wrongdoing and a hateful tragedy their due, the commemorations of the deportation and of Vichy contributed decisively to overturning the genetic functions of historical commemoration, hitherto based on celebrating our dead, the glorious chapters and 'founding moments' in the history of the nation. Such commemorations instilled doubt into what until then had been a linear narrative, bloody at times but always tending to the construction of the nation 'France'. This epistemological overturning made it possible to evoke, if not assimilate, these painful periods that were strongly present yet not discussed until the early 1980s (Rousso, 1990).

Memories of the colonial period (and of slavery) have not undergone the same processes of assimilation and integration into the systems of heritagization and commemoration. Quite the opposite. Elected representatives (the National Assembly and the Senate) and successive governments have demonstrated strong conservatism in this regard, instrumentalizing the colonial past for electoral and ideological purposes.[9] The notion of repentance also became an obstruction to this process of incorporation, first of all because 'anti-repentance' activism clouded any objective historical assessment. As historians Catherine Coquery-Vidrovitch, Gilles Manceron and Benjamin Stora rightfully observed in

Libération in 2007: 'The rejection of repentance serves to hamper the work of historians and provide unity to the Right' (Coquery-Vidrovitch *et al.*, 2007).

Indeed, maintaining the 'national greatness' narrative constitutes one of the main ideological constructs of the Right, in particular since the 'governmental Right' has worked to win over the constituency of the Far Right represented by the Front National (Perrineau, 2014). The bond between the various currents on the Right is founded on a defensive posture toward history 'aimed at negating a critical view of colonisation' (Coquery-Vidrovitch *et al.*, 2007). So much so that 'the simple fact of bringing up this reality becomes synonymous with a desire to denigrate France itself, which is posited as an indivisible whole' (ibid.). The political desire to build a unified, linear and positivist (not to say 'positive') view of French history is manifested by an attempt

> to smooth things over, leaving in the shadows all the complexity of events, all the power relations and social struggles that forged them, reducing thereby national identity to a matter of essence, when it is in fact a permanent construction,

writes Nicolas Offenstadt (Van Eeckhout, 2007). This consensus between the various Rightist currents on the colonial issue has its counterpart in their agreement on other issues, such as immigration, which is increasingly seen in the same terms by the 'governmental Right' and the Far Right (Bancel, 2011). It is clear that the nationalistic discourse rooted in a vision of the glorious past that expurgates the colonial episode is one of the concrete conditions for the unrestrained expression of xenophobia toward immigrants (especially postcolonial immigrants). After all, a frank examination of colonial racism could have reined in the reiteration of the kind of stereotypes and stigmatization that were developed to a great extent during the period of the French Empire. Such soul-searching could also have brought public attention to the ethnic discriminations that are widespread and largely ignored in France.

The built monuments and museum projects focusing on the colonial past have been marked by a nostalgic, if not downright pro-French Algeria perspective, sometimes even celebrating the OAS (Organisation de l'armée secrète; the Secret Army Organization). They are located for the most part in the south of France (from Nice to Marseille, from Toulon to Montpellier, from Aix-en-Provence to Béziers). Much the same can be said of the commemorations, although there are some local variations, depending on the municipality (as in 2009 in Paris,[10] Aubervilliers and Bobigny, for instance, concerning the commemorations of the Massacre of 17 October 1961, when the French police killed several hundred civilians during a peaceful demonstration of support for the National Liberation Front, FLN).

In the field of education, there has been considerable progress in the area over the past 15 years (see Lemaire, 2005; Lantheaume, 2003, 2007, 2009; Corbel and Falaize, 2003; Porte, 2006). And in fact education has become one of the major stakes in the debate on the colonial past. School programmes were at the heart of the act adopted in February 2005 and repealed after 11 months of recurrent debate.

In this context, Benoît Falaize and Laurence Corbel have defined the narrow framework within which this treatment of the colonial past would have to be lodged. As they argue, the colonial question is hard to digest in an educational institution that is confronted with it in two ways: first due to the students being taught there (heirs to this particular history) and second due to the years of near denial of a reality that, without being comparable in any way to the nature of the destruction of the Jews of Europe, nonetheless has decisive social repercussions in French society today (Corbel and Falaize, 2004: 43–55).

When it comes to bringing 'history to the general public' it is clear that the neo-conservative view is largely prevalent with prominent spokespeople in the media – for instance Paul-François Paoli, Max Gallo, Patrick Buisson, Daniel Lefeuvre, Marc Michel, Bernard Lugan, Pascal Bruckner, Guy Pervillé and Pierre Montagnon – and the ubiquitous presence of conservative views being aired on French stations specialized in history or on high-audience broadcasts on the main over-the-air channels (as opposed to programming on less popular stations such as Arte or France 5) (Veyrat-Masson, 2000, 2004).

A standoff between two camps

The militant struggle for recognition of the Massacre of 17 October 1961 and the struggle for recognition for the 'heroes' of the anti-slavery movements clearly indicate the longstanding suffering involved in the two issues. The fight for recognition of the October 1961 massacre was driven by the children of colonization, second and third generations of Maghrebian immigration. Not having achieved 'national recognition' through the 1983 Marche des Beurs movement (the first great movement of the second generation of Maghrebian immigration), they set out to achieve it for the crimes committed against their 'fathers'. The search for recognition for the heroes of the fight against slavery is constitutive of a 'black identity'. The first milestone in the development of this identity was the demonstrations in 1992 against the commemoration of the discovery of America. Then came the 23 May 1998 march that brought together numerous black organizations, followed by the Taubira Law of May 2001 and the formation of the CRAN in 2005.

These new social and political manifestations of a memory borne by the postcolonial wave of immigrants and their descendants sparked a strong reaction from those holding onto the memory of French Algeria or glorifying the 'civilizing mission' of colonialism. This backlash took the form of an increased hold on the memorial ground, through the media and commemorative spaces. This is the context in which the notion of 'repentant intellectuals' came to the fore. Between 2003 and 2005, conservative lobbying led to the passing of the February 2005 bill, to memory projects, special issues in magazines, websites and conferences.

At this point in time, the political epicentre of the struggle also shifted from the Front National (the party that traditionally glorified French colonialism) to the Republican and governing Right. The emergence of this unifying theme on the Right of the political spectrum (backed also by part of the 'Republican Left') was part of a return to identity-based nationalism. It was an active element in Nicolas Sarkozy's strategy to compete with the Front National on its own ground and thereby capture some of its constituency (a strategy that worked during the 2007 presidential election, when the Front National lost votes to Sarkozy's Union pour un Mouvement Populaire). Safeguarding 'the honour of France' with regard to the colonial past became one of the major themes of the Right, as unifying a theme as anti-Communism had been in the 1930s.

During the 2000s, the process of rehabilitating (or safeguarding) the past and colonial memory enjoyed widespread support from intellectuals in the media and writers. The weeklies *Le Point, Le Figaro magazine*[11] and *L'Express* all denounced the movement of repentance and praised colonial accomplishments. Similarly in September 2006 the magazine *Marianne* referred to the 'vices of repentance' and 'excessive victimization' and did not hesitate to praise outspoken 'anti-repentant' neo-conservative authors.[12]

In the wake of the 2001 publication of *Je ne demande pas pardon. La France n'est pas coupable* (*I don't ask for forgiveness. France is not guilty*) by Alain Griotteray, a conservative politician and advocate of the union between the Right and the Far Right, came a whole series of like-minded books and essays: Daniel Lefeuvre's *Pour en finir avec la repentance coloniale* (2006); Paul-François Paoli's *Nous ne sommes pas coupable. Assez de repentance!* (2006); Bernard Lugan's *Pour en finir avec la colonisation* (2006); Max Gallo's *Fier d'être Français* (2006); and Pascal Bruckner's *La Tyrannie de la pénitence. Essai sur le masochisme occidental* (2006). These books, which sold well, brought their authors much attention, in both print and broadcast media.

These publications followed on three decades of 'rehabilitationist' writings. There was, of course, Bernard Lugan, a specialist on South Africa whose work is informed by a racialist view of 'legitimate colonization'. But we can also cite Pierre Montagnon – a former member of the OAS and co-author with Daniel Lefeuvre and others of the special September 2009 issue of *Historia* bearing the revealing title *Colonisation. Pour en finir avec la repentance* – who wrote from the mid-1980s on over a dozen books on colonialism and Algeria. Then there were army officers like Maurice Schmitt or former militants like Roger Faulques, who acted as a bridge between a defence of the 'army's honour' and reactionary thinking. And one can hardly disregard the influential activist Dominique Venner, who as editor-in-chief of such journals as *Enquête sur l'histoire* (founded in 1991) and *La Nouvelle Revue d'histoire* (founded in 2002) brought together the whole spectrum of writers driven by nostalgia for colonial France. He was relayed in the meanders of the government and on the *Histoire* TV channel by Patrick Buisson, special advisor to then-president Nicolas Sarkozy. There were also writers like Pierre Pellissier, who was to become 'Monsieur Indochine' alongside Raymond Muelle. Thus we are dealing with a tendency with multiple branches and relays that, as historian Benjamin Stora observes in the communist newspaper *L'Humanité* (July 2005), became persuasive well beyond the confines of the Far Right: 'The survival of colonial memory has always been said to be anchored in the Far Right. This is true, but today it goes beyond this framework.'

Nostalgia for colonial Algeria

Bolstered by positions taken by the government for decades and supported by media intellectuals and some media outlets, many commemorative sites and monuments were put up in a spirit of nostalgia for the colonial period. So omnipresent are they in the south of France that Jean-Philippe Ould-Aoudia (2006) describes the region as a reduced model of French Algeria. The oldest, dating to 1965, is located in Aix-en-Provence and it is the site of official ceremonies organized every year by the municipal government (the 2007 ceremony was the occasion for Mayor Maryse Joissains Masini to denounce 'phoney historians', 'repentance' and 'anti-France' attitudes). Another was erected in 1973 in Nice by an organization of repatriates, with support from then-mayor Jacques Médecin (who became a member of Chirac's government in 1976), and is inscribed with a specific homage to Roger Degueldre, former leader of the OAS, sentenced to death in France and executed in 1962.

A new stage was reached in 1980 with the presence of local and national government representatives at the inauguration of such a monument in Toulon. This 'official' unveiling sparked protests in the National Assembly and within the government, but it nonetheless constitutes a pivotal moment that is worth examining more closely. Two metres in height and six in width, the monument shows a parachutist lying on the ground, his epaulettes torn off, and is inscribed with the words '*Pour une parole donnée*' (in reference to the promise made to keep Algeria French). It was destroyed in an attack on 8 June 1980, but unveiled nevertheless on 14 June 1980 in a ceremony held on the 150th anniversary of the arrival of French troops in Algeria (1830). Among the 2,000 people present were militants, but also prominent figures such as General Jouhau (honorary president of the Front National des Rapatriés), the State Secretary for Repatriates, Jacques Dominati, a Prefect of the Republic, plus elected representatives of the Right, such as Jean-Claude Gaudin (future mayor of Marseille), François Léotard (future Defence Minister under Jacques Chirac) and the deputy mayor of Toulon, who placed wreaths on the broken pieces of the monument. The rapprochement between the various currents of the Right on this issue marks the beginning of a tendency that was to develop over the next decade.

Twenty years later, the Toulon municipality once again manifested this spirit of nostalgia for French Algeria in naming an intersection after the army general and subsequently OAS-commander Raoul Salan. A few years later, in 2003, Hubert Falco, former minister and newly elected mayor of Toulon, transformed the name of the intersection subtly to 'Colonel Salan – Liberation of Toulon – August 1944'; but in May 2006 he authorized a surprising ceremony in a tribute to the 1830 'Algiers expedition'. A year later, in the same city, then presidential candidate Nicolas Sarkozy gave his speech praising the colonial enterprise. Few observers understood the solemn significance of this speech in this place, but the militant 'repatriates' and members of the National Front saw it as a veritable act of recognition for their struggle and for their loyalty to 'France's colonial undertaking', 45 years after the independences (1960–62). Sarkozy was making a call on National Front territory (the city had fallen into Front National hands in 1995 with the election of Jean-Marie Le Chevallier) during an electoral campaign, with the intent of winning over this constituency at the least cost and weakening the FN candidate in local and national elections.

Already by 1987, the movement had entered a new dynamic. The commemorative trend continued in Pérols in the Hérault with the unveiling of a monument in a local cemetery paying tribute to the executed of the OAS; the ceremony was held in the presence of André Santini, State Secretary for Repatriates, in a demonstration of approval from Chirac's government. Two years later, in the same region, a second monument was erected in Valras Plage, 'to the people of French Algeria executed by firing squad and to the *Harkis*'.

Then, after a lull of about 15 years (possibly resulting from debates on the Algerian War and the use of torture), the commemorative dynamic picked up again at the beginning of the twenty-first century.[13] In Théoule-sur-Mer in 2002, for the fortieth anniversary of 1962, an association of repatriates put up a replica, over ten metres high, of Notre-Dame-d'Afrique, with the inscription: 'To all our comrades who fell defending French Algeria.' The site has since become an annual pilgrimage place for those driven by nostalgia for French Algeria. At the same time, Perpignan became one of the main places of commemoration of the imperial past.

In 2003, a monument in memory of OAS combatants was unveiled in a Perpignan cemetery.[14] There was more and more talk at this time of building a Memorial of French Overseas Territories in Marseille and one specifically dedicated to Algeria in Montpellier. The following year, an official monument 'in memory of our servicemen and civilians who died overseas' was erected in the cemetery of Béziers. In 2005, a new monument was put up illegally in Marignane and was not removed until after a major campaign against it and official protests.

Throughout this period, the Algerian War was the subject of debate, as was France's colonial past (especially on the occasion of the fiftieth anniversary of the fall of French Indochina in 1954). Despite this context, veterans of the Algerian War did not succeed in setting a date for public commemoration: 19 March, proposed by the war veterans' organization FNACA (Fédération nationale des anciens combattents en Algérie, Maroc et Tunisie) was not accepted as an annual day of commemoration. Ultimately, the term 'war' to refer to the events in Algeria, was not recognized until 1999, and different currents commemorated it in different months: March, June, October or December. At the same time, veterans of sub-Saharan Africa and the *Harkis* made their entry into the debate on national memory (Bernard, 1998; Champeaux and Deroo, 2006), notably to achieve equality of pensions. Thus it seems that a specific memory, that of the repatriates, has a hold in the south of France, while what we are witnessing on the national level is silence and amnesia, or active conservatism or yet again a move to nostalgic commemorations.

The first truly Parisian (and national) monument of the postcolonial period – a sculpture of Lyautey inscribed with the words, 'For all those who died for France overseas' – dates to 1985. It is a discreet, understated and relatively unknown monument located behind the Invalides, but one that in circles cultivating nostalgia for the Imperial enterprise is regarded as a homage to the colonial past and as the nation's official recognition of this history. The monument to a colonial administrator – he was 'viceroy of Morocco' and one of the conquerors of Madagascar, an aristocrat seen at the time by the nationalist Right as anti-Republican – is lodged in a tradition of monuments to 'Empire builders' that was especially strong in the colonial period: the Duc d'Orléans in Alger in 1845, Bugeaud in 1852, Faidherbe in 1887 and 1896 in Lille, Garnier in 1891 and 1898 in Paris, Gallieni in 1923 and 1926 in Paris, Schoelcher in 1897 and 1904, Ferry in 1896 and 1911.

What is utterly remarkable is the way in which a tradition that seemed to have run its course after the independences resurfaced first with a plaque to French Algeria on the Arc de Triomphe in 1973 and then in Notre-Dame de Lorette in 1977 to continue with the statue of Lyautey in 1985 and a monument to Indochina in Fréjus in 1988.

These monuments are all still standing today and they remain the focus of official memorial ceremonies dedicated to one figure or another in the colonial pantheon (notably on the part of the Army, which keeps alive the memory of colonial campaigns). Finally, the 'Chirac period' was marked by a great deal of this kind of activity, notably with inauguration of the Mémorial national de la guerre d'Algérie et des combats du Maroc et de la Tunisie (National Memorial of the Algerian War and the Battles in Morocco and Tunisia) on Quai Branly in 2002.[15] This constitutes a pivotal moment because the memorial is lodged in a long tradition of French military monuments as then-president Jacques Chirac observed at the unveiling: 'Now the French soldiers who fought in North Africa, like their predecessors from 1914 and 1940, have finally been given the place that is theirs in the memory of our country.' The monument, which was originally Lionel Jospin's idea, commemorates the 'military' past while refusing to address the complexity of colonial conflicts and the colonial system itself.

This 2002 memorial, the 1985 monument and the Musée du Quai Branly inaugurated in 2006 together form a symbolic triangle – a triangle that remains a 'memory zone' for many French heirs to the colonial past who are hoping to see a full-blown colonial memorial that would take over from the Musée de la Porte Dorée (replaced in the early 1960s by the Musée des arts d'Afrique et d'Océanie and today housing the Musée national de l'historire de l'immigration, the National Museum of the History of Immigration). A *virtual memorial* of sorts has thereby come into being, fragmentary and spread out though it may be, as if to offer a subliminal response to those segments of the population that could decipher its signs.

There are not many counter-examples to such nostalgic memorials. A commemorative plaque was put up by the municipal government in 2001 in memory of the people killed in October 1961. In 2007, the 12th arrondissement town hall commemorated the 75th anniversary of the 1931 Exposition Colonial in the Bois de Vincennes with an exhibition of 60 'totems' critically tracing the history of an event that marked the apogee of French imperialism.

Thus we can see that the politics of commemoration tend to be informed more by nostalgia than by a critical remembrance of the past. The vast majority of monuments and places of remembrance provide glowing tributes to the colonial enterprise, sometimes to the point of glorifying gung-ho supporters of French Algeria and the 'martyrs of the OAS'. The more ambitious museum projects devoted to the subject find their underpinnings in this scattered but vast movement of building places of commemoration.

Memorials and monuments

Nicolas Sarkozy was the first to take an initially explicit and unambiguous stance on the colonial past, declaring on 7 February 2007 in an election campaign speech in Toulon:

> The European dream needs the Mediterranean dream. The horizons were narrowed when this dream was shattered – a dream that once sent knights from all of Europe on the roads of the Orient; a dream that drew so many emperors of the Saint Empire, so many kings of France, to the South; a dream shared by Bonaparte in Egypt, Napoleon III in Algeria, and Lyautey in Morocco. It was a dream not so much of conquest as of civilization. We must stop blackening the past. [...] We may disapprove of colonialism with our values of today, but we ought to respect the men and women of good-will who honestly believed their work was useful to achieving an ideal of civilization in which they believed. [...] To all the people of the Mediterranean who spend their time dwelling on the past and on old hatreds, I want to say that the time has come to look to the future. [...] France did not say to Germany: Expiate [your sins] first, and then we'll see [...]. The time has come not to forget but to forgive.
>
> (Sarkozy, 2007)[16]

Framed in this way, the debates animating French society for some years on the question of slavery (Vergès, 2006) and colonization (Bancel, Blanchard and Lemaire, 2015) are seen simply as ways of blaming the French and diminishing the vitality of the Nation.[17] This position was the culmination of a long series of developments that were mainly manifested in projects for memorials and museums dedicated to the colonial period.

There was no policy of addressing the colonial period in museums until the 2000s, when a series of projects were announced, from 2001 on, mainly informed by a nostalgic view of the period. These met with a triple difficulty: the controversy they triggered among professional historians; their geographical concentration in the south of France, where they gave rise to many questions concerning local circles of politics and civil society; and finally the ambivalent attitude of the government, busy assessing the political echo of controversies when the aim should initially be to answer a desire for consensus.

These local responses to the national debates, as manifested in museum projects, are worth analysing insofar as they reveal a political will to establish a certain memory of colonialism's 'civilizing mission'. A museum of the history of France in Algeria (1830–1962) was planned in Montpellier.[18] The project was led by Daniel Lefeuvre (historian of colonial Algeria and one of the spokesmen of the movement of repatriates against 'repentance') until his belated resignation as a result of the waves of protest from the scientific committee. The scientific committee was overhauled to comprise historians of indisputable authority, but the project was finally abandoned in 2014, testifying to the political sensitivity of such an enterprise. Another site dedicated to the Algerian War and the 'events' of decolonization in Morocco and Tunisia was planned in Montredon-Labessonnié in the Tarn – a project led by Jean-Charles Jauffret, a university professor. Finally, a national memorial of overseas France (Mémorial national de la France d'Outre-mer, MoM) in Marseille proposed to present the French colonial enterprise in North Africa and elsewhere, under the direction of two historians, Jean-Jacques Jordi and Jean-Pierre Rioux, and benefitting from substantial means and the support of pied-noir organizations. As we see, politicians, organizations of repatriates and historians came together around memorial sites with the intention of preserving the colonial past.

The Marseille project remains the most important and the one of greatest symbolic import due to the involvement of the national government, a major French city and the main leaders of the UMP. It was planned as a memorial of 'national' character, covering the whole colonial enterprise and not only Algeria. Furthermore, it was supported by several academics, including Lefeuvre, Rioux, Jordi and Marc Michel (2009).[19] The project triggered waves of protest, as much from historians who withdrew from it as from local organizations – protests that slowed down its progress and may well have put a definitive end to its construction. For all these reasons, the Marseille project makes a very interesting textbook case to understand the issues structuring the debate over colonial memory in recent years.

The aim of this project for a national memorial of overseas France was more to trace the history and keep alive the memory of the people who lived in the French colonies in the nineteenth and twentieth centuries than to develop a critical analysis of the colonial past. We are dealing here with a *tribute* to this civilizing enterprise. Thus, on the demand of organizations of repatriates active on the scientific committee and the few historians involved, Algeria was defined as the 'central focus of the memorial'. Interestingly the first draft of the governmental text submitted by Michelle Alliot-Marie in 2003, which led to the act adopted by the Assembly in February 2005 (presented by deputies Christian Kerk and Christian Vanneste), overtly linked the project of the memorial to the article of the bill on recognizing the 'positive values of colonialism'.

So, as we can see, the possibility of carrying through such a project is dependent on a number of factors. First of all, it must be politically acceptable.

In this respect, the shift in the positions of the Republican Right after 1995 is telling. Concretizing the glorification of the colonial past had become a 'political possibility'. This made it possible to even conceive of gratifying a demand that had never been satisfied before and to do so profitably, not only in political terms (the appeal to the repatriate constituency) (Savarese, 2007), but also because 'colonial pride' had become an acceptable, even desirable, argument in a section of the Republican Right. Furthermore, the theme had every chance of satisfying a large section of the Far Right constituency (Stora, 2007).

On the other hand, reactions against the project were vehement. Many historians actively mobilized against it and the vast majority refused to support it (Heméry, 2001). A conference was organized to denounce the project's biased agenda and the lack of serious historiography underpinning it.[20] As a result the Marseille project seems to have been suspended and has even disappeared from the website of the Mairie de Marseille, its main initiator.

Taken together, the Marseille memorial project, the ones in Montpellier and in Montredon-Labessonnié, and the memorial wall planned by the city of Perpignan manifest the will to assign a positive value to the French colonial presence, especially in North Africa, and even more so in Algeria. They also testify to the general direction of colonial memory politics in the 2000s. Interestingly, these projects have all been suspended or simply abandoned, in the wake of pressure from historians and various organizations.

What we are positing here is that these sites of remembrance – museums, memorials and commemorative monuments – are not isolated entities. They are embedded in a normative view of what collective memory on colonialism should look like and also, and more profoundly, what the history of France, the 'national narrative', should be. It is worth noting that these different projects were driven (at least in their initial phases) by academics, and this sheds light on the deep divergence of opinion between historians in French universities. It is also worth noting that this normative view is part and parcel of a vast movement of ideological regression manifested in the extension of the 'governmental Right' toward themes hitherto reserved for the Far Right. As observed above, these themes regard immigration first and foremost – conceived as a handicap and a threatening submersion at once biological (witness the current popularity of the theme of the '*grand remplacement*' of a white France by a mixed-blood France) and cultural, since the postcolonial immigrants are seen as capable of profoundly changing essentialized French culture and traditions. The rise of these ideas in public discourse can be attributed to deep-seated anthropological concerns about 'national identity' (Bancel *et al.*, 2015).

These concerns are evident in the desire to paint a positive picture of the 'French contribution' in the colonies, a desire that participates in a global view of the history of France wherein the emphasis is on appreciating, recognizing and teaching its merits, including as a colonial power. Glorifying the nation provides a form of reassurance with regard to forces (such as globalization, immigration and mixed populations) that appear destructuring and destructive. One of the most striking examples of this search for 'grandeur' in history can be seen in the project for the 'Maison de l'histoire de France'.

'Maison de l'histoire de France'

It was Nicolas Sarkozy's decision as presidential candidate to have a French History Museum built. It was a project that grew out of his conception of French history as the 'history of the great men who made France'. Not only did Sarkozy position himself as the culminating figure in this genealogy, he also appropriated historical figures from the Left in an effort to 'nationalise' history (De Cock *et al.*, 2008). Of course, this 'history of great men' (Poulot, 2007) has little to do with historical research. It applies instead the methods used to teach history to primary school children under the Third Republic, according to the precepts of Ernest Lavisse. In Lavisse's positivist view, history must be edifying (with the 'great men' setting an example); it must provide a moral and civil education, and thus it must be fundamentally normative (with the nation's glorious past underpinning the duties of its citizens); it must articulate a national 'essence' on continuity and constant progress (Comtean positivism) (Aprile, 2007) and on the homogeneity of its people, united by past trials and by a common sense of belonging (see Citron, 2008); finally it must be a glorious history, founded on the events 'that made France' or that exemplify its genius. Sarkozy did not hesitate to appropriate the moral legacy of the Left in support of his genealogy: the Revolution, of course, the patriotism of the First World War (in ceremonies marking the passing of the last *poilu*), and the Resistance (honouring Guy Môquet, the young Communist patriot whom the Germans executed by firing squad) (Azéma, 2007).

The glorification of the 'civilizing mission' overseas is lodged in this view of history, as was the report drafted by Hervé Lemoine (2008) on the project of building a French History Museum. Lemoine blames the collapse of the national narrative on Anglo-Saxon deconstructivism and the ensuing relativism that has swept away all identity references, thereby provoking a new crisis of collective representations. Seen from this standpoint, it is hard to imagine where there would be room for a dialectical or critical approach to colonial history.

Three times in his report, Lemoine reiterates the 'importance' of colonial history in the 'construction of France' but nowhere does he explain how the history of the French presence overseas can be integrated into this great narrative of French history. How can this complex period be addressed if the intent of the project is to reinforce national pride? By way of an answer, Lemoine chooses to emphasize three events as foundational in French history: the battle of Poitiers in 732 'that stopped the Arab invasion and thereby changed Western history'; the capture of Jerusalem in 1099, which shows 'the consolidation of Christian Europe and its aspiration of expansion', and the Revocation of the Edict of Nantes in 1685, which 'confirmed the long-lasting tendency in the history of France "to choose Rome"'. The symbolic import of this emphasis is to define France as exclusively Christian, but also as underpinned by an identity grounded in the exclusion of the other, mainly of 'Arabs' but also Protestants (see Lemoine, 2008).

That the historical narrative the museum was constructing would stress French military feats (colonial as well) as part of a glorifying picture of the 'construction of France' is evidenced by this choice of dates and also by a number of other elements: the fact that the report was commissioned by both the Ministry of Culture and the Ministry of Defence; the title of the report itself 'Pour la création d'un centre de recherche et de collections permanentes dédié à l'histoire civile et militaire de la France' (For the creation of a centre for research and permanent collections dedicated to the civil and military history of France); the many military professionals that Lemoine consulted while preparing the report; and the initial choice of Les Invalides for its location. We have here some of the major principles informing projects dedicated to the memory of colonialism. But this project, like most others of its kind, was abandoned after the election of François Hollande.

Polarized memories

This panorama of monuments, museums, homages and commemorations reveals, on the one hand, the limited institutional visibility of colonial-period history and its absence in museums and, on the other, the polarization of positions on the colonial past. The polarization goes hand in hand with what can be termed the growing socialization of this past (through organizations with memorial or communitarian agendas). Colonial history was sidelined until the beginning of the 1990s for two reasons: the need to forget a historical trauma that undermined the nation's self-image and the need to prevent a fallout from colonial confrontations. The colonial aphasia that characterized this period seems again to have become an interim solution, for want of anything better and after the many failed official projects informed by a nostalgic view of the colonial period. This is why there are no official commemorations, major places of learning or state-driven policies of research on the colonial and postcolonial periods.

Generation after generation, historians have done their work, as Benjamin Stora has demonstrated (2003). Over the past three decades they have considerably expanded our knowledge of colonial history. Various organizations – anti-racist such as the Ligue des droits de l'homme, educational such as the Ligue de l'enseignement and human rights groups – have fought for the recognition of colonial history as an essential chapter in French collective history, with the emphasis often placed on the most violent aspects of colonization, such as the use of torture in Algeria. Books, websites[21] and articles have been published on the subject, although major documentaries on colonialism have been few and far between, except for those taking up the Algerian War. Fiction films for TV or for theatrical release (see Lindenberg, 1994) nonetheless have reached the general public. This was the case for *Days of Glory* (*Indigènes*) (which received an award at Cannes in 2006) and *Intimate Enemies* (*L'Ennemi intime*) from 2007, *Nuit noire* on Canal + on the Massacres of 17 October 1961 (2005); TV films include *Capitaines des ténèbres* by Serge Moati (Arte, April 2006), after the three-part mini-series *L'Algérie des chimères* broadcast by Arte in November 2001 and a whole generation of movies from *Indochine* to *Coup de torchon*.

But these developments in addressing the colonial past have not shaken the silence of the government, which continues to look upon the past as a permanent resource for developing and teaching 'national values' (Citron, 2008). In any other terms, the colonial period and its postcolonial consequences are seen as being of no 'practical use'. They are even potentially counterproductive, given the controversies to which they give rise. Voice is given to the potential for conflict inherent in this historical period by the social groups that have a stake in colonial period issues – pieds-noirs, the *Harkis*, repatriates, colonial and postcolonial immigrants – driven as they are by radically different perceptions of colonial history. The current situation in France, marked by a lasting economic crisis, reinforces the government's tendency toward silence.

But the silence also contributes to frustration and the impossibility of transmission. The fact is that nearly ten million people in France have a more or less direct relationship with colonial history through their family background. Second- and third-generation children of colonial and postcolonial immigration in particular are essentially deprived of that genealogy. This is a form of discrimination, on top of the other more concrete and equally destructive forms, affecting young generations of immigrant background and their access to the job market (in poor quarters nearly 40 per cent of young people aged 18–25 are unemployed) and to housing (a young person with an Arabic or African sounding name has four times less chance of finding housing). Coming in addition to pronounced forms of ghettoization, these discriminations feed the construction of worlds separated from and rejected by the society at large. The combination of the refusal to take up colonial history with these forms of discriminations have without doubt something to do with the radicalization of an active, visible minority of these young people from postcolonial immigrant backgrounds, who reinvent this past and use it as an argument against their country of birth: witness the different forms of Salafism that have taken hold in poor areas over the last two decades. As France and the entire world experienced or witnessed on 13 November 2015, this type of radicalization can lead to extreme violence.

The difficulty that France has in examining its colonial history ultimately stands in the way of an understanding of the blind spots that exist in France today, and which can only be understood from the perspective of the history of the French Empire. To give one example among others, the systems of racialized representations of colonial populations are incomprehensible without knowledge of their genealogy during the colonial period, as are the discriminations that constitute today a blatant injustice but also a major social risk. In the face of these difficulties, new manifestations of a desire for recognition have emerged, through organizations such as the *Indigènes de la République* and the CRAN (Conseil représentatif des associations noires), seeking to make the colonial and postcolonial issue a matter of public debate. Their efforts so far have met with little success, since they have been kept out of the political and media spotlight. The question is, how long can the country continue to ignore a period that is part of its history and that therefore contributes to aspects of its contemporary identity?

Translated by Gila Walker

Notes

1 This chapter picks up some passages from 'Colonisation: Commémorations et mémoriaux' in Bancel *et al.* (2010).

2 Barcellini (2008) observes that the 1873 Act about honouring those who gave their lives for France is the first

> intervention of the State in what was to become the politics of memory. As the first French memorial act, the 1873 Act gave precise indications as to the status of the place of burial and the type of tombstone. It also allowed the State to channel post-Boulangist commemorative impulses. The great ceremonies organised by veterans of the 1870 war were held at these memorials and in particular at those in Bazeilles and in Mars-la-Tour.

3 These include the inauguration by the President of the Republic of the Vel' d'Hiv' memorial (1994); the creation of the Mémorial des Justes in Thonon (1997); the inauguration of the national memorial at the Camp des Milles (1997); the homage to the Righteous (2000); the President of the Republic's visit to Chambon-sur-Lignon (2004); the inauguration by the President of the Republic of the Memorial of the Shoah and the wall of names of the 76,000 deported Jews in Paris (2005 on the site of the Memorial of the Unknown Jewish Martyr from 1956); the inauguration of the 'Mur des Justes' (2006); the awarding of the Legion of Honour to the French Righteous (2006); and entry of the Righteous to the Pantheon (2007).

4 Two bills concerning the Armenian genocide accompany the creation of these memorial spaces: the first, recognizing the genocide, was discreetly adopted by the French National Assembly in January 2001; the second was a bill criminalizing its denial adopted in October 2006 but still awaiting application.

5 The author cited the book (plus DVD) by Patrick Buisson, advisor to the president, *La Guerre d'Algérie* (2009) and the novel by Norbert Multeau *Paul et Kader* (2009).

6 On 24 October 2009, Abdelaziz Belkhadem, secretary general of the National Liberation Front (FLN), called on France 'to recognize and provide reparations for the barbarian genocidal crimes committed by colonialism for 132 years in Algeria'. Speaking in Sétif at a conference for the 55th anniversary of the Revolution of 1954, he concluded that his demand 'was more popular and powerful than any of the measures adopted by the French government to glorify the colonial past' (a reference to the bill passed in February 2005).

7 It is worth noting that excessive attitudes to memory on the other side of the Mediterranean foster symmetrically polarized positions and their radicalization.

8 In 1983, with the extradition of Klaus Barbie from Bolivia, François Mitterrand unintentionally inaugurated a new phase of memory in France, the memory of the 'victims'. Two years later, Robert Badinter introduced an act identifying those who 'died after deportation'. Still, victory commemorations did not yet bring up this question, even after Mitterrand's visit to the Natzweiller-Struthof concentration camp. In the following years, attention was focused on the First World War and then on the bicentenary of the French Revolution in 1989. The turning point came in 1990, first with a bill defining the notion of 'victim' and then with the Gayssot Act, which laid down the government's role in the construction of a 'memory of the Shoah'. The ceremony for the 40th anniversary of the Vel' d'Hiv' Roundup, when Mitterrand was booed, was to play a major role. Finally, in 1993, a decree established 'a national day of remembrance of the racist and anti-Semitic persecutions committed under the authority of the so-called government of the French State'. Henceforth, the 'victims' hold a new place in the nation's collective memory. The final step was Jacques Chirac's 1995 speech, cited above.

9 As have been the case with the act of February 2005 or the founding of the CNHI, the National Museum of Immigration History and Cultures, in the Palais de la Porte Dorée.

10 The mayor of Paris unveiled a plaque in the capital on 17 October 2001 in memory of the 1961 events.

11 The traces of 'human blood' will have to be wiped away, Jacques de Saint-Victor wrote in the *Le Figaro* in January 2004, 'to attain a serene nostalgia for the colonies'.

12 At the same time, a series of articles in other magazines and journals analysed this debate. See, for example, 'Le trou de mémoire' in *Hommes & Libertés* (LDH), summer 2005; 'Repenser le passé colonial' in *Nouveaux regards* (FSU, no. 30, July–September 2005); 'La vérité sur la colonisation' in *Nouvel Observateur*, 8–14 December 2005; 'France coloniale, deux siècles d'histoire' in *Histoire & Patrimoine*, September 2005; 'La question postcoloniale' in the 30th anniversary special issue of *Hérodote* in 2006 (though critical of some of the new research published in 2005–06); 'La colonisation en procès' in *L'Histoire*, October 2005; 'Colonies, un débat français' in a special edition of *Monde2*, May 2006.

13 In addition to the monuments, plaques were added to religious monuments in the Sacré-Cœur d'Antibes church or Saint-Nicolas du Chardonnet – commemorating those who were killed in March and July 1962.

14 The bronze monument erected in the Perpignan cemetery, called the '*stèle des fusillés*', depicts a man attached to a post collapsing, with the inscription '*Terre d'Algérie*' and the name of former combatants of French Algeria.

15 Then President Jacques Chirac was the one who decided to situate this national memorial to French soldiers who died in North Africa right near the soon to be opened Musée des Arts premiers, or the Musée du Quai Branly. The monument to the dead consists of three columns in the colours of the French flag, bearing the names of the 22,959 French and *Harkis* who died for France displayed on light panels. At its unveiling in December 2002, Chirac declared: 'Our Republic must fully meet its duty to remember.' Three months later, on an official trip to Algeria, after a major speech by the French ambassador, Chirac again brought up the conflict and this 'still painful' past.

16 Sarkozy's speech was far more explicit than Valéry Giscard-d'Estaing, Jacques Chirac or François Mitterrand, all of whom defended France's colonial activities. It is worth noting that Chancellor Adenauer acknowledged Nazi crimes and apologized in the name of the German nation. Even though France did not ask for this 'acknowledgement', it contributed to paving the way to bilateral French–German relations.

17 Sarkozy's speech seems to borrow on the writings of Max Gallo (2006).

18 This project was at the centre of a controversy in 2006, after a declaration made by Georges Frêche, then mayor of the city and initiator of the project, who called the *harkis* 'sub-humans'.

19 Marc Michel and Daniel Lefeuvre are founders of the Études coloniales association and website, providing active support for these different projects.

20 See the programme for the conference: 'Mémorial de l'Outre-mer ou Historial du colonialisme?', Marseille, 21 October 2006, organized by the Faculté St Charles (unpublished).

21 See the comprehensive website of the Toulon section of Ligue des Droits de l'Homme (LDH): http://ldh-toulon.net/

Bibliography

Aprile, S. (2007) 'L'histoire par Nicolas Sarkozy: le rêve passéiste d'un futur national-libéral'. Comité de Vigilence face aux Usages publics de l'Histoire (CVUH). 30 April. [Available at: http://cvuh.blogspot.se/2007/04/lhistoire-par-nicolas-sarkozy-le-reve.html]

Azéma, J.-P. (2007) 'Guy Môquet, Sarkozy et le roman national', *L'Histoire*, 323 (September), p. 6.

Bancel, N. (2011) 'La Brèche. Vers une racialization des discours publics?' *Mouvements* (Special Issue), 1, pp. 13–28.

Bancel, N. and Blanchard, P. (2010) 'Colonisation: Commémorations et mémoriaux'. In: Bancel, N., Bernault, F., Blanchard, P., Boubeker, A., Mbembe, A. and Vergès, F. (eds), *Ruptures postcoloniales*. Paris: La Découverte.

Bancel, N., Blanchard, P. and Boubeker, A. (2015) *Le Grand repli*. Paris: La Découverte.

Bancel, N., Blanchard, P. and Lemaire, S. (eds) (2005) *La Fracture coloniale. La société française au prisme de l'héritage colonial*. Paris: La Découverte.

Barcellini, S. (2008) 'L'État républicain, acteur de mémoire: des morts pour la France aux morts à cause de la France'. In: Blanchard, P. and Veyrat-Masson, I. (eds), *Les Guerres de mémoires. La France et son histoire*. Paris: La Découverte.

Bernard, P. (1998) 'Le dernier de la "Force noire"', *Le Monde*, 12 November.

Blanchard, P. and Veyrat-Masson, I. (eds) (2008) *Les Guerres de mémoires. La France et son histoire*. Paris: La Découverte.

Bruckner, P. (2006) *La Tyrannie de la pénitence. Essai sur le masochisme occidental*. Paris: Grasset.

Buission, P. (2009) *La Guerre d'Algérie*. Paris: Albin Michel.

Champeaux, A. and Deroo, E. (2006) *La force noire: Gloire et infortune d'une légende coloniale*. Paris: Tallandier.

Citron, S. (1987/2008) *Le mythe national. L'histoire de France revisitée*. Paris: L'Atelier.

Coquery-Vidrovitch, C. (2009) *Enjeux politiques de l'histoire coloniale*. Marseille: Passé Présent Agone.

Coquery-Vidrovitch, C., Manceron, G. and Stora B. (2007) 'La mémoire partisane du président', *Libération*, 13 August.

Corbel, L. and Falaize, B. (2003) *Entre mémoire et savoir: L'enseignement de la shoah et des guerres de décolonisation*. Rapport de recherche de l'équipe de l'académie de Versailles. Lyon: Institut National de Recherche pédagogique.

Corbel, L. and Falaize, B. (2004) 'L'enseignement de l'histoire et les mémoires douloureuses du XXe siècle. Enquête sur les représentations enseignante', *Revue française de pédagogie*, 147 (April, May, June), pp. 43–55.

De Cock, L., Madeline, F., Offenstadt, N. and Wahnich, S. (eds) (2008) *Comment Sarkozy écrit l'histoire de France*. Paris: Agone.

De Saint-Victor, J. (2004) 'Nostalgie. Le rêve de nos ailleurs perdus', *Le Figaro*, 2 January.

Folch, A. (2009) 'Pieds-noirs, une blessure française', *Valeurs actuelles*, 22 October. Available at: www.valeursactuelles.com/politique/pieds-noirs-une-blessure-francaise-25643 [accessed 4 February 2016].

Gallo, M. (2006) *Fier d'être Français*. Paris: Fayard.

Gilzmer, M. (2009) *Mémoires de pierre*. Paris: Autrement.

Griotteray, A. (2001) *Je ne demande pas pardon. La France n'est pas coupable*. Paris: Editions du Rocher.

Heméry, D. (2001) 'À propos du "Mémorial de l'œuvre française outre-mer" – Lettre de Daniel Heméry', *Outre-mers, revue d'histoire*, 88 (330), pp. 309–10.

Hilberg, R. (1961) *La destruction des juifs d'Europe*. Paris: Fayard.

Klarsfeld, S. (1978) *Le Mémorial de la Déportation des Juifs de France*. Paris: AFFDJF.

Lantheaume, F. (2003) 'Enseigner l'histoire de la guerre d'Algérie: entre critique et relativisme, une mission impossible?', In: Liauzu, C. (ed.), *Tensions méditerranéennes*. Paris: Cahiers Confluences Méditerranée-L'Harmattan, pp. 231–65.

Lantheaume, F. (2007) 'Manuels d'histoire et colonisation: Les forces et faiblesses de la polyphonie de l'auteur-réseau, ses effets sur la formation de l'esprit critique', *Revue de linguistique et de didactique des langues*, LIDIL, 35 (3), pp. 159–75.

Lantheaume, F. (2009) 'Fait colonial et religion dans les programmes et les manuels scolaires'. In: Borne, D. and Falaize, B. (eds), *Religion et colonisation*. Paris: Éd. de l'Atelier.

Lefeuvre, D. (2006) *Pour en finir avec la repentance coloniale*. Paris: Flammarion.

Lemaire, S. (2005) 'Colonisation et immigration: des "points aveugles" de l'histoire à l'école?'. In: Lemaire, S. (2006) 'Une loi qui vient de loin'. *Le Monde diplomatique*, janvier.

Lemoine, H. (2008) La maison de l'histoire de France. Pour la création d'un centre de recherche et de collections permanentes dédié à l'histoire civile et militaire de la France. Rapport à Monsieur le ministre de la Défense et Madame la ministre de la Culture et de la communication. [Available at: www.culture.gouv.fr/culture/actualites/rapports/rapporthlemoine.pdf].

L'Humanité (2005) [Interview with Benjamin Stora:] 'C'est un mouvement profondément réactionnaire', 6 July.

Lindenberg, D. (1994) 'Guerres de mémoire en France', *Vingtième Siècle. Revue d'histoire*, 42 (April–June), pp. 77–95.

Lugan, B. (2006) *Pour en finir avec la colonisation: l'Europe et l'Afrique XVe-XXe siècle*. Monaco: Rocher.

Michel, M. (2009) *Essai sur la colonisation positive. Affrontements et accommodements en Afrique noire, 1830–1930*. Paris: Éditions Perrin.

Multeau, N. (2009) *Paul et Kader*. Paris: Télémaque Editions.

Ould-Aoudia, J-P. (2006) *La Bataille de Marignane 6 juillet 2005: La République, aujourd'hui, face à l'OAS*. Paris: Editions Tiresias.

Paoli, P-F. (2006) *Nous ne sommes pas coupable. Assez de repentance!* Paris: La Table Ronde.

Paxton, R. (1973) *La France de Vichy (1940–1944)*. Paris: Seuil.

Perrineau, P. (2014) *La France au Front*. Paris: Fayard.

Porte, A.-C. (2006) *L'esclavage dans les programmes scolaires*. Lyon: Institut National de Recherche pédagogique.

Poulot, D. (2007) 'Le musée d'histoire en France entre traditions nationales et soucis identitaires', *Anais do museo paulista*, 15 (2), pp. 293–316.

Rousso, H. (1990) *Vichy, l'événement, l'histoire, la mémoire*. Paris: Gallimard.

Sarkozy, N. (2007) 'Déclaration de M. Nicolas Sarkozy, ministre de l'intérieur et de l'aménagement du territoire, président de l'UMP et candidat à l'élection présidentielle, sur son souhait de voir se réunifier l'espace méditerranéen pour le remettre au coeur de la civilisation occidentale et de la mondialisation', Toulon 7 February. Republique Français. Direction de l'information légale et administrative, DILA. Available at: http://discours.vie-publique.fr/notices/073000533.html [accessed 4 February 2016].

Savarese, É. (2007) *Algérie: la guerre des mémoires*. Paris: Non Lieu.

Stoler, A.L. (2010) 'L'aphasie coloniale française: l'histoire mutilée'. In: Bancel, N., Bernault, F., Blanchard, P., Boubeker, A., Mbembe, A. and Vergès, F. (eds), *Ruptures postcoloniales*. Paris: La Découverte.

Stora, B. (2003) 'Guerre d'Algérie: 1999–2003, les accélérations de la mémoire', *Revue Hommes et Migrations*, Dossier 'Français et Algériens', 1244 (July–August), pp. 83–95.

Stora, B. (2007) 'La Guerre des mémoires – Entretien réalisé par Marie Poinsot', *Revue Hommes et migrations*, 1268–69 (July–October), pp. 208–16.

Van Eeckhout, L. (2007) 'Opposé à la repentance, M. Sarkozy participe à la commémoration de l'abolition de l'esclavage', *Le Monde*, 9 May.

Vergès, F. (2006) *La mémoire enchaînée: Questions sur l'esclavage*. Paris: Albin Michel, 2006.

Veyrat-Masson, I. (2000) *Quand la télévision explore le temps. L'Histoire au petit écran, 1953–2000*. Paris: Fayard.

Veyrat-Masson, I. (2004) *Télévision et Histoire, le mélange des genres. Docudramas, docufictions et fictions du réel*. Brussels: INA-de Boeck.

4 The selective forgetting and remodelling of the past

Postcolonial legacies in the Netherlands

Esther Captain

The Netherlands is a small country.[1] Yet, no one can deny the sheer magnitude of the historical Dutch presence overseas (Captain and Jones, 2007a). Beginning in 1682 with the foundation of the West Indische Compagnie (WIC), or the Dutch West Indies Company, Dutch trade, exploration and – when it came to colonization and slavery – exploitation stretched across the entire globe. In North America and the Caribbean, Dutch possessions ranged from New York, a city founded by the Dutch as New Amsterdam, to countries and islands in the West Indies, including Surinam and the Antillean islands of Aruba, Bonaire, Curaçao, Sint Maarten, Sint Eustacius and Saba. In the Old World, in addition to the Indonesian archipelago, the Dutch claimed trading posts on the coasts of Africa, in India and in Ceylon (Sri Lanka), and Dutch Boers established major settler colonies near the Cape of Good Hope in southern Africa. Still today, the Antillean entities are still part of the Kingdom of the Netherlands: Aruba, Curaçao and Sint Maarten as separate countries, Bonaire, Sint Eustacius and Saba as 'special' Dutch municipalities.

Colonization enriched the Netherlands in many ways: from the fortunes made by private individuals and money earned for the national treasury, to the birth of new population groups of mixed ethnic descent and thus an increased demographic diversity in the country. The foreign relations of the Netherlands have been characterized as an intriguing mixture of peace, profits and principles (Voorhoeve, 1985). Since the violent decolonization of Indonesia in 1949 and the peaceful independence of Surinam in 1975, two of the greatest colonial assets of the Netherlands, the Dutch have promoted human rights and development aid for other countries in global affairs. The Dutch pursuit of peace and its principles has attracted various NGOs, such as Amnesty International, Clean Clothes Campaign, Friends of the Earth International, Greenpeace and War Child, to establish their head offices in Amsterdam, making it the international capital for NGOs. As a free-trade nation and an active member of international organizations, the Netherlands is often eager to set an example to other states, sometimes forgetting its own complex history of exploration as well exploitation. In order to be aware of this complex and sometimes controversial heritage, I would like to focus in this chapter on the way in which contemporary crisis and decline prompt a selective forgetting and remodelling of the Dutch past. I will do so by discussing two case studies: on the one hand, the celebration and commemoration of the Treaty of Utrecht of 1713 by the Utrecht city council in 2013; on the other hand, the precarious situation of cultural institutions such as museums and libraries that deal with the Netherlands' colonial past and postcolonial present, which in recent years have been closed or become short of funding.

The first case study, on the Treaty of Utrecht, demonstrates how the commemoration of a historical date is used to launch a heroic and homogeneous story about the past of the Dutch city, in which less gratifying parts of its history, notably its colonial involvement in the slave trade and slavery, is occluded. It also shows how colonial history can today be instrumentalized as a city branding event, that is, retold, reinvented and relaunched for political as well as commercial purposes. The second case study, on postcolonial heritage institutions, illustrates the dynamics between the ways in which the Dutch colonial past is displayed to the general public and the simultaneous dismantling of the infrastructure of specialized knowledge in collections and libraries, which leads to an increasing unavailability of sources on the Dutch colonial past. It is my aim to try to understand how our views, interpretations and representations of the colonial past affect and shape our present society. The case studies can be considered topical practices of how colonial history, colonized people, minorities and migrants are represented in museums and memory culture in the Netherlands. I will juxtapose my two cases with actual developments in Dutch historiography, notably in museology and history, working from the premise that there is a continuity in the way the Netherlands has manifested itself towards its subjects in the colonial past and towards its citizens in the postcolonial present.

Case study 1: the Treaty of Utrecht (1713)

In July 2013, together with Rosi Braidotti, professor in philosophy at the Centre for the Humanities of Utrecht University, I co-organized a two-day international conference on 'The Colonial Legacy of the Treaty of Utrecht' at Utrecht University. The background to the conference was a decision by the Utrecht city council to designate the Treaty of Utrecht as a historical event to be commemorated in ways that would, as stated in the programme, 'reinforce the (inter-) national reputation of Utrecht as a city and a province of knowledge and culture' (Treaty of Utrecht, 2013). The city council established the Treaty of Utrecht Foundation, which was tasked to organize a cultural programme that aimed to promote the city's cultural infrastructure in a sustainable way. In order to understand these ambitions, let us briefly elaborate on the Treaty of Utrecht itself.

In 1712 and 1713, representatives of the countries involved in the War of the Spanish Succession convened in Utrecht to negotiate a peace treaty. After two centuries of religious wars and bloody conflict, the most powerful countries in Europe gathered in the city hall and signed the Treaty of Utrecht on 11 April 1713. It was probably the first time a large-scale war did not end on the battlefield with a winner and a loser, but was settled at the negotiating table. The parties re-divided Europe and their possessions in the Americas and elsewhere in a deal whose contours are still visible today (Schnabel, 2012). The Treaty of Utrecht confirmed the end of the French quest for hegemony in Europe and established the United Kingdom's position as world hegemon. In continental Europe, the British presence remained limited to Gibraltar, but in North America it acquired the French possessions of present-day Canada, and the slave trade became a largely British monopoly. Yet, however significant the Treaty of Utrecht was as an international accord, principally shaping eighteenth-century political and constitutional relationships, it had barely any impact on the city in which it was signed, nor on the Dutch Republic itself. The major impact of the Treaty of Utrecht was that the Dutch themselves had lost a great deal of political power and influence to the British.

If the Treaty of Utrecht was a symbol of the definitive decline of the Dutch Republic as an international superpower, one may wonder why the city council of Utrecht chose to 'celebrate' its tercentenary in 2013. One possible answer is that the historical event could be used to promote an image of the city that conforms to present-day European ideals and commercial programmes. 'It was diplomacy, rather than war, that had brought peace to Europe', stated the Treaty of Utrecht Foundation.

> The visit of this colourful company of international diplomats also brought a boost to the (creative) economy of Utrecht, at a cultural as well as financial level. All the more reason, then, to celebrate the tercentenary of this diplomatic success 300 years later with an international programme filled with musical performances, theatre, festivals, conferences, exhibitions and many other events.
>
> (Treaty of Utrecht, 2013)

While the Treaty of Utrecht Foundation preferred to turn a blind eye to less gratifying aspects of the Treaty, the Centre for the Humanities sought to consider the colonial dimension of the Treaty of Utrecht as a fundamental aspect of the event, and as one of its most enduring legacies.

The conference 'The Colonial Legacy of the Treaty of Utrecht' was devoted to an exploration of the links between three commemorative years:

- 1713: signing of the Treaty of Utrecht on 11 April
- 1863: abolition of slavery by the Netherlands on 1 July
- 2013: commemoration of the 300th anniversary of the Treaty of Utrecht and the 150th anniversary of the abolition of slavery.

The conference's exploration of the three events was motivated by the conviction that it was necessary to interpret the commemorations of 2013 not only along strictly historical lines, but also ethically and politically in terms of their relevance for the world of today. As its starting point, the conference considered the actual history of the Treaty of Utrecht. On the one hand, the Treaty marked the end of religious wars and conflicts in Europe; for the first time in modern history armed conflict was resolved by diplomacy and not on the battlefield (Bély, 2007). On the other hand – and this was the emphasis of the conference – the Treaty of Utrecht confirmed and consolidated Europe's colonial grip on Africa, Asia and the Americas. In the Treaty of Utrecht – and this was practically unknown in the Netherlands, as the Treaty is much better known outside the country – Spain granted Great Britain the so-called *asiento de negros*, which can loosely be translated as 'agreement on blacks' (Williams, 2006). Literally, *asiento* means stipulation or agreement related to commercial monopoly. The *asiento de negros* entailed the right to deliver slaves to the Spanish for a period of 30 years. The Treaty of Utrecht thus gave British slave traders and smugglers access to Spanish markets in the Americas that had formerly been closed to them (Weindl, 2008).

Countering city marketing

The Treaty of Utrecht is a very peculiar treaty: on the one hand providing peace, freedom and prosperity *within* Europe, and on the other hand establishing a regime of enslavement and trade in human beings *outside* Europe. In this sense, the two events commemorated in 2013 – the 300th anniversary of the signing of the Treaty of Utrecht in 1713 and the 150th anniversary of the abolition of slavery by the Dutch in 1863 – could no longer, as had previously been the case in standard Dutch historiography and memory culture, be treated separately. On the contrary, it became important to investigate the links between them. The implications of these century-old ties between 'motherland' and 'colony' needed to be accurately and systematically mapped out. At the centre of these ties was the institution of slavery, a pervasive influence on societal organization from antiquity to the nineteenth century, progressively elaborated and codified into the legal frameworks of European state powers (Aldridge, 2007).

Colonial slavery and the slave trade are part and parcel of the construction of modern Europe and may have implications that are still relevant. This may be seen, for instance, in modern forms of slavery and human trafficking, but also in the debates about recovery, reparation and reconciliation – after painful episodes in our pasts. This relevance was actualized in one of the events organized by the Centre for the Humanities, titled *Traces of Slavery in Utrecht, A Walking Guide*, which demonstrated that slave trade and slavery was not a phenomenon from long ago and far away (Captain and Visser, 2012). The walking guide features formerly enslaved people, as well as plantation and slave owners and abolitionists, all of whom once were living in the city of Utrecht. It made clear that the city of Utrecht itself had been involved in slave trade and slavery in various ways. After the abolition of slavery in 1863, Utrecht slave owners claimed compensation for their lost 'goods' (Captain, 2013). They usually received a financial compensation of 300 guilders per liberated slave, equivalent to €3,045 today. More research is needed to establish the exact number of slave owners in Utrecht, but a preliminary estimation is that a total of 406,650 guilders have been paid to former slave owners, or approximately €4 million today.

In this light, the decision of the Utrecht city council to launch the Treaty of Utrecht as a city-branding event appears remarkable indeed. Whereas the Treaty of Utrecht Foundation preferred to *celebrate* the date of the historical signing of the Treaty on 11 April 1713, the Centre for the Humanities wanted to *commemorate* the content of the Treaty and its implications for persons that became enslaved and were trafficked across the world. It is a phenomenon that occurs frequently in today's Netherlands and Europe: economic and commercial interests privilege a certain narrative of a national (in this case Dutch) or European past, whereas other parts of the cultural heritage are weeded out. What is obscured in this display of a heroic and homogeneous story about the past are the global perspectives and cultural pluralities that are also embodied or symbolized by the Treaty of Utrecht. The same pattern dominated at the 400th anniversary of the Verenigde Oost-Indische Compagnie (VOC) [the *Dutch East India Company*], organized by a governmental committee and other official institutions. The celebrations were contested by various private initiatives all the way from symposia featuring highly critical appraisals of Dutch colonialism by persons of Eurasian, Dutch, Indonesian and Moluccan descent to a committee called 'Celebration of 400 Years VOC? No!' (Captain and Jones, 2007b). In the Netherlands as in other former imperialist nations, strong critical voices have been raised against colonialism and colonial institutions. It is important to pay attention to these postcolonial voices. Their critical expressions are a necessary counterweight to city-branding initiatives that rely on a one-dimensional image of the past that mainly serves to make profit in the present.

Case study 2: postcolonial institutions

In anticipation of the 150th anniversary of the abolition of slavery by the Netherlands on 1 July 1863, the Dutch Council of Churches offered, on 14 June, their official apologies for their active role in the slave trade. They acknowledged that slavery had partially been sustained and legitimized by the church on theological grounds. This recognition by the Church reinforced hopes by the descendants of enslaved people that the Dutch government would follow suit on 1 July and offer an official apology for its involvement in the slave trade and slavery. The commemoration in Amsterdam was attended by the Dutch King Willem Alexander with Queen Máxima, as well as Lodewijk Asscher, Vice Prime Minister of the Netherlands. While the Vice Prime Minister spoke of 'sincere regrets', the word 'apology' was not used. And while King Willem Alexander and Queen Máxima sang along with 'Redemption Song' by Bob Marley, which surprised some of the people in the audience, the King and Queen kept silent after the song. The singing along with 'Redemption Song' also was not followed by official apologies by the Dutch government. Sadly enough, this should not have come as a surprise. Considering the analogies between redemption, reconciliation and reparation in a royal as well as colonial context, an interesting and symptomatic phenomenon can be distinguished here. From a historical point of view, the psychological and political distance between the Dutch royal family and the colonies has been big (Oostindie, 2006). Nevertheless, the Dutch royal family presents itself as closely connected to the population of the Antilles and of Surinam, whether during state visits overseas or at official occasions in the Netherlands. King William III (1849–90), for example, signed the Emancipation Law in 1863, which ended slavery in Surinam and the Antillean islands, although the King himself never was in favour of the abolition of slavery. He signed simply because the King signed all Dutch laws. However, the news of abolition was communicated to the people in the colonies as a direct message from William III to his faraway subjects. It made him the King who liberated the enslaved, and the royal family very popular, a popularity that is still continued today by Antillean and Surinamese citizens.

The changed Dutch sociopolitical landscape, and especially the situation of institutions devoted to the study of colonial and postcolonial history and culture, is an indicator of the current state of affairs in the Netherlands. Studying colonialism and its long-term ramifications has been a firm tradition in the country. On a governmental level, colonial and postcolonial studies have been supported by an essential institutional infrastructure, consisting of museums, collections and libraries. This institutional landscape was intact until approximately 2012 and can be related to an important shift in the Dutch political landscape. After the elections in 2010, Prime Minister Mark Rutte of the Liberal Party could only form a minority government with the confessional party. They needed electoral support from a third party in order to reach a majority in the Dutch parliament. Rutte found a partner in the populist right-wing party of Geert Wilders, which agreed to support the minority government. The influence of Geert Wilders, who advocates an anti-migrant and anti-Islam policy, can also be found in the fact that many postcolonial institutions have been diminished, dismantled or, worse, liquidated. The National Institute for the Study of Dutch Slavery and its Legacy (NiNsee) in Amsterdam, established in 2003, was closed down in 2012 as the Dutch government decided to withdraw its annual funding. It is noteworthy that according to the government, one of the criteria by which the decision on the continued funding of the NiNsee was judged was 'support of the community'. This is to say that 'the community' had to show interest in and support for NiNsee by gathering the financial resources necessary for a continuation of the institution's activities. The 'community' referred to here was reduced to people of Surinamese-Dutch and Antillean-Dutch descent in the Netherlands. Contrary to scholarly insights that slavery is a past commonly shared by *all* Dutch inhabitants, the criterion on funding introduced by the government confirms the disconnection between 'Dutch' citizens on the one hand and 'Surinamese-Dutch' and 'Antillean-Dutch' citizens on the other. Moreover, the appeal to community support seems to be a doubtful argument, because every citizen of the Netherlands should be able to see themselves reflected in Dutch museums and heritage institutions. All citizens have been funding these public utilities by paying taxes, as is the case, for instance, with the renovation of the *Rijksmuseum*, the Dutch National Museum of Art and History. But whether the Rijksmuseum adequately reflects colonial history, and whether it offers a space of recognition also to

Surinamese- and Antillean-Dutch citizens, remains a question with which I will finish this chapter.

NiNsee is only one item on a long list of Dutch institutions that recently have been terminated or faced severe budget cuts and hence have been partially closed or forced to transfer some of their institutional tasks to others. The Museum Maluku in Utrecht (devoted to the history and culture of the Moluccan), the Museum Nusantara in Delft (devoted to the history and culture of Indonesia) as well as Kosmopolis Utrecht, Kosmopolis Den Haag, Kosmopolis Rotterdam, three city platforms devoted to intercultural dialogue, art and culture; all have been abolished in 2012. Also, the Royal Netherlands Institute of Southeast Asian and Caribbean Studies in Leiden (KITLV) has had to transfer its collections (library and archives) to Leiden University in order to ensure its continuity as a research institute dedicated to colonial and postcolonial studies.

Another important case is the Royal Tropical Institute in Amsterdam, which I will analyse in greater detail since it is at the heart of the debate on postcolonial institutes and infrastructure. The Royal Tropical Institute was founded in 1910 as the 'Colonial Institute' for the purpose of studying the 'tropics' and promoting trade and industry in the (at that time) colonial territories of the Netherlands (Legêne, 2005). The decolonization period resulted in a broadening of the institute's mission, from studying the 'Dutch Overseas Territories', to the tropics in general, including 'cultural, economic and hygienic issues'. In 1926, Queen Wilhelmina opened the new museum complex in Amsterdam, which took 11 years to construct. In 1967, new additions were added: a theatre, Tropenmuseum Junior (an exhibition for children) and a new exhibition hall. During the 1970s and 1980s, the focus of the museum shifted towards the Third World, with thematic exhibitions on poverty, health, hygiene and development (Van Duuren, 1990). With the appointment of anthropologist Susan Legêne as head of the curatorial department in 1997 and museologist Wayne Modest as her successor in 2010, the Tropenmuseum has developed into a site for the critical study of colonialism. The interconnectedness of Dutch colonial expansion with the development of museums as sites for civic education was analysed, thus pointing out how Dutch culture was created as a representation of us versus others (Legêne, 2004).

These days of glory are over. As from January 2013, the Ministry of Foreign Affairs withdrew its structural financial support for the Royal Tropical Institute. Profitable departments such as biological research on tropical diseases will remain, while other non-profitable departments have to close, such as the theatre and library. In total, 90 employees have lost their jobs, among which are 32 of the 33 employees working at the library. The library of the Royal Tropical Institute, which dates to 1777, contained 900,000 books, maps, magazines and other documents: in total ten kilometres of material. The oldest document dates from 1469. The material pre-dating 1950 has been transferred to the library of Leiden University, as the Dutch government is obliged to care for this material as a public duty. Post-1950 material – nine kilometres – 'does not generate money' according to Dutch newspaper *Trouw* (25 October 2013) and, if other libraries turned out not to be interested in taking over the collection, would be 'recycled', a euphemism for ending up in the paper shredder. However, in November 2013, the Biblioteca Alexandrina in Egypt, known as the oldest scientific library in the world, became the new owner of 400,000 books and 20,000 magazines, in total seven kilometres of publications and documents, previously housed in the Royal Tropical Institute. The Biblioteca Alexandrina was renovated and re-opened in 2002. The money for the renovation came from UNESCO and a considerable donation by former Iraqi leader Saddam Hussein. Other parts of the collection went to Dutch institutions, such as the library of the Peace Palace in The Hague, Rijksmuseum Amsterdam, Maritime Museum Rotterdam and the medical archive of a private foundation.

Austere Histories and Forgetting

The example of the Royal Tropical Institute leads to a number of observations. First, the 'library case' is a perfect illustration of the erasure of the Dutch colonial archive. Although it did not go as far as documents containing the collective memory being destroyed in the paper shredder, the Dutch colonial archive has been moved out of what was once the country's most prestigious postcolonial institute, and even out of the country itself. International experts were baffled. As Jeffrey Shane, librarian of Ohio University and chair of Cormosea (Committee on Research Materials on Southeast Asia), an association of scientific libraries devoted to Southeast Asia, stated in the Dutch newspaper *Trouw* (26 October 2013): 'The demolition of this enormous collection was done with very little consideration of the immense investment in books as well as in the time and energy of the employees. It is extremely reckless.' As the deliberate erasure of the Dutch involvement in the colonial project, it can be considered an act of destroying historical evidence. For scholars, students, journalists, citizens and others interested, this will obstruct the reconstruction of the colonial past and its repercussions in the postcolonial world, as collections and expertise have disappeared and been dispersed, or are severely fragmented.

Second, the fact that institutions were abolished or threatened by severe budget cuts is partly related to the economic crisis of 2008 and its long-term consequences. But the choices made by Dutch political and administrative policymakers when cutting budgets are highly significant. From the viewpoint of austerity policies, it does not make sense to give up 700,000 expensive books that have already been purchased with government money (*Trouw*, 26 October 2013). Obviously, reasons of efficiency do not apply here: politicians have made a political decision that sends a clear message. The colonial and postcolonial legacy of the Netherlands is not considered valuable enough to be preserved for the purpose of scientific research and information to the broader public.

The implications of such choices in austerity politics are not neutral and may have to do with a particular topic that has not been addressed so far: the legacy of Dutch racism (Essed and Hoving, 2014). The legacy of Dutch racism on the one hand translates into a sense of pride in the achievements of imperialism.

For example, in a parliamentary debate in 2006 former Prime Minister Jan-Peter Balkenende literally endorsed the mentality of the Dutch East India Company (VOC): 'Let's be happy with each other. Let's say: "The Netherlands can do it again!" That VOC mentality: looking behind the borders! Dynamics!' (loosely translated from footage of *NOS Journaal*, 28 September 2006). On the other hand, the legacy of Dutch racism also causes a deliberate silence on difficult parts of colonial history, as the case study of the Royal Tropical Institute as well as the abolishment of other institutions has indicated.

This deliberate silence can be understood in many ways. Melissa Weiner has called the Dutch case 'a unique form of racism, which is rooted in racial neo-liberalism, anti-racialism (i.e. the denial of race), racial Europeanization and the particular Dutch history of colonial exploitation' (Weiner, 2014). Within the context of this chapter, the silence may be interpreted within the broader frame-work of the erasure of colonial memories in the Netherlands. Dutch policy-makers investigating the state of diversity at cultural institutions have not only signalled a lack of diversity but also observed that awareness of this lack of diversity is missing in the Netherlands. They speak of this lack of diversity at cultural institutions as ' "the elephant in the room": everybody sees the elephant, but nobody is acknowledging it' (Netwerk CS, 2009). Anthropologist Ann Laura Stoler has suggested, in the context of French history, the term 'colonial aphasia' for the silence surrounding the colonial past. It operates through a discursive and epistemological disconnection of colonial history and national history:

> In aphasia, an occlusion of knowledge is the issue. It is not a matter of igno-rance of absence. Aphasia is dismembering, a difficulty of speaking, a diffi-culty generating a vocabulary that associates appropriate words and concepts with appropriate things. Aphasia in its many forms describes a difficulty retrieving both conceptual and lexical vocabularies and, most important, a difficulty comprehending what is spoken.
>
> (Stoler, 2011)

Anthropologist Guno Jones used the term colonial aphasia in 2012 to understand the place of slavery in the collective memory of the Netherlands (Jones, 2012). In my own historical work on memories about the transfer of the colony of the Dutch East Indies to the independent country of Indonesia, I have used the term 'whispering' about the colonial past, as I argued that the postcolonial migrants actually *did* talk about their experiences, histories and memories, but could not find a willing, listening ear in the receiving Dutch society (Captain, 2002). Under the cliché of 'silence', many variations on the scale of silence and speaking can be discerned. First, if people were silent, it is often because postcolonial migrants 'generally do not spread the word about experiences of paternalistic attitudes from social workers, of discrimination when trying to find a job or housing, or about the feeling of alienation while living in the so-called motherland' (Captain, 2014). 'Whispering' seems more adequate to me since these migrants, being the opposite of uncritical and docile, had their own views about and defiance of the receiving Dutch country. This can be seen in the literary and cultural expressions of three generations of postcolonial migrants from Indonesia. Other metaphors have also been introduced, such as 'forgetting and repression' by anthropologist Gert Oostindie (Oostindie, 2010). Yet regardless of whether we prefer to speak of 'the elephant in the room', 'aphasia', 'whispering', or 'forgetting and repression' as we seek an adequate metaphor for the place of colonial memory in the Netherlands and its recent erasure, most would agree with historian Susan Legêne that 'the transnational dimension of being Dutch [...] after 1949 disappeared from public discourse, as being something of the past. [...] This silence in fact should be interpreted as a deeply felt crisis in thinking about the Dutch nation' (Legêne, 2009).

The loss of the colonies with the proclamation of independence of Indonesia in 1945 and the transfer of sovereignty from the Netherlands to Indonesia in 1949, as well as the s*refidensi* (independence) of Surinam in 1975, turned out to have serious effects on the historiography of the Dutch nation. After 1945, (post) colonial history and national history have become divided from one another and have been developed as objects of separate academic fields. Sometimes, this division has also been accompanied by a problematic colour division in terms of researchers and perspectives: it is 'about them, but without them', as Kwame Nimako has suggested (Nimako, 2012). As Legêne observes, the relationship between colonial history and national history was and still is complex by definition. This complexity is reflected by the fact that memories from the Dutch colonial past keep coming back, sometimes to inspire, sometimes to haunt life, culture and politics in present-day Netherlands.

Collective memory and crisis of identity

These observations point to a beginning of an answer to the question why crisis and decline in the Netherlands have triggered selective forgetting and remodelling of the past. For centuries, the Dutch national identity has centred on images of the country boasting a history as a progressive, open, internationally oriented, aid-giving, tolerant guide for other countries in the world. However, after the 9/11 attacks in 2001 and their impact on the Netherlands, the murders of right-wing populist party leader Pim Fortuyn in 2002, and of writer and film-maker Theo van Gogh in 2003, boundaries have been drawn between 'us' and 'them', between the 'real Dutch' and 'Others' within the nation-state of the Netherlands (Captain and Jones, 2007b). Dutch and international scholars, journalists and other opinion-makers have therefore claimed that the first decades of the third millennium will be a test case for Dutch identity.

It is true that testimonies and counter voices of a Dutch past, experienced by persons and their descendants originating from the peripheries of the Kingdom of the Netherlands, have also been expressed. Yet, it may still be concluded that Dutch postcolonial citizens from Indonesia, Surinam and the Antilles from the first, second and third generations, who nowadays make up about one million individuals in a Dutch population of 16 million inhabitants, are virtually unheard and unrepresented in political discourses. The economic and political crisis, as well the crisis in Dutch national identity, is partly grounded in an insufficient public discourse on the history of the Dutch colonial past and its postcolonial citizenry. Moreover, the complexities and ambiguities that are inherent in public discourse on Dutch colonial experience affect current debates on migration and the fear and hatred of 'the other'. In order to understand this current Dutch predicament, it is instructive to make a short historical detour that exposes the treatment of Dutch colonial and postcolonial subjects.

In the 1980s, political consensus in the Netherlands was established on the acceptance of religious and cultural differences and manifest xenophobic rhetoric was condemned. The twenty-first century has seen the implementation of restrictive immigrations laws, which have been increasingly legitimized by a discourse that posits migration and migrants as a threat to the 'Dutch community'. Dutch right-liberal governments have implemented policies aiming to expulse 'undesirable aliens', regardless of whether they have been socially integrated in Dutch society or not. In drawing boundaries between the global and the national through restrictive migration policies, the Dutch government has become a contender against an international migration regime founded on international law, of which it was once a fierce proponent. Cultural and religious diversity, advocated and institutionalized as routes to integration in the 1980s, are thus today perceived as obstacles to integration and as a threat to the reified Dutch nation. In the new political consensus, Islamic minorities have been painted as enemies within the borders of the nation-state. Apart from much more restrictive migration policies, integration policies have increasingly held up assimilation, or the compliance with an essentialized and mystified notion of a uniform 'Dutch culture', as a remedy. So-called non-Western newcomers have therefore been subjected to 'integration programmes', even before entering the Netherlands.

Despite all these efforts, colonial episodes still haunt the Netherlands as the former Dutch colonies keep reminding us of our shared past. This may be related to the changed Dutch political climate of the last decade, in which the Netherlands have changed from being a progressive and open country to being one of Europe's most introvert nations. The more Dutch politicians are trying to suppress reminders of our colonial past, the more these reminders pop up. For instance, the war of decolonization between the Netherlands and Indonesia (1945–49) literally still hides many skeletons in the closet. In 2011 and 2013, the Dutch state lost two court trials to Indonesian widows whose husbands were murdered by the Dutch army in 1946 and 1947 (Court Ruling The Hague, 2011). In 2012, pictures of executions of Indonesian men by Dutch militaries were saved from a trash bin. It made headlines in the Dutch newspapers: 'First pictures ever of executions by Dutch army in the Indies' (*De Volkskrant*, 10 July 2012). In 2013, war crimes in Indonesia committed by Captain Raymond Westerling and Second Lieutenant Jan van der Meulen were revealed and acknowledged. Dutch newspaper *Trouw* wrote on 16 November 2013: 'The Netherlands have their own My Lai', referring to the massacre of Vietnamese citizens by the American army in 1968. Two days later, *Trouw* published the 'news' that historian William Frederick had called the massacre of Dutch and Indo-Dutch by the Indonesian freedom fighters 'a forgotten genocide'. The scoop was based on an article that Frederick published a year before in the *Journal of Genocide Research* (Frederick, 2012).

After these eruptions of a repressed postcolonial past into the present, it could have been expected that an examination of the Dutch–Indonesian relations during 1945–49 would be one of the most urgent tasks for historical research in the Netherlands. In June 2012, a proposal was submitted to the Dutch government by the Royal Netherlands Institute of Southeast Asian and Caribbean Studies (KITLV), the Netherlands Institute for Military History (NIMH) and the Netherlands Institute for War, Holocaust and Genocide Studies (NIOD). These three institutes proposed a combined contribution of €1.2 million and asked the Dutch government for co-financing. However, the Minister of Foreign Affairs and the Minister of Defence concluded that no money would be made available for such a research programme, as there would be no support in Indonesia for such research. A letter from the Minister of Foreign Affairs and the Minister of Defence on 14 January 2013 pointed out that the government considered this of 'crucial importance at a time when the Netherlands and Indonesia are working together on a future-oriented agenda'. This seems to be yet another way of silencing the past, as it is a public secret that, up until now, the government of Indonesia has not been inclined to sustain such research because focusing on the violence of the years 1945–49 would include not only Dutch, but also Indonesian, atrocities.

Just recently (we are writing in September 2015), the Dutch-Swiss historian Remy Limpach concluded that the violence of the Dutch colonial army during the years 1945–49 had not been restricted to a number of incidents, but could be characterized as extreme and structural (Limpach, 2015).

Conclusion

So where does this leave the Netherlands? I would like to end this chapter by looking at the way in which the colonial past is represented by the Rijksmuseum, the National Museum of Art and History in Amsterdam. In my opinion, curators translate academic insights into the public realm, just as a museum can be considered an intervention in the public space. The Rijksmuseum reopened in March 2013 after nine years of renovation for a total cost of €375 million. In the new exhibition art, crafts and history are presented in an integrated exhibition. Historians, and notably historians specializing in colonial and postcolonial history, have received the new exhibition critically: 'In the new Rijksmuseum, it is true that history is present, but it is not "living history". Aesthetics are dominant' (Drieënhuizen, 2013).

Others were more specific and argued that the Rijksmuseum presented an inward-looking, jubilant representation of the Netherlands and its colonial past. The national history interpreted by the Rijksmuseum is about imposing 'awe' in an 'unproblematic nostalgic framework'. The integration of art and history is viewed by them very critically:

Downright bizarre is the public presentation on the twentieth century. The few objects connected to our colonial past are presented without context. Plaster casts from faces of inhabitants of the island Nias are an artistic installation. The colonial framework, the power relations in which these masks were made, as well as its consequences seem to be irrelevant. Although decolonisation itself is mentioned, every visual or material reference to it is missing.

(Bloembergen *et al.*, 2013)

The words of historian Frank van Vree seem therefore crucial:

We are witnessing a fundamental and irreversible change in our culture. Knowledge and understanding of cultural heritage are no longer obvious, because slowly we are disconnected from its origins. [...] Because of this lack of true understanding, mostly an aesthetic experience remains.

(Van Vree, 2013)

That the colonial past is reduced to a spectacle, such as presented by the Rijksmuseum, is a development that needs a strong counterweight. Knowledge and awareness of the colonial legacy is not an optional extra, but a fundamental building block for sustainable societies in Europe in the twenty-first century. It is not only the case that people who ignore their history are condemned to repeat it, but also that the tragic-comic repetition is never productive and seldom instructive.

Note

1 I am grateful to Dr Guno Jones (Leiden University), Nancy Jouwe MA (former programme director of Kosmopolis Utrecht) and Wim Manuhutu MA (former director of Moluccan Museum Utrecht) for sharing their thoughts with me on the topic of this chapter.

Bibliography

Aldridge, R. (ed.) (2007) *The Age of Empires. Overseas Empires in the Early Modern and Modern World*. London: Thames and Hudson.

Bély, L. (2007) *L'Art de la Paix en Europe. Naissance de la Diplomatie Moderne XVI–XVIII Siècle*. Paris: PUF.

Bloembergen, M., Schulte Nordholt, H. and Eickhoff, M. (2013) 'Koloniale nostalgie in Rijksmuseum'. In: *NRC*, 21 June.

Captain, E. (2002) *Achter het kawat was Nederland. Indische oorlogservaringen en –herinneringen 1942–1995*. Kampen: Kok.

Captain, E. (2013) 'Driehonderd gulden per vrijgelaten slaaf. Slaveneigenaren in Utrecht en de afschaffing van slavernij in 1863'. *Oud Utrecht. Tijdschrift voor geschiedenis van stad en provincie Utrecht*, 86 (2), pp. 38–43.

Captain, E. (2014) 'Harmless Identities: Representations of Racial Consciousness among Three Generations Indo-Europeans'. In: Essed, P. and Hoving, I. (eds), *Dutch Racism*. Amsterdam/New York: Rodopi, pp. 53–70.

Captain, E. and Jones, G. (2007a) 'The Netherlands: A Small Country with Imperial Ambitions'. In: Aldridge, R. (ed.), *The Age of Empires. Overseas Empires in the Early Modern and Modern World.* London: Thames and Hudson, pp. 92–111.

Captain, E. and Jones, G. (2007b) 'A Passport is a Piece of Paper, or the Enrichment of the Netherlands'. In: Braidotti, R., Esche, C. and Hlavajova, M. (eds), *Citizens and Subjects: The Netherlands, for Example. A Critical Reader.* Dutch contribution to the 52nd International Art Exhibition La Biennale di Venezia. Utrecht/Zürich: BAK/JRP Ringier, pp. 87–97.

Captain, E. and Visser, H. (2012) *Wandelgids Sporen van slavernij in Utrecht/Walking Guide: Traces of Slavery in Utrecht.* Utrecht: Utrecht University/Centre for the Humanities.

District Court of The Hague (2011) Court Ruling: Foundation of Dutch Honorary Debts versus the Ministry of Foreign Affairs.

Drieënhuizen, C. (2013) 'Terug naar af? Het nieuwe Rijksmuseum en de Nederlandse koloniale geschiedenis'. Blog, 25 April 2013. Open Universiteit. Available at: www. ou.nl/web/erfgoedplatform/terug-naar-af-het-nieuwe-rijksmuseum-en-de-nederlandse-koloniale-geschiedenis [accessed 3 February 2015].

Essed, P. and Hoving, I. (eds) (2014) *The Legacy of Dutch Racism.* Amsterdam: Rodopi Publishers.

Frederick, W.H. (2012) 'The Killing of Dutch and Eurasians in Indonesia's National Revolution (1945–49): A Brief "Genocide" Reconsidered'. *Journal of Genocide Research*, 14 (3–4), pp. 359–80.

Jones, G. (2012) 'Slavernij is onze geschiedenis (niet). Over de discursieve strijd om de betekenis van de NTR-televisieserie De slavernij'. *Bijdragen en Mededelingen betreffende de Geschiedenis van Nederland (BMGN)*, 127 (4), pp. 56–82.

Legêne, S (2005) *Nu of nooit. Over de actualiteit van museale collecties.* Amsterdam: Vossius Pers.

Legêne, S. (2009) 'Dwinegeri – Multiculturalism and the Colonial Past (Or: the Cultural Borders of Being Dutch)'. In: Kaplan, B., Carlson, M. and Cruz, L. (eds), *Boundaries and their Meaning in the History of the Netherlands.* Leiden/Boston: Brill, pp. 223–42.

Limpach, R. (2015) 'Ook de kok wilde wel een Indiër martelen'. *Trouw*, 23 September.

Netwerk CS. (2009) *De olifant in de kamer. Staalkaart culturele diversiteit in de basisinfrastructuur.* Amsterdam: Netwerk CS.

Nimako, K. (2012) 'About Them, but Without Them. Race and Ethnic Relations Studies in Dutch Universities'. *Human Architecture. Journal of the Sociology of Self-Knowledge*, 10 (1), pp. 45–52.

NOS Journaal, 28 September 2006.

Oostindie, G. (2006) *De parels en de kroon. Het koningshuis en de koloniën.* Amsterdam: De Bezige Bij.

Oostindie, G. (2010) *Postkoloniaal Nederland. Vijfenzestig jaar vergeten, herdenken, herinneren.* Amsterdam: Bert Bakker.

Schnabel, P. (2012) 'An Epilogue to Serve as a Preface'. *Knowledge, Peace, Freedom. The Treaty of Utrecht Revisited.* Utrecht: Center for the Humanities.

Stoler, A.L. (2011) 'Colonial Aphasia: Race and Disabled Histories in France'. *Public Culture*, 23 (1), pp. 121–56.

Treaty of Utrecht. (2013) *Utrecht celebrates peace.* Utrecht: Treaty of Utrecht.

Trouw, 26 October 2013.

Trouw, 15 November 2015.

van Duuren, D. (1990) *125 jaar verzamelen.* Amsterdam: Tropenmuseum.

Volkskrant, 10 July 2012.

Voorhoeve, J. (1985) *Peace, Profits and Principles. A Study of Dutch Foreign Policy.* Leiden: Martinus Nijhoff.

Vree van, F. (2013) Lecture at the opening of the academic year of the Faculty of Humanities of the University of Amsterdam, 5 September.

Weindl, A. (2008) 'The *Asiento de Negros* and International Law'. *Journal of the History of International Law*, 10 (2), pp. 229–57.

Weiner, M.F. (2014) 'The Ideologically Colonized Metropole: Dutch Racism and Racist Denial'. *Sociology Compass*, 8 (6), pp. 731–44.

Williams, H. (2006) *Days That Changed the World. The 50 Defining Events of World History.* London: Quercus.

5 From austerity to postcolonial nostalgia

Crisis and national identity in Portugal and Denmark

Elsa Peralta and Lars Jensen

In Europe the notion of 'austere' has since the beginning of the global financial crisis become inextricably linked to the austerity measures demanded by the EU Commission, a number of member states, and the European Central Bank of countries whose short-term financial survival were undermined by the financial market's attack on their ability to secure new loans. In the financial market media and in the national media of the more affluent parts of Europe, the derogatory acronym PIGS (Portugal, Italy, Greece and Spain) or PIIGS (if Ireland was included) came to symbolize an attitude that, although an immediate product of the current crisis, was also a case of the resurfacing of a much deeper-rooted representational history – a re-materialization of domestic European orientalism (Said, 1978/95; Dainotto, 2007; Gramsci, 1926/1978).

This domestic orientalism produces Europe's South as occupying a liminal space in relation to a northern-centred European rational (economic) self and has been fed by a long history of travellers, intellectuals and, more generally, public discourse in Europe's North (Rota, 2012; Moe, 2002). The South produced by this discourse is characterized by lacks – of responsibility, productivity and rationality. The North, through the verbalizing of the shortcomings of the South, comes to operate as an invisible and hence uncontested model of the perceived ideal characteristics.

While Europe's North has its own history of being produced as marginal, it is here the extreme North that has been subjected to 'orientalized' representations (Sami people and Greenlanders as 'others', and Faroese and Icelanders as displaced, exoticized or 'othered' northern selves). Significantly, these representations are produced in the North itself, as a discourse about an aberrant 'Northern North' projected against a normativized European North. Paradoxically, the extreme North has also been depicted in terms of purity, partly influenced by racialized discourses projecting an aspirational pure whiteness as characteristic of the North, with which the metropolitan cultures of the North have identified as part of a northern continuity. Here 'pure' North operates in contrast to a 'tainted' discourse about the liminal – or questionable – European southerner (and easterner[1]), which cannot operate as a parallel ideal.

As such, the North has worked as an ambiguous space for projections of a displaced and idealized Europeanness in which the European North has had a determining degree of agency. The European southerner has not been assigned a comparable agency in relation to representations of the South. This imbalance between North and South in terms of representational power has been explained by a number of scholars as resulting from a historic shift from the 'first modernity', or the Renaissance, based in the Mediterranean area, to the 'second modernity', the Enlightenment, based in northwest Europe (see most notably Dussel, 1998; Mignolo, 2000; and Dainotto, 2007). Some scholars discuss this primarily or exclusively in terms of internal or domestic European power shifts, while others see it as intrinsically linked to Europe's global history.

In this chapter we engage with the intersection between 'domestic' and 'global' Europe, and we begin with the domestic European context. Thus we seek to place the current crisis in the *longue durée* of a European modernity (Braudel, 2009) informed by two significant spaces that still inform European self-perceptions and political agendas: the national space and the former colonial space. In the context of the crisis, these two spaces gain a new momentum in the mediation of the common understandings of the 'us' (with a growing enclosure of the national space) and of the 'other' (reinforcement of conservative views regarding the colonial past and attitudes and policies towards migrants). We will contextualize our arguments through the comparative analysis of two cases, respectively placed (geographically and symbolically) in Europe's South and North: Portugal and Denmark. While there are many ways in which Portugal and Denmark can be seen to occupy different if not polarized positions, they also have overlapping histories when it comes to their histories as colonial powers and in relation to their self-perception as historically peripheral to the centripetal forces of pan-European history.

The Portuguese history as a colonial power can arguably be dated back to the conquest of Ceuta in 1415, but colonialism is not a leitmotif that can be identified from that point onwards. A more obvious starting point is Vasco da Gama because his journey to India led to the establishment of the first Portuguese empire. Yet, in terms of our search for historical continuity from the colonial to the postcolonial, it is the rise, stagnation and collapse of the third[2] Portuguese colonial empire in Africa that represents the most interesting phase. Historically, the collapse of empire culminates with the colonial liberation wars in the Portuguese African colonies and the 1974 revolution in Portugal, leading to a reorientation towards Europe with the accession of Portugal to what became the EU.

Danish colonial history (discounting the Viking era) dates back to the decision to participate in the lucrative spice trade in the 1600s. The dismantling or demise of the Danish colonial empire, in contrast to the Portuguese, began with the sale of the 'tropical' colonies in Africa and Asia in the mid-nineteenth century, culminating with the sale of the Danish Virgin Islands in 1917. What is often forgotten in the Danish context is that the possessions in the North Atlantic (Greenland, Faroe Islands and Iceland) were also colonies, which extends Danish colonial history in the North Atlantic to Iceland's independence in 1944 and beyond, since Greenland and the Faroe Islands still today remain integral, autonomous parts of a Danish defined realm. Hence, while the Portuguese colonial history ended with the transfer of Macau to China in 1999, Denmark still wields significant influence over its former colonies in the North Atlantic.

Situating the current crisis

The currently unfolding European economic crisis and its accompanying austerity measures have revealed the biggest cracks in the EU since its foundation, to which have recently been added the issue of border protection as a result of the refugee crisis continuously unfolding at the time of writing. In the crisis discourse the agency of the European South has been dramatically circumscribed as accusations of laziness, unaccountability, corruption and clientelism have been routinely directed at the peoples of the EU's southern member states by countries in the North, but also by certain parts of the South itself. The 'high' North of Europe – in this case Denmark, Sweden and Finland (Norway is of course not in the EU) – is clearly a part of the current power centre of the EU (dominated by the European Commission, the European Central Bank and the German government) and has allied itself with the discourse of the centre. The lack of agency in responding to accusations (acquiescence does not really constitute agency), and the absence of a space within the institutionalized structures of the EU for formulating alternative solutions to the austerity regime that is spreading poverty across Europe, has led to emerging alternative platforms in Europe's South directed against the austerity measures. These counterstrategies have targeted the EU itself and its central power brokers. Here agency is clearly identifiable, not least in the Greek Syriza-led government's insistence on not only renegotiating a debt that is indisputably unserviceable (even according to the IMF) (Nardelli, 2015), but also on redefining what Greece's debt is actually about. An equally important development is the parallel process of political formation that has transformed the Spanish *indignados*' protests into the political movement Podemos.

The Greek and Spanish interventions clearly reveal how the neoliberal order, which produces these crises, is met overwhelmingly by grass-root counterstrategies emerging from Europe's South.[3] The North, by contrast, remains largely complicit with the austerity regime, while anti-austerity and anti-neoliberal sentiments have until now mainly been channelled into right-wing populism focusing on anti-immigration. Since the current situation is marked by crisis, it is an open question if the counterstrategies of the South will continue to take the form of counter-movements, as in the case of Greece and Spain (and, more controversially, Italy). It is equally difficult to predict if these movements will become real alternatives to the European political order or lead to the return to earlier forms of patron–client relations in which the weaker part (the South) negotiates with, and at the same time resists, the dominance of a powerful North (Scott, 1990).

In a more optimistic vein, collaboration could also develop between austerity measures resistance in the South and groups in the North who have also been targets of neoliberal reforms even before the global financial crisis, such as working poor in affluent Germany. At present, however, it is difficult to escape the conclusion that the crisis will continue to unfold since, even according to the lending institutions themselves (IMF, 2015), the austerity measures are merely prolonging and deepening the crisis, rather than solving it.

Crisis comes to Denmark

The reductionist narrative of the global financial crisis, according to which the failure of southern European countries to service and refinance debt resulted from an irresponsible spending beyond their means, reveals how quickly the crisis discourse latches on to the history of stereotypical conceptualizations of Europe's North and South. When the crisis emerged in 2007–08, it was the spectacular failures of the financial system to prevent speculation and exploitation of financial ignorance that dominated the headlines. In fact, 'financial pillars of society' were revealed to participate in and exacerbate speculative bubbles. In other words, it was the privatization agenda (installed since the early 1980s and gathering momentum from the 1990s) of Western economies, supported by the neoliberalist creed to limit state intervention because the market is self-regulating, that in this case quite literally broke the bank.

The crisis, of course, originated in the far North, where Iceland had eagerly embraced the neoliberal economic agenda and deregulated its banking sector, abrogating in the process the state's responsibility of supervision. The Icelandic economy collapsed in spectacular fashion in October 2008 (Danielsson, 2009; Bergmann, 2014; see also Loftsdóttir, 2014, for a discussion of the conceptualization of the many aspects of the crisis in Iceland). Iceland is of course a former Danish colony, and some of the private bankers had spent part of their windfall in the boom years leading up to the crash by acquiring symbolic Danish national 'treasures' in the form of Copenhagen landmarks such as the Hotel D'Angleterre and the department store Magasin. The Icelandic economy was profoundly differently geared in comparison with the Danish and those of the other Nordic countries, even if their economies were also being transformed according to the logics of deregulated capitalism. In the other Nordic countries, economic constraints were mainly caused by the EU's stipulated maximum budget deficit of 3 per cent of GDP (euro convergence criteria), which forced EU governments to curb public expenditure through measures that led to a dramatic rise in unemployment and welfare cuts. Privatization of welfare services, which had already paved the way for the erosion of social benefits, health care and education, was now replaced by the outright elimination of certain welfare services.

In affluent Denmark, which does not belong to the Eurozone but has tied its currency to the euro, the crisis caused an estimated loss of 200,000 jobs (Confederation of Danish Employers, 2013). This is dramatic in a small country of 5.5 million people, and the job losses were accompanied by further restrictive measures, such as drastically reduced periods of unemployment benefit entitlement. Even so, it is important to remember that the Danish crisis unfolded against a backdrop of being one of the most affluent and equal societies in the world, albeit also a society with a paltry record in securing equal opportunities for its migrant population (see for example *Big Gaps ...*, 2014). Hence the crisis has been relatively mild at a national level in comparison with the cutbacks experienced by other European countries, not least in the South. There is a danger, however, in reductively portraying the Danish reaction as a set of emergency policies aimed at containing a crisis threatening to undermine the entire economy. One look at the history of the Gini coefficient (which works as a measuring tape for inequality) reveals a longer history of rising inequality that predates the crisis. The Gini coefficient for Denmark was stable throughout the 1980s and early 1990s, but from the mid-1990s it began to rise and the crisis has not bucked this trend, placing Denmark as a middle-ranking OECD country rather than the country with the highest degree of equality (Eurostat, 2015; CEVEA, 2014). Rising inequality therefore cannot be seen only as a result of the crisis, even if job losses clearly contributed to it, but must instead be seen as the result of government initiatives also prior to the crisis, for example the deregulation of the real estate market. This illustrates the real problem is neoliberalism itself, rather than the crises it produces. In the longer term, it reveals a more profound crisis in the state's ability to redistribute wealth. This again undermines the prevailing discourse in Europe according to which crisis is coming to the North from a European South plagued by economic mismanagement.

Currently, the crisis is discursively constructed in Denmark as petering out with rising employment figures. Yet, particularly, the losses of unskilled jobs incurred during the initial crisis years are far from being recovered. The Gini coefficient has not changed correspondingly, suggesting a situation similar to that of other countries in the global North: slow and largely jobless economic growth. While there is widespread dissatisfaction with political leadership in Denmark, there has not yet been anything amounting to the widespread anti-austerity demonstrations in Europe's South. In fact, Denmark, similar to the other Nordic countries, has instead seen the rise of populist anti-globalization sentiment linked to an anti-immigration agenda, dissociated from any critique of the austerity regime. Even if there have been protracted conflicts over implementations of some parts of the economic reforms in Denmark, these conflicts have been isolated to disputes between employers and employee groups and have rarely ignited any broader movements of solidarity. The economic crisis in Denmark has thus had very concrete but also very elusive manifestations. It has had devastating consequences for some people, yet it also remains, at a broader level, somewhat intangible. This sits well with the neoliberal project of individualizing the effects of the crises produced through the concentration of wealth.

Crisis comes to Portugal

Although Portugal has been facing a severe financial crisis since 2010, leading to the intervention of the IMF and other financial agencies in order to prevent the insolvency of the country, the structural roots of the actual crisis are much older. They can be traced through the country's long history of inhabiting a peripheral position, both in relation to Europe and to the modern capitalist system. Hence part of the Portuguese financial crisis is a problem of contagion. When the global financial crisis of 2008 hit Europe, the Portuguese economy soon emerged as one of the most vulnerable. Nine years later this is still the case. The Portuguese economy had already weakened since the late 1990s due to a number of factors: the preparation of the entry into the Eurozone (in 1999); the enlargement of the EU; and the expansion of the emerging economies.

When the crisis began, the level of Portugal's debt, although serious, was closer to that of Spain or Italy and the country was not subjected to the same pressures as Greece or Ireland from international markets. However, the situation deteriorated rapidly from the beginning of 2010, when Greece's dire circumstances became apparent. Also, the crisis in the Eurozone worked as an opportunity for market vultures such as hedge funds to speculate against the ability of southern Europe to service its debt, which again raised the interest on new loans. As such, the crisis has undermined the idea, widely entertained in liberal and social-liberal circles, that the market acts rationally and in the interest of the common economic good. The abandonment of (social-) liberal explanations leads inevitably to the perception that the market is geared towards maximising short-term profiteering, and has no interest in the social-economic costs brought on by negative speculation (Epstein and Habbard, 2011), let alone long-term destructive effects of economic reforms.

The contagion of the Greek problem affected the most vulnerable Eurozone economies: Spain, Ireland and Portugal. Portugal and Spain responded to the market pressure by implementing austerity measures aimed to reduce government expenditures and employment costs. While this led to a temporary relief of market pressures on Portugal, in 2010 concerns about the Irish banking sector again subjected already weak economies to financial market speculation. With Greece and Ireland under the umbrella of international aid programmes, attention now turned to Portugal. In November 2010, the Portuguese Parliament adopted the toughest austerity budget in 30 years. Wages in the public sector suffered an overall reduction of 5 per cent, recruitment in public administration was essentially blocked and career promotions and salary progressions were banned. Subsidies and social benefits have been reduced and pensions frozen. The National Health Service and other public programmes were subjected to cuts. On the revenue side, the measures included an increase of two percentage points in the standard VAT rate and one percentage point in employee contributions to the General Pension Fund (Lourtie, 2011: 89). In early 2011, the Portuguese economy began to show signs of recovery, but the markets maintained the view that Portugal would have to ask for urgent financial help, partly due to the negative speculation as argued above. The fact that Portugal is a small economy in the European context, along with structural economic weaknesses and the related susceptibility to financial contagion effects, made it very difficult to ward off market pressures.

Portugal's economic and political weakness within Europe was for centuries compensated by its imperial economy and policies, with Portugal often being in a position of vulnerability vis-à-vis other European imperial powers, not least the British, from which it often sought protection. With the revolution of 1974 and the subsequent collapse of the colonial empire, Portugal experienced a period of political and financial instability. The IMF provided financial assistance to Portugal in 1978, and again in 1983. After this period of political and financial turmoil, the 1980s finally brought democratic consolidation and economic development, especially after Portugal's entry into the European Economic Community in 1986. There was a substantial improvement in the standard of living, accompanied by a complex process of social transformation. The urban middle class enjoyed considerable economic growth and could embrace a cosmopolitan, European lifestyle. Yet the economy as a whole remained fragile and susceptible to global market shifts. When the crisis hit, it became clear that the fate of Portugal was not for Portugal itself to make. Recovery would depend on the world economy in general, on the actions of other EU member states and 'the market'.

Moreover, the EU needed to respond to the actual crisis with structural changes in economic governance as well as with political consensus, both of which have been extremely difficult to achieve. Economic indicators differ considerably inside Europe, and markedly between Europe's North and South, with Germany and some northern and central European countries regarded as strong economies. The discrepancy between economic performances has been matched by sharp differences in the perceptions of the crisis and how to fix it. While the populations of the countries most affected by the crisis have to cope with harsh austerity measures, a significant part of electorates in northern and central Europe see the crisis almost exclusively as the result of bad budget management carried out by irresponsible southern spendthrifts. These negative perceptions are not only entirely wrong, as the problem does not lie with the disregard of rules (by many members of the Eurozone) but with the lack of rules. This lack of rules has further contributed to the worsening of the problem in the sense that it has increased market pressure on vulnerable economies such as the Portuguese.

The Portuguese government tried to reverse the negative perceptions and avoid an international bailout by implementing tough austerity measures. Eventually, these austerity measures were rejected by the Portuguese Parliament, with the inevitable consequence of the government's fall. Markets reacted immediately to this political instability. In just over a week Fitch downgraded the Portuguese credit rating from A+ to BBB– and Standard & Poor's from A– to BBB– (Lourtie, 2011: 96). Given the collapse of financing conditions, in April 2011 the Portuguese government called for international financial assistance from the EU and the IMF. Financial help (€78 billion) was granted on the condition that Portugal would implement a vast economic and financial adjustment programme.

Portuguese society responded to the austerity measures by social upheaval and protest. A social movement called *Que se Lixe a Troika* (To Hell with the Troika) was created in 2012 as a response to 'the humanitarian disaster that befalls the country'. The movement organized the protest of 15 September 2012, through the internet and social networks that mobilized around one million people against the government and the Troika. Three years later, however, the government that was under siege in 2012 did not lose by the predicted landslide in the October 2015 national elections. The government's fortune has been helped by the opposition's inability to present a consistent proposal for an alternative policy to the austerity regime. One million unemployed, the continuing rise of the taxation level, the 300,000 Portuguese who have had to leave the country in search of jobs, are just a few figures that make up the crisis statistics in Portugal. Yet, the government is seeking to distance Portugal from the image of 'chaotic' Greece and to convince the rampantly impoverished Portuguese people that they are better off without too much contestation of the European policies. Moreover, the public treasury has improved and the country's financing capacity has been partly restored, much due to rising export incomes, which increased by 24 per cent after the entry of the Troika and in 2015 accounted for 41 per cent of GDP. Markets such as Cape Verde, Angola and Mozambique, along with Spain and France, are among the countries where Portugal has the largest market shares. This shows the extent to which the former colonial world is still pivotal to the Portuguese economy.

While Portugal left the bailout programme in 2014, the recovery remains fragile and the European Commission and the IMF have both warned about the vulnerability of the Portuguese economy. And even if the country has managed to keep afloat, the consequences have been dramatic. There has been a forced impoverishment at all levels of the middle classes due to reduced or frozen wages, a tremendous increase in the tax burden and a sharp cut in pensions. In social and public life, poverty is often an unspoken issue, masked by shame or endured only through help from family. Yet it remains deep-seated in Portuguese society. Hence, the pattern of cutbacks affecting the poor and middle classes, while the rich have continued to accumulate wealth, is an experience that Portugal shares with Denmark, even if the degrees of severity are markedly different.

Crisis and the reimagining of the global nation

What we have detailed so far is the deep crisis currently swamping all of Europe, yet often perceived as a collection of national crises. In a less nation-specific and more pan-European perspective it has become apparent that the failure of crisis management threatens the institutional cohesion of Europe itself. As such, Europe's crisis is far more than an accumulation of national crises. But it is also far more than a domestic *European* crisis.

Indeed, the juxtaposition of the national and continental dimension of the crisis fails to take into consideration that Europe is not the only relevant factor beyond the nation. Nor, as mentioned earlier, is the North–South discursive divide in Europe merely a by-product of the present austerity agenda. The *longue durée* of the representational history has also had and continues to have global repercussions. Indeed, European ideas of selfhood at both national and pan-European levels are defined by European colonial and postcolonial discourses about colonial and postcolonial others. Although this division has been disguised by the European post-war 'continental developmentalism', or modernization process, and after the fall of the Berlin Wall by post-Cold War neoliberalism, it was wrought by colonial modernity, whether it established its classification inside of Europe or outside its borders throughout its colonial domains. Yet very rarely have 'national' European scholars devoted attention to this. One exception is Kristin Ross (1995), who discusses the overlaps between a modernization craze in 1950s and 1960s France and the Algerian War of Independence. She argues that the post-war Americanized commodification of a French selfhood cannot be understood outside France's relationship with colonial Algeria and to a lesser extent other parts of the French empire. Her work remains one of a few instances where connections between a domestic national order and the late colonial world are made explicit and seen as integral to a national framework.

In this perspective, the current crisis can be seen as the end of one order and the beginning of a new. During the accompanying transformation process a whole set of old classificatory apparatuses and ideologies that used to lie dormant under the neoliberal market ideology again come to the fore as tentative frameworks. These frameworks can ideologically place and enable responses to the new crisis mentality. Because of their tentative nature they do not stabilize themselves in the shape of a clear political agenda to cope with the crisis. Instead they feed on pre-existing stereotypical assumptions and relations both between the European North and South (the 'modern North' vs the insufficiently 'modern South') and between Europe and its former colonial others.

In the context of the crisis, the colonial other occupies an ambivalent space. It is both an object of attack (migrants as a manifestation of the crisis and perpetrators responsible for anti-immigration laws) and an object of desire (longing for the colonial past and a willingness to economically and politically engage with the former empire as a way of coping with crisis). In both Denmark and Portugal of the 1980s and 1990s, the national imagination was aligned with a perception of belonging to a wider European identity, also because Europe was seen to provide stability and greater affluence. This identification with Europe, which was never unequivocal, paved over other patterns of identifications associated with both nations' previous engagements with the world outside.

Denmark had emerged from the Second World War with a damaged reputation, which it worked to restore through a solid investment in the role as international actor in development aid (similarly to Norway and Sweden). At the same time, it sought to preserve its foothold in the two remaining colonies, Greenland and the Faroe Islands. The Danish neo-colonial presence in the North Atlantic is complex, but one of its most important features was the massive investment in Greenlandic society, aimed at transforming it from a traditional Inuit hunting society to a modern economy based on a fishing industry. However, the modernization period, as it was officially labelled in the 1950s and 1960s, led to a profound crisis in Greenlandic society in the 1970s, forcing a Danish recognition of a limited Greenlandic home rule in 1979 and self-government 30 years later.

Portugal in similar fashion sought to preserve its colonial realm in Africa after 1945 through its declaration of the colonies as overseas provinces in the Constitutional Revision of 1951 (Denmark made Greenland and the Faroe Islands an integral part of the Danish realm in 1953). In a context of an ever-swelling anti-colonialist tide, Portuguese colonial policy directed its attention to the rhetorical construction of 'Portugal's Ultramarine', conceived as a multi-continental nation and the orchestrator of an exemplary colonization marked by miscegenation, cultural fusion and lack of racial prejudice. It reinscribed its African colonies as overseas provinces (Castelo, 1999) alongside its 'European' island provinces (Madeira and the Azores). Portugal furthermore boosted white settlement in its colonies, and the white population in Angola rose dramatically from 44,000 in 1940 to 79,000 in 1950 and 173,000 in 1960 (Castelo, 2012; Clarence-Smith, 1985). The rise in 1947 of the world market coffee price was no doubt an incentive for migration to Angola, but the determining factor was the political and economic ambitions of Portugal's authoritarian, nationalist-imperialist Estado Novo[4] and its efforts to legitimize its colonies as 'overseas provinces', against the tide of the post-war international order that saw successive waves of independent former colonies across Africa and Asia.

Denmark also experienced a sizeable migration of Danes to Greenland to 'help' with the modernization process, but here the preferred model was the posting of Danes in Greenland for a shorter or longer period of time. The reasons were partly the quickly rising affluence of Danish society, which dampened the desire for migration, partly the Greenlandic Arctic climate which cooled the desire. Some Danes nonetheless decided to stay on, and in Greenland, just as in Portuguese Africa, migrants and settlers became a group to be reckoned with by the administrations in Lisbon and Copenhagen. Again, this serves as an important reminder that in the broader European context this migratory form of colonialism, or settler colonialism, was not unique to Denmark and Portugal, nor to the post-war period. Germany exported citizens to its colonial world during its short-lived imperial reign, as did Italy in East Africa, Belgium in the Congo, the Dutch in Indonesia and the French in Algeria (Palumbo, 2003; Frankema and Buelens, 2013; Ross, 1995).

In both Denmark and Portugal these colonial strategies were intrinsic to the national imagination. In both countries, presence in the colonial world, also post-1945, was regarded and projected as natural. This naturalization was built on a colonial archive of representations where nostalgia and benevolence – directed from the civilized North to the uncivilized South – were central ingredients. Yet, this symbolic geography presents some particular features in the Portuguese case stemming from Portugal's double condition of being at once a peripheral, sub-altern, Western country and a European, colonizing nation (Santos, 2008). In this perspective, Europe appears as a continent before which Portugal needs to affirm the greatness of its empire in order to compensate for its fragile political and economic position within the political landscape of Europe. (In a similar but more restricted fashion, Denmark used its possession of Greenland as an entrance ticket to NATO and disproportionate American influence.)

Lacking the administrative and economic resources needed to establish an indisputable political presence in the colonial territories, Portugal made extensive use of rhetorical devices to legitimize its colonial domain. Unlike the colonial discourses coming from the 'North', which mainly appealed to the rule of a civilizing reason, Portuguese imperial and colonial discourses were, particularly after the Second World War, constructed around an affective or emotional rationale, which stressed the nation's 'intimate' relationship with 'its' empire, sometimes even to the point of rejecting ideas of racial superiority. Instrumental as they were in the post-war geopolitical scenario, these ideas contributed to symbolically place Portugal as belonging simultaneously to the 'North' and the 'South': to the colonial order of the 'North' and to the affective, non-materialistic cultures of the 'South'.

These ambivalent ideas drew a more positive picture of Portuguese colonialism than the ones that portrayed European states as rejecting the colonial subject as a human subject. The Portuguese attitude to its former empire remains largely intact. Yet, Portugal's ideas were of course elaborated in the historical context of colonialism. They offered moral legitimacy for colonial rule and the perpetuation of racial inequality, and in this sense they did not differ from the structures of the imperial centres in Europe's centre and north.

Even as the colonies of both Denmark and Portugal were relabelled, largely in response to UN pressures to strengthen the decolonization process, the colonial apparatus continued to inform racialized discourses about Greenlanders, Angolans, Guinea Bissauans, Cape Verdeans and Mocambicans. Anti-colonial protests in the colonies took quite different forms, but they were driven by the same demand for recognition. In Portuguese Africa a protracted colonial war ended with the withdrawal of Portugal, and the enforced repatriation of somewhere between half a million and one million Portuguese settlers between 1974 and 1979, in the wake of decolonization.

In Greenland the process towards autonomy was, by comparison, non-violent. Yet although there was no colonial war, many Greenlanders condemned the modernization period as an attack on Greenlandic identity and way of life that caused severe social problems, such as alienation, alcoholism and suicide. The anti-colonial pressures led to the formation of Greenlandic political parties and a negotiated process of transferring parts of the local Danish administration into Greenlandic hands. This process continued with the achievement of Greenlandic self-government in 2009. No Danes stationed in Greenland, however, were forcefully repatriated. In fact, the colonial practice of Danes occupying key positions in the Greenlandic administration continues.

The Danish entry into the then EC in 1973, and the Portuguese in 1986, can be seen as a confirmation of the two nations' privileging of their attachment to Europe in a postcolonial world. Yet, the long-held stakes in the colonial world were not abandoned in either case. Important examples of the sustained emotional investment in the colonial world are, in the case of Portugal, migration between the different parts of the former Lusophone empire and, in the case of Denmark, the continued stationing of Danes in Greenland. Monetary investment also continues with Denmark investing in the protection of Danish sovereignty over Greenland (military and research). In the case of Portugal the crisis has seen the flow of funds in particular from Angola into Portugal – even if Portugal also remains the biggest investor in Angola (Fidalgo, n.d.).

At the time Portugal was entering the European Economic Community, a commemorative culture towards empire started to emerge, with the democratic regime again making use of the emotional attachments to the former colonial world to negotiate a symbolic positioning in the new European identitarian space. A prominent example of this is the 1998 World Expo in Lisbon. Expo'98 redeemed the notion of Portugal's imperial history, as the exhibition alluded strongly to the 'discoveries' of the fifteenth and sixteenth centuries, but not to colonialism. Furthermore, the discourse was updated and provided with a gloss of modernity through the extended use of 'European' ideas of multiculturalism and cosmopolitanism. The catchwords of the new 'postcolonial' rhetoric were tolerance and cultural contact, appropriate to globalizing languages and branding operations of a 'Portugality' linked to tourism, trade between Portugal and the former colonial territories and the designs of the so-called economic diplomacy. Gentrification, urban development, interventions in heritage assets, all processes typical of postmodern consumption on the one hand, and of post-imperial nostalgia on the other, nourished an industry and a policy based on the 'heritagization' of history.

In Denmark one could draw parallels to the emotional investment in the Danish West Indies as a tourist destination,[5] where sightseeing of Danish colonial buildings and streets with Danish names was uneasily positioned alongside the history of slavery without which this colonial architecture would never have existed. Hence, colonialism has not simply been replaced by a new and more intimate relationship with Europe, but still provides strong fantasies and objects of identification that periodically come to the fore.

The European crisis, and the shaken confidence in continental identification, has renewed the interest in opportunities offered by the 'ex'-colonial world. In the Danish case, this pattern has been very clear in the recent years' preoccupation with Greenland in Danish public discourse. In the Portuguese case, because of the austerity measures implemented in the country, both private interests and political agencies have increased their attention to the former colonies as preferred markets for Portuguese investments – and as sources of investment. At the same time, the country struggles to overcome the crisis and save its reputation as a state belonging to Europe. Portugal makes use – symbolically, politically and in economic terms – of its bonds with its former colonial world as a way towards financial recovery. This reorientation is also related to a wider global restructuring. Angola and Brazil's emergence as countries that can offer financial relief to Portugal's crisis-stricken economy is illustrative of this change, even if the Brazilian economy has recently developed its own economic crisis. The same applies to Denmark's boosting of its Arctic presence, through its 'duty' to uphold Danish sovereignty in Greenland in an era where the neoliberal scramble for the earth's diminishing resources has refocused attention on remote parts of the globe. The Arctic has received sizeable attention on this account, which is partly related to the presence of the unexploited resources, partly to climate change in the anthropocene which makes their extraction more possible, even if not necessarily less risky.

Contemporary migrancy

Migrancy has a long convoluted history in Europe including a large exodus of people from Europe to the colonial world and, later on, during decolonization, from the colonial world again back to Europe (Smith, 2003). The earlier exodus from Europe is often conveniently forgotten in the context of the migrancy crisis that has been unfolding in recent years. In this concluding section we explore how migrancy exists in the shadow of the contemporary economic crisis. Denmark and Portugal occupy polarized positions in the current European migrancy crisis. Denmark has – apart from a brief spell in the late 1960s and early 1970s – for decades sought to stem the flow of migrants into the country, and yet it remains one of the more desired destinations for the contemporary largely illegalized migrants.[6] The economic crisis in Portugal has by contrast led to a massive emigration of over 100,000 people annually, some to the former colonies. This mass emigration follows a brief period towards the end of the twentieth century where Portugal attracted a considerable number of migrants. In the context of the broader European crisis management of migration, Portugal represents an anomaly in terms of its absence of recent immigration, not least in view of neighbouring Spain's role as an at times important recipient of illegalized migrants. Furthermore, Portugal is not a transit country, in contrast to other European southern nations which have been or are facing large flows of illegalized migrants – including the most adversely affected crisis country, Greece.

In Denmark, migrants have been subjected to ever more negative scrutiny and circumscribing legislation, aimed squarely at discouraging immigration, or, for those who have already arrived, at encouraging assimilation. Policies have targeted different groups at different times, from anti-Tamil procrastination in relation to treating their right to family reunion in the late 1980s (a scandal that caused the prosecution and conviction of the then Minister of Justice), to reduced public allowances for migrants and refugees who have lived less than three years in Denmark (introduced in 2002, abolished in 2012, then reintroduced in 2015). The list of anti-immigration laws and regulations have come in a steady stream since the 1970s, but have been a major national preoccupation since the 'race election' of 2001.[7]

In Portugal the crisis has not been accompanied by anti-immigration laws nor by an aggravation of the social attitudes towards immigrants. This is directly related to the particular features of immigration to Portugal. Historically, Portugal is a country of emigration, with Portuguese people moving to several parts of the world to look for an improvement of their living conditions. The immigrants coming to Portugal started to arrive in the aftermath of decolonization and were mostly former imperial subjects fleeing from war or political instability in their newly independent countries.[8] The flow of migrant labour from the Portuguese-speaking countries increased from the late 1980s onward, especially from Cape Verde, Angola, Guinea-Bissau, and particularly Brazil, which soon became the largest immigrant community in Portugal. The expansion of the labour market in Portugal was then being encouraged by a period of relative economic growth, thanks to the integration into the EU and to the entry of the country into the global market economy (Vasconcelos, 2012). Apart from a large flow of immigrants from Eastern European countries, the greatest numbers of immigrants in Portugal originate from its former colonial domains.[9] Language, culture and social ties maintained between the former metropolitan centre and colonial periphery paved the way for postcolonial migration flows, often reproducing the power relations and the racialized classifications established under colonialism. Nonetheless, these are for the most part read in the light of the anti-racist and humanist orientation of the old imperial ideology that still mediates postcolonial relations in contemporary Portugal, thus somehow preventing the harshening of the relations in the social field, even if these are marked by several material and racial barriers.

At the same time, the effects of the economic crisis and the ensuing austerity policies have had consequences for both Portuguese nationals and immigrants, making it difficult to firmly separate the two. Portuguese nationals were encouraged to emigrate by the government, and some did. Around 110,000 Portuguese left the country in 2013 alone, some heading for Angola and Brazil, where a growing economy absorbed unemployed or underpaid Portuguese qualified professionals. Brazilians working in Portugal have also been leaving in large numbers, often returning to Brazil, where the economic growth presented new opportunities.[10] The ambivalent migratory space occupied by Portugal (caused by both the peripheral positioning of Portugal within Europe and the colonial and postcolonial relations established by the Portuguese) helps to explain the absence of a political discourse directed against immigrants and immigration, even if the reality in which immigrants live in Portugal is, as in other places, generally marked by poverty and exclusion.

Conclusion

We have sought to establish links between the current economic crisis as a challenge to an existing domestic European order and as an opportunity to reinvent the idea of a nation as shaped by its non-European colonial history. We have done this by examining two European countries localized at opposite ends, both in terms of their respective location in the North and the South, and in terms of their polarized positions in relation to how the European crisis has impacted on individual countries through the austerity regime. Both countries have a history as largely forgotten empires, both countries have orchestrated imperial narratives of exceptionalism and benevolence, which are resurrected as the two countries have recently started to reinvent their relations with the now ex-colonial world as a safety measure against the uncertain future of the pan-European project of continental nation-building.

The intersection between the nation as participant in a pan-European project that is now threatened by the unfolding crisis and the nation's re-identification with its postcolonial contemporaneity entails both a renegotiating of relations with a far less submissive ex-colonial world and a coming to terms with a wider postcolonial reality. The most profound aspect of this reality is the difficulty presented by the arrival of migrants from the general ex-colonial world, a process that inevitably transforms Europe's contemporary history. But this is by no means a unidirectional transition. As the case of Portugal shows, the movement of people and market opportunities is also directed towards the ex-colonial world. Indeed, the global financial crisis has underlined this double process. While it has prompted a renewed focus on the national space – a space seen to partly belong to Europe and thus subjected to European challenges in the current austerity climate – it has also reinvigorated the attention on the ex-colonial world. The postcolonial economic and political space inherited from colonialism constitutes an instrumental and symbolic reference point from which the positioning of each nation within the European context is negotiated and reinforced.

Notes

1 Even if Eastern Europe is not the subject of this chapter, it is clearly possible to argue for a similar process of questioning Europeanness in relation to Eastern Europeans. But, as we will argue, there is also a particularity of representations surrounding the South, and it is the contextualization of this that is the focus here, rather than a more general conceptualization of Europe's centre and margins.
2 Portuguese colonial historiography divides the Portuguese empire into three periods; the colonial empire in the east following Vasco da Gama's journey to India; the Brazilian colonial state until its independence, and the colonial empire in Africa evolving from the late nineteenth century (see Clarence-Smith, 1985).
3 The crisis in the EU, both as a purely economic crisis and as a broader crisis of identification and recognition, is subject to rapid changes. While writing this chapter in the autumn of 2015, it is almost impossible to imagine Greece prior to the January 2015 election that brought Syriza to power. The Syriza-led government could be history before the end of the year, however. It is equally impossible to project what will happen after that. In the same way, the success of the Podemos movement in Spain is impossible to project, just as few would have imagined its rapid transformation from a protest movement to a political movement. Finally, the currently unfolding refugee crisis has shifted attention in many parts of Europe towards border protection, away from the effect of austerity measures. Clearly, these two crises are linked, for example by adding another layer to the under-siege-mentality that haunts contemporary Europe, but that is not the focus of this chapter.
4 Estado Novo (New State) was an authoritarian regime, 1932–74. It envisioned a nationalist, Catholic and imperialist Portugal standing against anti-fascist ideologies and anti-colonialism. It identified Portugal as a pluricontinental country which 'naturally' ruled over its African colonies.

5 In 2013 the number of hotel guests in the US Virgin Islands with a Danish passport reached more than 16,000. According to the United States Virgin Island Bureau of Economic Research (2013), Danish visitors made up two-thirds of the entire number of visitors from Europe.

6 We are using the term 'illegalized' here to point out that technical distinctions between migrants, legal migrants and refugees have been displaced by discursive strategies aimed at making all migration appear illegal, except for the EU's internal mobility and various forms of labour migration (usually for high-skilled professionals) that are regulated by 'green card' arrangements and specific EU directives. This also includes the right of asylum for refugees. This is a right which signatories to the 1951 Geneva Convention on the Status of Refugees have pledged to uphold, but which the vast majority of nations in the global North have increasingly and systematically sought to ignore and undermine in every conceivable way – from Australia to Denmark.

7 Though the Danish media reported the 'tougher tone' in political discourse leading up to the election, it was left to international media (Belgian, *Le Soir*; see also Anders Lindberg's article in *Aftonbladet*, 16 June 2015, where he discusses the 2015 election in the context of the watershed 2001 election) to openly refer to racism as an undertone during the election campaign.

8 As early as 1975, new legislation laid down rules for keeping Portuguese nationality following the independence of the overseas territories under Portuguese administration (Decree Law 308-A, of 24 June, 1975). The criterion of *jus soli* was abandoned in favour of *jus sanguinis*, which meant the loss of nationality for all who were born or domiciled in those territories but not direct descendants of individuals born in mainland Portugal and adjacent islands. Nationality – and Portuguese citizenship – was hence largely reserved for the white population, whether born in Portugal or not, as well as for individuals of mixed ancestry and one parent from the metropole, and for migrant workers that had resided in Portuguese territory for at least five years prior to 25 April 1974. In 2006 this law was amended and a mixed status was adopted whereby the *jus sanguinis* criterion was combined with the category of nationality by acquisition (naturalization).

9 Of the 417,042 immigrants registered by the *Serviço de Estrangeiros e Fronteiras* (SEF) in 2012, 25.3 per cent were from Brazil, 10.3 per cent Cape Verdean, 4.9 per cent Angolans, Guinean 4.3 per cent, and 2.5 per cent from São Tome). The migrant population coming from these countries who have become naturalized Portuguese must be added to these figures to get a complete picture of migrants from the former colonies (*Serviço de Estrangeiros e Fronteiras*, 2013).

10 The use of the past tense here signals the dramatic downturn in economic conditions in Brazil since 2013. The consequences for Portuguese migrants of this new situation is too recent to be dealt with at the time of writing this chapter.

Bibliography

Bergmann, E. (2014) *Iceland and the International Financial Crisis: Boom, Bust and Recovery*. London: Palgrave Macmillan.

Braudel, F. (2009) 'History and the Social Sciences: The Longue Durée', trans. Wallerstein, I., *Review*, 32 (2), pp. 171–203.

Castelo, C. (1999) *O Modo Português de Estar no Mundo: O Luso-tropicalismo e a Ideologia Colonial Portuguesa (1933–1961)*. Porto: Afrontamento, 1999.

Castelo, C. (2012) 'Colonial Migration into Angola and Mozambique: Constraints and Illusions'. In: Morier-Genoud, E. and Cahen, M. (eds), *Imperial Migrations: Colonial Communities and Diasporas in the Portuguese World*. New York: Palgrave Macmillan, pp. 137–56.

CEVEA (Centrum Venstre Tænketanken) (2014) 'Uligheden stiger mest i Danmark', 24 March. Available at: www.cevea.dk/files/materialer/analyser/140324notat_ulighed_stiger_mest_i_danmark.pdf [accessed 15 August 2015].

Clarence-Smith, G. (1985) *The Third Portuguese Empire: 1825–1975: A Study in Economic Imperialism*. Manchester: Manchester University Press.

Confederation of Danish Employers (DA) (2013) *Labour Market Report 2013. Employment in Denmark*. Copenhagen: DA Forlag. Available at: /www.da.dk/bilag/LABOUR%20MARKET%20REPORT%202013.pdf [accessed 15 August 2015].

Dainotto, R. (2007) *Europe (in Theory)*. Durham, NC: Duke University Press.

Danielsson, J. (2009) 'The First Casualty of the Crisis: Iceland'. In: *The First Global Financial Crisis of the 21st Century, Part II, June–December 2008*. London: Centre for Economic Policy Research, pp. 9–14.

Dussel, E. (1998) 'Beyond Eurocentrism: The World-System and the Limits of Modernity'. In: Jameson, F. and Miyoshi, M. (eds), *The Cultures of Globalization*. Durham, NC: Duke University Press, pp. 3–31.

Epstein, G. and Habbard, P. (2011) *Speculation and Sovereign Debt – An Insidious Interaction*. TUAC [Trade Union Advisory Committee to the OECD], October. Available at: www.tuac.org/en/public/e-docs/00/00/0C/74.

Eurostat (2015) 'Gini Coefficient of Equivalized Disposable Income'. Available at: http://ec.europa.eu/eurostat/tgm/table.do?tab=table&language=en&pcode=tessi190 [accessed 15 August 2015].

Fidalgo, J. (n.d.) 'The Impact of the Historical Influence of Portugal in Angola.' *The International Banker*. Available at: http://internationalbanker.com/comment/impact-historical-influence-portugal-angola/ [accessed 3 March 2016].

Frankema, E. and Buelens, F. (eds) (2013) *Colonial Exploitation and Economic Development: The Belgian Congo and the Netherlands Indies Compared*. London: Routledge.

Gramsci, A. (1926/1978) 'Some Aspects of the Southern Question.' In: Hoare, Q. (ed.), *Selections from Political Writings (1921–1926*. London: Lawrence and Wishart.

International Monetary Fund (IMF) (2015) 'Greece: An Update of IMF Staff's Preliminary Public Debt Sustainability Analysis'. IMF Country Report no. 15/186, 14 July. Available at: www.imf.org/external/pubs/ft/scr/2015/cr15186.pdf [accessed 15 August 2015].

Lindberg, A. (2015) 'Det Danmark vi inte känner', *Aftonbladet*, 16 June. www.aftonbladet.se/ledare/ledarkronika/anderslindberg/article20978951.ab

Loftsdóttir, K. (2014) ' "The Enemy Outside and Within": The Crisis and Imagining the Global in Iceland'. In: Loftsdóttir, K. and Jensen, L. (eds), *Crisis in the Nordic Nations and Beyond: At the Intersection of Environment, Finance and Multiculturalism*. London: Ashgate, pp. 161–80.

Lourtie, P. (2011) 'Portugal no contexto da crise do euro', *Relações Internacionais*, 32, pp. 61–105.

Mignolo, W.D. (2000) *Local Knowledges/Global Designs: Coloniality, Subaltern Knowledges and Border Thinking*. Princeton: Princeton University Press.

Moe, N. (2002) *The View from Vesuvius: Representations of the South in Nineteenth-Century Italy*. Berkeley: University of California Press.

Nardelli, A. (2015) 'IMF: Austerity Measures Would still Leave Greece with Unsustainable Debt', *Guardian*, 30 June.

Palumbo, P. (ed.) (2003) *A Place in the Sun: Africa in Italian Colonial Culture from Post-Unification to the Present*. Berkeley and Los Angeles: University of California Press.

Ross, K. (1995) *Fast Cars, Clean Bodies: Decolonization and the Reordering of French Culture*. Cambridge, MA: The MIT Press.

Rota, E. (2012) 'The Worker and the Southerner: The Invention of Laziness and the Representation of Southern Europe in the Age of the Industrious Revolutions', *Cultural Critique*, 82, pp. 128–50

Said, E. (1978/1995) *Orientalism*. New York: Penguin.

Santos, B. de S. (2008) 'Between Prospero and Caliban: Colonialism, Postcolonialism and Inter-identity'. In: Moraña, M. and Jáuregui, C.A. (eds), *Revisiting the Colonial Question in Latin America*. Madrid: Iberoamericana, pp. 139–84.

Scott, J.C. (1990) *Domination and the Arts of Resistance: Hidden Transcripts*. New Haven, CT: Yale University Press.

Smith, A.L. (ed.) (2003) *Europe's Invisible Migrants*. Amsterdam: Amsterdam University Press.

The Local (2014) 'Big Gaps Remain Between Immigrants and Danes', 26 November. Available at: www.thelocal.dk/20141126/significant-gaps-remain-between-immigrants-and-danes [accessed 11 February 2016].

United States Virgin Island Bureau of Economic Research (2014) Hotel Guest Origin, 2012. Available at: www.usviber.org/HotelGuestOrigin13.pdf [accessed 15 August 2015].

Vasconcelos, J. (2012) 'Africanos e afrodescendentes no Portugal contemporâneo: redefinindo práticas, projetos e identidades', *Cadernos de Estudos Africanos*, 24, pp. 15–23.

6 Austere curricula

Multicultural education and black students

Robbie Shilliam

Introduction

Austerity is not simply a macro-economic policy.[1] Rather than a neoliberal invention, austerity has a long history of racializing certain bodies as dangerously excessive to requirements. To be specific, austerity has always informed the sensibilities of postcolonial governance in the imperial heartlands. In recent decades the UK has experienced a growth in peoples from ex-colonies settling in the 'mother country' at the same time as mainstream British culture has come to be marked by melancholia over the loss of empire (Gilroy, 2006). Melancholic sensibilities resonate with austere ones, connoting severity, strictness, frugality and unadorned simplicity that are at odds with the rich, complex and diverse peoples and relations that make up postcolonial UK society. In other words, the austere sensibility works through existing frameworks of mono-ethnic national belonging to render multiculturalism an indulgent embellishment and dangerous excess.

It is no surprise, then, that current economic austerity measures interact with and strengthen existing structures of racialized inequality (see for example Runnymede Trust, 2015). In the UK these structures have been at least somewhat ameliorated by multicultural policies and equality statutes. As John Holmwood and Gurminder Bhambra (2012) point out, education acts as a crucial site for the amelioration of inequalities in liberal societies. Indeed, in the struggles to integrate the rich and diverse social relations that postcolonial peoples bring to the UK, one of the key ameliorative strategies has been the introduction of multiculturalism into school curricula. However, from the austere point of view, multicultural education is necessarily a subversive indulgence of excess cultures. And sure enough, there has recently been a high-level attempt by government to extricate Britain's colonial history from the school curriculum in the context of a wider moral panic over the loss of 'British values' in an increasingly multicultural education experience (see Spafford, 2013; Holmwood, 2015).

Whilst secondary education in the UK has at least entertained a struggle to address structures of racialized inequality by introducing multicultural principles, tertiary education has hardly begun to consider the problem. Only recently, with initiatives such as the Race Equality Charter (which seeks to address the racial inequalities that affect staff and students), has a systemic challenge to monocultural practices and pedagogies reached the higher levels of university management. Nevertheless, the level of awareness, enthusiasm and commitment to change by management remains extraordinarily low. In this context, and by reference to the UK context, I want to ask: how are universities and academics complicit in an austerity project that seeks to contain the dangerous multicultural excesses of a postcolonial society? And what is the relationship between an austere sensibility, racialized inequality and the university curriculum?

To address these questions I look specifically at the experience of British students of African-continental heritage. These students share the racial appellation of 'black' with their African-Caribbean peers. However, African-continental students diverge from African-Caribbean students in achieving higher attainments at secondary school (11–16 years old). Nevertheless, African-continental students experience a subsequent reversal of their upward mobility at university so that upon leaving tertiary education they by and large come to share the broad racialized inequalities suffered by their African-Caribbean peers.

In order to explain this mobility/dis-mobility I engage with the so-called deficit model of education, which itself contains deep austere sensibilities and has its origins in the containment of enslaved and colonized peoples in the metropoles of imperial rule. I consider how the conventional curriculum at the university level undertakes similar containment policies with deleterious consequences for the social mobility of African-continental (as well as other black) students. In making this argument I am seeking to remind scholars that while they might critique austere measures 'out there', they could be complicit in these same measures through their own professional practices. In making this argument I wish to suggest that austere curricula are integral to the production of austere histories and that this relationship facilitates wider austerity measures.

Austere thinking and the deficit model

The deficit model of education has primarily been used as a sociological explanation of differential achievements between groups of students. When engaging with the deficit model nowadays it is difficult not to address Pierre Bourdieu's (1986) concept of 'cultural capital', which marks the mechanism whereby privilege is transferred inter-generationally, but in a site that is presumed to be meritocratic in essence – public education. For Bourdieu, the embodied affections and dispositions of the dominant culture, that is to say the ways in which individuals 'get on' socially, are transmitted through a particular knowledge base that is unavailable to lower-class families. In other words, only privileged families can inculcate their children with the requisite cultural capital required to achieve and attain, and in this way the education system reproduces the unequal 'structure of the distribution of cultural capital among classes' (Bourdieu, 1973). Bourdieu's thesis spoke to a particularly French delineation of 'high' and 'low' culture. But subsequent work has mobilized the concept of cultural capital to look at alternative contexts wherein the lines of cultural division are congenitally racialized (for example Kingston, 2001; Roscigno and Ainsworth-Darnell, 1999).

Arguably, it is the question of race that gave rise to deficit thinking in education in its contemporary form. In the USA, concerns over the failures of African-American students arose in the 1960s during Lyndon Johnson's 'war on poverty' and, more importantly, at the moment when Black Power was seen to be overtaking a failing Civil Rights movement. Speaking to the abiding post-civil war problematique of the place of African-Americans in the civic life of the USA, educationalists and policymakers invoked the deficit model to explicate the cultural deprivation of African-Americans caused by the segregated schooling system (famously called to order in *Brown* v. *Board of Education* in 1954). The stakes were high because the liberal promise of egalitarianism rested upon education acting as an effective ameliorative instrument for meritocratic advancement regardless of race or social status (Gutiérrez and Rogoff, 2003: 19; United States Department of Labor, Office of Policy Planning and Research, 1965: 2).

Central to the deficit model, in this respect, was the assumption that the lack of contact by low-income African-American children with middle-class white children curtailed a transfer of positive cultural values that would support attainment. Such an assumption placed the African-American family at the centre of the deficit problem. Daniel Patrick Moynihan, sociologist and assistant secretary of labour during Johnson's 'war on poverty', articulated these assumptions in his influential report on 'the Negro family':

> The white family has achieved a high degree of stability and is maintaining that stability. By contrast, the family structure of lower class Negroes is highly unstable, and in many urban centres is approaching complete breakdown.
>
> (United States Department of Labor, Office of Policy Planning and Research, 1965: 5)

Effectively, Moynihan's report sought to redeem the ideal of liberal egalitarianism not by questioning the normativities of mono-cultural analysis but by sociologically comparing a structurally disadvantaged racial minority with a structurally privileged racial majority and imputing the 'norm' to the latter and the 'deviance' to the former (Kirk and Goon, 1975: 606). And by developing policy prescriptions that targeted structural racialized inequality, Moynihan pathologized African-American family life, pointing out for example that, compared with white families, more African-American marriages dissolved, more births were illegitimate, and more households were female headed and in welfare dependency (United States Department of Labor, Office of Policy Planning and Research, 1965: 6). For Moynihan, African-American children possessed no cultural capital to achieve at school; their familial and community heritages held no value in or for the public sphere.

I would argue that the pathologization of African-American familial and community heritage was directly linked to a fear of integration by white Americans in general but also, specifically, to a fear of failed integration and its consequence – namely, the rise of Black Power. The deficit model was thus both a prescription for assimilation and, if that was not possible, then a tool for the continued pacification of a historically resident yet structurally excluded people.

The deficit model emerged in the UK at roughly the same time as in the USA. But here the model was mobilized principally (albeit not only) to address the failings of African-Caribbean children in school. Similar to the racialized defence of mono-culturalism in the settler-colony, the defence of mono-cultural British nationalism required postcolonial arrivants to the 'mother country' to assimilate or be contained. However, while fears of the social consequences of failed assimilation bridged both societies, in the UK there was no equivalent of the Moynihan report and so considerations of egalitarianism in education did not, at this point in time, significantly shape policy discussions towards African-Caribbean children. Indeed, by the late 1960s it had become clear that the UK education system refused to countenance any substantive accommodation of the long-term presence of African-Caribbean families in the post-imperial heartland. Instead, schools became one more site wherein a racist austere sensibility was practised.

Very similar arguments made by Moynihan regarding the black family also took root in the UK.[2] Henceforth, educationalists talked of the corrosive hyper-patriarchal or hyper-matrifocal nature of the 'West Indian family', its lack of proper English language and its poverty-stricken status (see Carby, 1999). Deficit thinking assumed that African-Caribbean children possessed no cultural capital with which to achieve at school. Indeed, attempts by African-Caribbean children born in the UK to actively address the trauma of racism was read by educationalists as the display of innately negative cultural traits such as disinterestedness and disruptiveness (John, 2014). Thus, instead of acknowledging and addressing visceral and institutional racism in schools, commentators opted to explain the suffering of African-Caribbean children via an austere deficit model: their familial and community heritages lacked any cultural capital that could be mobilized to achieve in the English education system. (And in any case, these children were presumed to genetically lack a sufficient IQ.)

At the time, Bernard Coard (1971) wrote an influential thesis that sought to critically detail the making-sub-normal of African-Caribbean children in the school system (see also Warmington, 2014: 66). But it was not until the Swann Report of 1985 that the science of eugenics was officially discredited and declaimed as being able to explain the differential attainments of African-Caribbean children vis-à-vis the white majority (Committee of Enquiry into the Education of Children from Ethnic Minority Groups, 1985: 68). As an alternative and more plausible explanation, the report identified teachers' low expectations of African-Caribbean children as a key contributor to unequal attainment. Moreover, the report suggested that, rather than a simple prejudice, these expectations were part of a wider social and economic system of racial discrimination that resulted in 'cumulative disadvantage' (Committee of Enquiry into the Education of Children from Ethnic Minority Groups, 1985: 66–7). In many ways the Swann Report was incisively damning of the deficit model used to justify the status quo at schools, charging those who believed in its austere tenets as failing in their professional duty:

> Any teacher who sought to explain away, or who expected low achievement as the inevitable result of poor circumstances, would be failing in his task as an educator.
>
> (Committee of Enquiry into the Education of Children from Ethnic Minority Groups, 1985: 76)

The Swann Report reflected at least a decade of more or less serious attempts to implement multiculturalism in school curricula, albeit usually attenuated to aesthetic diversification rather than an intellectual transformation of teaching and learning which would moot political consequences (see Carby, 1999: 203–4, and in general Warmington, 2014). In contrast, black community responses to racist education had long sought to address the problem at its root. The late 1960s, for example, witnessed the emergence of weekend 'supplementary schools', independently run by African-Caribbean parents (especially mothers), intellectuals and community activists (see Mirza and Reay, 2000; Andrews, 2013). These voluntary schools imparted basic skills. But some also taught what would nowadays be called an 'Afrocentric' curriculum that allowed the student to utilize their familial and cultural heritage within the wider learning process in contrast to its active exclusion from mainstream school curricula. Gus John (2014), professor of education and one of the initiators of the supplementary school project in the late 1960s, argues that the majority of supplementary schools 'never operated a "deficit model" with regard to the needs of Black children'.

Likewise, a number of critical education scholars have confronted the deficit model, asserting that black families and communities in the USA and the UK possess a wealth of cultural capital, albeit capital that is garnered from and transmitted through heritages that might not be shared or valued by majority groups. For example, black children might cultivate aspirational attitudes from the pursuit of dreams in the face of societal barriers, navigational tools from the need to work through hostile institutions, and linguistic abilities where more than one language or register of communication is quotidian to family and community life (Yosso, 2005; Wright, Standen and Patel, 2010; Goulbourne, 2006). Hence critics of the deficit model argue that black children do not enter the classroom deficient in (or entirely lacking) the affections, dispositions and basic techniques required for learning – at least, no more than students from majority groups. The deficit does not lie with black heritages – familial and community – but in the racist structures that devalue, demean and exclude the sources of cultural capital that black children carry with them into the classroom.

Despite such critical responses by practitioners and academics to the deficit model, its associated racial stereotypes still circulate today. In recent years, the deficit model has returned to the USA as part of the 'No Child Left Behind' agenda, where poor and minority children are singled out for special pedagogical and cultural interventions (see Dudley-Marling, 2007). In the UK, meanwhile, many teachers still interpret the actions of African-Caribbean children as disrespectful regardless of the intentions of the student. For example, the cultural practice of looking down as a sign of respect when talking to adults is often interpreted as a display of defiance. Moreover, these black stereotypes can travel and proliferate; the same cultural misreading is made now of Somali children (Gillborn, 1992: 62; Coretta, 2011: 180–82). What is more, African-Caribbean students still suffer a disproportionate amount of exclusions relative to any other ethnic group. Crucially, the reasons for exclusion are less to do with actual infringement of rules but the perception by teachers of a bad attitude exhibited by the student (see in general Strand, 2012).

In sum, deficit thinking presumes that black families and communities have no cultural capital to gift their children as an inheritance, or, that the only 'gift' that black children receive is a transmission of pathological behaviour. Deficit thinking is a technology that reproduces structural inequalities along racial lines in so far as it polices which heritages – and struggles – can be seen as a worthwhile matter for education. Deficit thinking is congenitally austere, and, in its implicit defence of the racial hierarchies and exclusions of mono-culturalism, of colonial/postcolonial provenance. If, as Holmwood and Bhambra (2012) argue, the liberal egalitarian function of education is to provide a meritocratic opening for the partial disturbance of inherited privilege, deficit thinking mitigates against even this ameliorative impulse (see Kingston, 2001).

In what now follows I explore how students from African-continental heritages have confounded the expectations of the deficit model at secondary school level in England specifically. But I will also argue that their success and upward mobility has been neutralized at tertiary-level education. Having detailed this trajectory I will, in the final section, suggest that the mono-cultural university environment and especially the 'conventional curriculum' is complicit in making deficits where there are none and thus contributing to the racialized effects of austerity.

Black students and the making of a deficit

Answering a call for labour by the British state in the aftermath of the Second World War, African-Caribbean families began to settle in large numbers as adults took on predominantly public sector work. For some while, these communities defined the 'black experience' in the UK and suffered the formative racist pathologization that I have glossed above. More recently, however, African-continental families have arrived (once more) in large numbers as part of a new post-Cold War era of postcolonial migration. The route of African-continental peoples into the UK is in general markedly different from that of African-Caribbean peoples, especially in terms of their insertions into the national economy and their experiencing of the formative pathologization of blackness in Britain. These differences do not stop both groups from falling under the broader label of black. Do the educational experiences and outcomes of African-continental and African-Caribbean students reflect these divergences? Or do black students share a common fate?

Structural inequalities in the English school system are measured primarily from attainment gaps. A key measure, in this respect, is the achievement of five General Certificate of Secondary Education (GCSE) qualifications (from A* to C grade) including the subjects of English and maths. Although students take GCSEs at the age of 16, this is also an important indicator for prospective tertiary education because often times General Certificate of Education Advanced Level (A-level) qualifications, taken at the age of 18, are not yet completed when universities make admission decisions. African-continental students have improved significantly in this measure over the past ten years. For the 2009/10 year, 54.8 per cent of white British pupils achieved five such GCSEs, and this figure was also the national average, in comparison with 48.9 per cent of African-continental students (Department of Education, 2011). However, for the 2013/14 year, 56.4 per cent of white British pupils achieved this measure, just under the national average of 56.6 per cent, while 56.8 per cent of African-continental students achieved the same measure (Department of Education, 2015). Therefore, although African-continental students are by no means the highest-achieving ethnic minority, they are now slightly outperforming their white British peers – the majority group – and are just above the national level.[3] What is more, they are outperforming their black peers from an African-Caribbean heritage by nearly 10 per cent.

One reason offered for this success lies in the putative difference between being an 'immigrant' or a 'diaspora'. Many educationalists argue that immigrants arrive with cultural capital that translates into high aspirations for social advancement of their children through educational achievement (see Strand, 2014: 162). In other words, migrant parents are presumed to especially value schooling and so will forge productive relationships with teachers and be far more directive with their children's education. Meanwhile, 'settled' diaspora groups, especially the African-Caribbean community, are assumed (as we have discussed above) to lack similar levels of aspirations due to the inter-generational transfer of disadvantage and/or the familial absence of such cultural capital. The Minister of Education in the 2010–15 coalition government certainly believed in the explanatory power of the immigrant paradigm as well as the putative deficit suffered by other disadvantaged students (House of Commons Education Committee, 2014: 27, 37).

The immigrant paradigm does partly describe some of the reality of attainment in secondary education. For example, many commentators have noted, over the last few years, a 'London effect' wherein attainments from children in the capital city are significantly higher than in the rest of the country. Moreover, this effect is shared widely across socioeconomic divides and ethnic groups. Some argue that the general rise in attainment might be driven by the high percentage of students from immigrant parents who have made a new home in the city and are now spreading their aspirational attitudes to 'settled' groups (Burgess, 2014). The London effect is especially noteworthy because of the fact that a relatively high percentage of African-continental students arrive in the UK between the ages of five and 14 (Strand, Malmberg and Hall, 2015: 11) and a significant percentage of these students live in the capital city (Mayor of London, 2013: 17–19). A recent report in the Lambeth borough of London found that 71 per cent of African-continental students attained the five GCSE measure – significantly higher than the national average for the group (Demie, 2013: 6).

Nevertheless, while the immigrant paradigm might hold descriptive validity, its explanatory power can sometimes rest on a premise that reintroduces deficit thinking as a way of explaining the divergence between two minority groups that share the codification of 'black' in the British racial schema. African-continental families, despite being black, are said to enjoy migrant cultural capital, while African-Caribbean families, as part of a historically 'settled' and, as we have seen, demonized diaspora, are presumed to suffer from a lack of this capital. However, such binary presumptions have been critiqued in studies by the Joseph Rowntree Foundation, which have found little actual correlation between aspiration (considered to be a key attribute of cultural capital) and socioeconomic background/ethnic minority group (Cummings *et al.*, 2012). In fact, as a number of scholars have argued, the diminution of aspiration occurs not when students enter school but when they observe that their aspirations do not fit with the reality of so many of their group peers who do not or cannot enter into university or apprenticeships. In other words, it is not initial low aspirations that cause lower attainment but rather the subsequent demonstration effect of structures of racialized inequality and other intersectional determinants, which often take particular forms in particular locales (see in general Kintrea, St Clair and Houston, 2011).

I would therefore suggest that any binary contrast of 'good' immigrant families with 'bad' settled minority families necessarily draws upon the modalities of the deficit model. Nevertheless, it is the case that, as a group, African-continental students do seem to be fulfilling the upwardly mobile aspirations of their parents, despite the historical pathologization of black heritage as deficient in cultural capital and hence requiring austere remedies. So let us now follow these students through university.

Over the past decade increasing numbers of black youth have entered university: 6.3 per cent of the UK-national student population in Britain is now black, and amongst first-year students this rises to 6.7 per cent.[4] For the sake of perspective, the 2011 UK census reports that blacks make up 3.3 per cent of the general population. Hence, black students are significantly over-represented at university. The bulk of this growth has come from students with an African-continental heritage, who make up 4.4 per cent of the UK-national student population, with those from an African-Caribbean heritage making up 1.5 per cent and 'other' black heritage 0.3 per cent. This growth doubtless reflects not just a population increase, but also demonstrates that, at secondary school, African-continental students aspire and attain. As I have argued above, it is difficult to argue that such students enter into the university system with a deficit – cultural or otherwise. Yet despite this over-representation, university life for black students in general (including those from African-continental backgrounds) is marked by differential experiences from that of white students and, in some cases, from many other minority groups.

First, black students tend to attend institutions that are considered by industry and government to be less 'prestigious'. I want to parse this term through Bourdieu's argument about cultural capital. Rather than acting as a neutral mark of excellence, prestige should be understood much more as a marker of cultural capital and therefore its use is implicated in the unequal reproduction and transference of inherited privilege through tertiary education. In the most prestigious Russell Group of universities, black students have remained at 2.7 per cent of the student population in recent years (it should be remembered that black students constitute 6.3 per cent of the UK-national student population). Compare the Russell Group to the least 'prestigious' Million+ Group of universities wherein black students make up 11.9 per cent of the student population. This placement of black students is not simply down to personal choice, nor is it only an outcome of lesser achievements at secondary school. One recent study (Boliver, 2013) has found that, controlling for other variables such as attainment, ethnicity exercises a discrete and negative effect on the chances of black students being admitted into prestigious universities. In sum, having achieved at secondary school, black students, including those with African-continental heritages, are funnelling themselves and being funnelled into institutions that are relatively disadvantaged in the broader valuation of undergraduate degrees and subsequent pursuit of social mobility.

The second difference lies in the route that students take at the end of each academic year. At present, 92.2 per cent of white students continue to the next year, 1.5 per cent transfer institutions and 6.4 per cent leave higher education. In comparison, 86.8 per cent of African-continental students continue, 4.1 per cent transfer and 9.1 per cent leave higher education. While comparatively more African-Caribbean students (10.8 per cent) exit higher education than their African-continental peers, over the last couple of years the number of African-Caribbean students exiting is declining and the number of African-continental students exiting is increasing. Suddenly, then, at university, African-continental students seem to be demonstrating more 'deficit behaviour' than white students while approximating that of their African-Caribbean peers.

But third, and most importantly, end-of-degree attainment statistics starkly demonstrate racialized differences. In the English university system, degrees are classified in terms of first class honours (1st), second class upper division honours (2:1), second class lower division honours (2:2), third class honours (3rd), pass and fail. In the 2012/13 academic year (the most recent data available at the time of writing), 20.3 per cent of white female and 20.6 per cent of white male students attained a 1st classification in comparison with just 7.4 per cent of black women and 7.7 per cent of black men. 74.7 per cent of white female students and 71.2 per cent of white male students achieved either a 1st or a 2:1 classification compared with just 44.1 per cent of black female and male students. I want to make it clear, again, that this difference cannot be simply explained by reference to the educational deficits that black students bring with them to university vis-à-vis the merits that white students arrive with. For instance, a recent report by the Higher Education Funding Council for England (HEFCE, 2014) found that 72 per cent of white students who entered university with three 'B' grade A-levels attained a 1st or 2:1 classification degree compared with only 53 per cent of black students who entered university with the same A-level results.

Despite these divergences we would expect that African-continental students specifically, and given their relative success at secondary school, would not suffer significant divergence from the white norm. Indeed, we would imagine that they are comfortably outperforming their African-Caribbean peers. Yet neither is the case. In the 2012/13 academic year, 48.7 per cent of African-Caribbean students attained a 1st or 2:1 classification degree compared with 46.4 per cent of African-continental students. And while, in 2011/12, African-continental students just outperformed African-Caribbean students in the attainment of a 1st classification, in 2012/13 these attainments were on a par (both groups being within 0.1 per cent of each other). In 2012/13 African-Caribbean students attained 2.5 per cent more 2:1 classifications than their continental counterparts, 1 per cent less 2:2 classifications and 1.4 per cent less 3rd classifications. One might argue that this might all be due to a 'lag' in the time it takes for the superior-performing African-continental students to work their way through to the third year of their degree. And yet for the past ten years African-Caribbean students have *outperformed* African-continental students in attaining 1st and 2:1 classifications.

Remember that in secondary school African-continental students in general comfortably outperform their African-Caribbean peers. There seems to be no discernible improvement in the attainments of African-continental students in higher education that would match their improvements in secondary education. And remember, when it comes to university degrees, black students attain *significantly* below the levels of all other ethnic groups.

The significance of differential undergraduate attainment combined with the relative 'prestige' of the awarding university cannot be overestimated. It is a well-established fact that the major employers of graduate students do not look below a 2:1 classification when recruiting (Snowdon, 2012). Additionally, the prestige factor directly influences employability, especially with regards to professional jobs (Boliver, 2013: 345). The combined effects, therefore, are very detrimental if we consider that less than half of black students are graduating with a sufficient classification *and* those that do tend to graduate from less prestigious institutions. For example, six universities accounted for almost one quarter of black male undergraduates in 2012/13. All these universities are considered less prestigious. The average 'career score' for these six institutions was 52 per cent, compared with the six most prestigious universities, which scored 79 per cent yet wherein black males made up only 0.7 per cent of the student population (Black Training and Enterprise Group, 2014: 15).

It seems, then, that the upward mobility of African-continental students has lost much of its momentum by the time that their degrees have been attained.

And this immobilization needs to be contextualized within the era of austerity, which has impacted negatively upon racialized minorities at a rate proportionately greater than that suffered by the white majority (see in general Fisher and Nandi, 2015). Between 2009 and 2012, the years that saw the entrenchment of austerity measures in the UK, the employment gap between young white men aged 16–24 and young black men has grown even wider: 13 per cent of young white men were unemployed in 2009 compared with 28 per cent of young black men, while by 2012, 22 per cent of young white men were unemployed in contrast to 50 per cent of young black men (Black Training and Enterprise Group, 2014: 11–12). Moreover, young black men have, on average, higher rates of post-16 education than their white counterparts, but this has made no dent in the increasing divergence of employability along ethnic lines during the era of austerity.

Tellingly, these racialized differences in employment prospects are also evident in the graduate population specifically. 47.3 per cent of white graduates find professional full-time work compared with 38 per cent of black graduates and 5.2 per cent of white graduates are unemployed compared with 12.1 per cent of black graduates. Crucially, African-continental graduates share the same outcomes as the black population in general, although the differences are also instructive. Slightly fewer African-continental graduates find professional full-time work (37.7 per cent) than African-Caribbean counterparts (38.8 per cent) and more African-continental leavers are unemployed (13.2 per cent) than African-Caribbean (9.1 per cent). This suggests that job prospects are less favourable to African-continental graduates than for their African-Caribbean counterparts, although both groups fall significantly below the baselines of the white norm. I say all this in light of a recent study on inter-generational (im)mobility published by the Centre on Dynamics of Ethnicity (2014), which reports that African-continental men and women are in general less upwardly mobile and more prone to socioeconomic decline than not only their white but also African-Caribbean counterparts.

What we might now be witnessing is the university operating for some as a site that does not just reproduce privilege – as in Bourdieu's model – but a site that is complicit in *creating* racialized disadvantage. By the time that they leave university, African-continental graduates have lost much of the social mobility that was promised to them through their attainment record at secondary education. They have even lost their mobility relatively more than African-Caribbean counterparts, who they had outperformed at secondary school, and who, in the quotidian racial schema of the UK, are far more of a historical 'deficit problem' than recent arrivals. And so, despite being an increasingly 'model' migrant group, despite not sharing the same intimate and historical entanglement with deficit thinking as the African-Caribbean community, African-continental students are still suffering from the same (and sometimes worse) negative outcomes upon exiting university as black students in general.

The reasons for this dismobilization are doubtless complex and interlocking. In what now follows I will focus on one plausible contributing factor – the austere nature of the 'conventional curriculum'. Here, it has to be said, I am talking specifically about the curriculum of the social sciences and humanities.

An austere curriculum

At this point we must revisit the relative success of African-continental students at secondary school. Certainly, the aspirations enjoyed by these students are an important part of the reason for their improved attainment record. However (as I noted above), aspirations are not the exclusive domain of immigrant families. And, conversely, African-continental students do not entirely escape the pathologizations of blackness suffered by their African-Caribbean peers. For instance, Steve Strand has recently demonstrated that African-continental students are relatively more advantaged in cultural capital than white British students and yet this advantage does not translate into a proportionately greater attainment of GCSEs. In short, African-continental students are doing well, but should be doing even better (Strand, 2011; see in general Solorzano, 1992). Thus, I would argue that in order to identify the reasons for African-continental students' success at secondary school, we must focus upon structural transformations in education that have attempted to displace the mono-cultural logics that breed austere notions of black deficit.

Some secondary schools – especially in London – have embraced multicultural models that go beyond the strictly aesthetic pluralization of education environments. A fundamental aspect of this shift has been the mobilization of a curriculum that 'reflects the African pupil's heritage, culture and experience' (Demie, 2013: 20). Through a multicultural curriculum multiple heritages can be mobilized as a matter for learning in general: as one school puts it, 'we will use what children know and understand about themselves in our teaching' (Demie, 2013: 29). In this way children are able, with their families and communities, to engage meaningfully in UK life *through* their familial and community heritages. Rather than considered a deficit that must be discarded, these heritages are seen, in principle, as positive cultural capital that can feed an aspirational education process. A multicultural curriculum along these lines holds the potential to provide a countervailing meritocratic influence upon inherited and racialized hierarchies and inequalities. It is therefore painful to witness the current overhaul of the national curriculum that is intended to curtail multicultural pedagogies for the sake of returning to ostensibly traditional 'British values' alongside a retrenchment of race equality funding for schools (see Alexander, Weekes-Bernard and Arday, 2015).

As partial and contested as they are, these innovations in secondary education stand in stark contrast to the elitism and conservatism of most universities. In order to meet the statutory duties of the Equalities Act 2010 (a piece of legislation that brings together many previous equalities acts, including 'race relations'), the Higher Education Funding Council for England expects universities to ensure not just an equality of opportunity but even – and this surpasses the 2010 Act – to demonstrate compliance to this duty via equality of outcome amongst racialized groups (not individuals). But despite these benchmarks, the university sector has never received anything similar to the Swann Report, and the levels of reception of the problem of racialized discrimination and stratification amongst senior management remain extremely low (see ECU, 2011). This is not just a question of ignorance, but much more evidence of the institutional mono-culture culture of higher education. One of the key pillars of this culture is the tradition of readings, arguments, registers and debates that form the conventional curriculum.

More than simply a professionally selected portmanteau of edifying knowledge, the conventional curriculum makes manifest what might be called in Bourdieuan terms institutional habitus: the unchallenged social and cultural practices as well as forms of tacit knowledge that invest the academic with professional competency (Thomas, 2002). And perhaps the best way to understand the mono-cultural exclusivities of the conventional curriculum is to inquire into the nature of the conventional student body that it is designed to edify. Influential British philosopher Michael Oakeshott (2004), debating in 1950 on the purpose of higher education within the pages of the BBC's *Listener* magazine, argues that university study should not be for an 'ulterior purpose' but for the sake of a scholarly conversation that is its own purpose. Oakeshott is careful to point out that the privilege of taking part in the conversation should not depend on any external privilege, including financial ability. However, Oakeshott is just as clear that the student should be understood to occupy a position in between that of a child and adult so that the scholarly conversation takes place through 'the gift of an interval' (Oakeshott, 2004: 29–30).

To this portrait I want to add an influential argument by John Searle (1993). Writing after the confrontation of black, First Nations, feminist and Latino/a struggles within the American academy, Searle wishes to defend the 'traditional canon' against what he deems to be this 'multicultural' challenge. Specifically, Searle bemoans the entrance of 'politics' into disciplinary inquiry, especially the politicization of the racial, gendered and class characteristics of those thinkers included in the canon and also of those who teach the canon. While Searle is writing in the US context, his argument is useful to place next to Oakeshott's in so far as it suggests that the ability and availability to disavow political attachments and/or commitments – that is, taking the 'interval' – is also racialized. An interval requires you to unencumber yourself from familial, social, cultural and political commitments, duties and ties. But is it possible to unencumber yourself if your very bodily presence in the academy is unavoidably political in so far as it viscerally references not only a struggle over integration but just as much the problem of deficiency itself?

Here I want to argue that race is a great and perverse downward democratizer. Black is black is black – just as much for the children of African-continental migrant parents as it is for their African-Caribbean peers. And in a racially structured society such as the UK, including its public higher education system, black connotes extreme deficit, regardless of the disparate routes one takes to arrive and the diverse heritages that one holds onto upon settlement.

One technique to make 'troublesome' minority students compliant in secondary school is to 'decontextualize' their (deficient) family and community heritages via a focus on training standardized skills and methods (Dudley-Marling, 2007; Haberman, 2010). At university, compliance and decontextualization is achieved through the deployment of particular canons that are presumed to prepare the student for impartial and detached inquiry – that is, Oakeshott's scholarly conversation (see Morley, 1997: 232). Yet these thinkers, traditions and narratives are anything but impartially selected and pedagogically detached: they are epistemically white. By this terminology I mean to say that what counts as adequate frameworks of cognition and useful knowledge is racialized as exclusively white in order to then be rendered as neutral, transparent, universalizable and, increasingly, a marker of international 'excellence' (Hong, 2008: 104–5; see also De Sousa Santos, 2014). By contrast, black heritages – historical, intellectual, cultural – cannot be made transparent as in the racial schema of society they are constitutive of struggle, deviance from the norm and deficit. Indeed, when black students (and staff) critique the whiteness of the conventional curriculum, their actions are more likely to be 'instinctively' apprehended by academic institutions, in the finest traditions of postcolonial austerity, as at worst 'uncivil behaviour' or at least evidence of 'dumbing down' (Margolis and Romero, 1998: 21; Berry and Loke, 2011: 15, 51).

Black is black is black. And so for black students, whose bodies speak of deficit regardless of their different roots and routes into the UK, to be made unencumbered is to be made austere: your 'excess' – the heritage that necessarily entangles you, regardless of intention, with extra-academic material – must be stripped. What, we might ask, is then left for scholarly conversation except a black hole? There does, though, exist a special kind of student who does not require compliance to an austere process of decontextualization in order to prepare him for the scholarly conversation: the white student whose very heritage is a privilege that constitutes the apparently impartial, detached and universal conventions of the curriculum. And this remains the case, even though this student increasingly shares the halls of higher education with racialized minority students. It is entirely plausible, then, to consider that the racialized exclusions that deeply structure the conventional – mono-cultural – curriculum have a negative impact upon the experiences and even attainments of many black students. This is certainly the connection made in a number of recent reports that advocate a movement towards multiculturalism – or a more 'inclusive curriculum' – in order to address inequalities – including racialized ones – in degree attainment (Berry and Loke, 2011: 15; Haggis, 2006; Hockings, 2010; Mountford-Zimdars *et al.*, 2015: 24–5; 67–71).

To demonstrate these connections a little more, I want to reflect on the comments made by African-continental students in a recent focus group that I personally organized for BME students.[5] I should add that it is not uncommon to discover similar sentiments in the wider literature. In terms of their attempted engagement with a social science curriculum, students commented that 'I've been omitted', and 'you don't see yourself in the learning' (see also Jones,

2001). It seems that this structured – and not random or incidental – absence resulted in students feeling that their heritages could not be 'brought in' to the teaching and learning process. These comments align with the notion that, for some, the conventional curriculum provides an austere rather than enriching experience. Such epistemic exclusions understandably produced a crisis of investment in students: 'It's so boring. It limits the way I think'; 'I have an opinion but I have to translate it so that it becomes tedious and I am disengaged.' Of course, a crisis of investment can easily result in alienation: '[I'm] just writing essays to get the grades'; 'I've learned to give people what they want. And leave me behind' (see also NUS, 2011: 21). Interestingly, considering my argument above, at least one of the participants explained that her experience of multicultural learning at secondary school was far more challenging than her confrontation with a mono-cultural curriculum at university: 'I would [actually] like to be exposed and challenged to diversity.'

The absence, forced disinvestment and alienation that the conventional curriculum produces is, whilst not the only cause, nevertheless central to understanding the drastic drop in attainment collectively suffered by black students in general, but in particular by African-continental students whose collective attainment record, prior to university, displays no evidence of 'deficit'. The conventional curriculum is a rich one for white students who can draw upon their family and societal heritages that constitute the *particular* matter for scholarly conversation; in principle, they are able to mobilize their cultural capital. But for African-continental students, as for black students in general and many other marginalized groups (including poor white students, but in different ways), the conventional curriculum is an austere one. Many academics claim their curriculum to be an impartial and universal tool of edification. But its whiteness speaks – sometimes subtly, usually corrosively – to black students of their deviance, or even deficit. To those who have been on an upward academic trajectory the experience can be disorienting and disheartening.

Conclusion

Austerity is not just an economic project but a broader sensibility that structures exclusions and inequalities across the many dimensions of social life. The austere sensibility, now rampantly deployed as part of a neoliberal agenda, is also, and more foundationally, a postcolonial sensibility long used to contain the presence of formerly enslaved and colonized peoples in metropoles that were never designed for them. Education has been one of the major battlegrounds of austerity, wherein the deficit model has pathologized particular storehouses of cultural capital. At university, racialized minorities are required to unencumber themselves of the heritages that fill these storehouses. The process of unencumberment does not reveal the conventional student underneath the cultural baggage, now freed to adequately tackle the conventional curriculum; rather, in this process black students especially tend to become absent, disinvested and alienated as they confront these curricula. My evidence strongly suggests that the racialized differentials of degree attainment testify to the effect of this austere process.

I have also provided evidence that the austere nature of university environments do not just impact negatively upon teaching and learning, but are rather implicated in a wider phenomenon wherein racialized minorities, especially black peoples, are disproportionately made to bear the brunt of society-wide austerity programmes. How far academia is implicated can be gleaned from the fact that although university education is supposed to ameliorate inequalities-at-birth, it is instead not only reproducing inequalities (as Bourdieu argued) but is now complicit in *creating new* racialized inequalities.

Well-meaning commentators on the Left often argue that the real problem with racialized inequality in education lies not in academia but in broader socio-economic structures. Yet, counterintuitively, this Leftist strategy can all too easily accommodate austere sensibilities that assume deficits where there are none. Moreover, this strategy might mitigate against well-meaning academics taking a sober investigation of their own complicity in the reproduction and even creation of racialized inequalities through higher education. If the problem is 'out there', it is not necessary to critically account for our academic practices and all too easy to rail, instead, against 'falling standards' and the 'declining quality' of the character and abilities of our students.

In conclusion, I would suggest that it is in austere curricula that our colonial histories and our austere presents collide. Although the austere sensibility is currently mobilized by neoliberal ideologues, its provenance lies in the racialized governance of colonial and postcolonial peoples. In part, this form of governance requires the outlawing of certain familial and community heritages that are necessarily entangled with struggles over European colonialism by design or by fate, and which inevitably present a deep challenge to white supremacy in its current neoliberal expressions. But surely, stories of (post)colonial provenance must edify all of us who inhabit empirically multicultural societies? If so, then as long as a foundational and principled engagement with multiculturalism is disavowed by austere sensibilities, we are all the poorer in thought and in action.

Notes

1 Thanks to Gurminder Bhambra, John Holmwood and the editors for constructive comments.
2 In his inquiry into the Brixton riots of 1981, Lord Scarman was directly influenced by Moynihan's work (Kushnick, 1993: 18). For a comparative analysis of USA and UK contexts, see Majors (2001).
3 It should be noted that it tends to be English-speaking African-continental families that perform at this level (see Hollingworth and Mansaray, 2012).
4 Unless stated otherwise, all statistics in this section are sourced from the Equality Challenge Unit (ECU, 2015).
5 To preserve the anonymity of the participating students, I will not disclose the university or the programme that the focus group was drawn from.

Bibliography

Alexander, C., Weekes-Bernard, D. and Arday, J. (2015) 'The Runnymede School Report: Race, Education and Inequality in Contemporary Britain'. Runnymede Trust. Available at: www.runnymedetrust.org/projects-and-publications/education/the-school-report.html [accessed 7 February 2016].

Andrews, K. (2013) *Resisting Racism: Race, Inequality, and the Black Supplementary School Movement*. London: Trentham Books.

Berry, J. and Loke, G. (2011) *Improving the Degree Attainment of Black and Minority Ethnic Students*. Equality Challenge Unit. Available at: www.ecu.ac.uk/wp-content/uploads/external/improving-degree-attainment-bme.pdf [accessed 7 February 2016].

Beverley, B., Dadzie, S. and Scafe, S. (1985) *The Heart of the Race: Black Women's Lives in Britain*. London: Virago.

Black Training and Enterprise Group (2014) *Action Plan to Increase Employment for Young Black Men in London*. Available at: www.bteg.co.uk/sites/default/files/Action%20Plan%20To%20Increase%20Employment%20Rates%20For%20Young%20Black%20Men%20In%20London%20BTEG%202014.pdf.

Boliver, V. (2013) 'How Fair Is Access to More Prestigious UK Universities?' *The British Journal of Sociology*, 64 (2), pp. 344–64.

Bourdieu, P. (1973) 'Cultural Reproduction and Social Reproduction'. In: Brown, R. (ed.), *Knowledge, Education, and Cultural Change: Papers in the Sociology of Education*. London: Tavistock, pp. 71–112.

Bourdieu, P. (1986) 'The Forms of Capital'. In: Richardson, J. (ed.), *Handbook of Theory and Research for the Sociology of Education*. New York: Greenwood, pp. 241–58.

Burgess, S. (2014) 'Understanding the Success of London's Schools'. Working Paper 14/333. The Centre for Market and Public Organisation.

Carby, H. (1999) 'Schooling in Babylon'. In: Carby, H. (ed.), *Cultures in Babylon: Black Britain and African America*. London: Verso, pp. 189–218.

Centre on Dynamics of Ethnicity (2014) *Addressing Ethnic Inequalities in Social Mobility*. University of Manchester. Available at: www.ethnicity.ac.uk/medialibrary/briefings/policy/code-social-mobility-briefing-Jun2014.pdf [accessed 7 February 2016].

Coard, B. (1971) *How the West Indian Child is made Educationally Sub-normal in the British School System*. London: New Beacon.

Committee of Enquiry into the Education of Children from Ethnic Minority Groups (1985) *The Swann Report: Education for All*. London: Her Majesty's Stationery Office.

Coretta, P. (2011) 'Institutional Racism and Ethnic Inequalities: An Expanded Multilevel Framework', *Journal of Social Policy*, 40 (1), pp. 173–92.

Cummings, C., Laing, K., Law, J., McLaughlin, J., Papps, I., Todd, L. and Woolner, P. (2012) 'Can Changing Aspirations and Attitudes Impact on Educational Attainment?' Joseph Rowntree Foundation. Available at: www.jrf.org.uk/report/can-changing-aspirations-and-attitudes-impact-educational-attainment [accessed 9 February 2016].

De Sousa Santos, B. (2014) *Epistemologies of the South: Justice Against Epistemicide*. Boulder, CO: Paradigm Publishers.

Demie, F. (2013) *Raising Achievement of Black African Pupils: Good Practice in Schools*. Lambeth Research and Statistics Unit.

Department of Education (2011) *GCSE and Equivalent Results: England – 2009 to 2010*. Available at: www.gov.uk/government/statistics/gcse-and-equivalent-results-england-academic-year-2009-to-2010-revised [accessed 9 February 2016].

Department of Education (2015) *Revised GCSE and Equivalent Results: England – 2013 to 2014.* Available at: www.gov.uk/government/statistics/revised-gcse-and-equivalent-results-in-england-2013-to-2014 [accessed 9 February 2016].

Dudley-Marling, C. (2007) 'Return of the Deficit', *Journal of Educational Controversy*, 2 (1), article 5. Available at: http://cedar.wwu.edu/jec/vol. 2/iss1/5 [accessed 9 February 2016].

ECU (Equality Challenge Unit) (2011) *The Experience of Black and Minority Ethnic Staff in Higher Education in England.* Available at: www.ecu.ac.uk/wp-content/uploads/external/experience-of-bme-staff-in-he-final-report.pdf [accessed 9 February 2016].

ECU (Equality Challenge Unit) (2015) *Equality in Higher Education: Statistical Report 2014.* Available at: www.ecu.ac.uk/publications/equality-higher-education-statistical-report-2014/ [accessed 9 February 2016].

Fisher, P. and Nandi, A. (2015) 'Poverty across Ethnic Groups through Recession and Austerity'. Joseph Rowntree Foundation. Available at: www.jrf.org.uk/report/poverty-across-ethnic-groups-through-recession-and-austerity [accessed 9 February 2016].

Gillborn, D. (1992) 'Citizenship, "Race" and the Hidden Curriculum', *International Studies in Sociology of Education*, 2 (1), pp. 57–73.

Gilroy, P. (2006) *Postcolonial Melancholia.* New York: Columbia University Press.

Goulbourne, H. (2006) 'Families, Communities and Social Capital', *Community, Work & Family*, 9 (3), pp. 235–50.

Gutiérrez, K.D. and Rogoff, B. (2003) 'Cultural Ways of Learning: Individual Traits or Repertoires of Practice', *Educational Researcher*, 32 (5), pp. 19–25.

Haberman, M. (2010) 'The Pedagogy of Poverty versus Good Teaching', *Phi Delta Kappan*, 92 (2), pp. 81–7.

Haggis, T. (2006) 'Pedagogies for Diversity: Retaining Critical Challenge amidst Fears of "Dumbing down"', *Studies in Higher Education*, 31 (5), pp. 521–35.

HEFCE (Higher Education Funding Council for England) (2014) *Differences in Degree Outcomes: Key Findings.* Available at: www.hefce.ac.uk/media/hefce/content/pubs/2014/201403/HEFCE2014_03.pdf [accessed 9 February 2016].

Hockings, C. (2010) 'Inclusive Learning and Teaching in Higher Education: A Synthesis of Research'. Evidence Net. April. Available at: www.heacademy.ac.uk/sites/default/files/inclusive_teaching_and_learning_in_he_synthesis_200410_0.pdf [accessed 9 February 2016].

Hollingworth, S. and Mansaray, A. (2012) *Language Diversity and Attainment in English Secondary Schools: A Scoping Study.* The Institute for Policy Studies in Education.

Holmwood, J. (2015) 'Schooling "British Values": Threatening Civil Liberties and Equal Opportunities', *Open Democracy*, 20 July. Available at: www.opendemocracy.net/ourkingdom/john-holmwood/schooling-%E2%80%98british-values%E2%80%99-threatening-civil-liberties-and-equal-opportunit [accessed 9 February 2016].

Holmwood, J. and Bhambra, G.K. (2012) 'The Attack on Education as a Social Right', *South Atlantic Quarterly*, 111 (2), pp. 392–401.

Hong, G.K. (2008) '"The Future of Our Worlds": Black Feminism and the Politics of Knowledge in the University under Globalization', *Meridians*, 8 (2), pp. 95–115.

House of Commons Education Committee (2014) *Underachievement in Education by White Working Class Children: Government Response to the Committee's First Report of Session 2014–15.* Available at: www.publications.parliament.uk/pa/cm201415/cmselect/cmeduc/647/647.pdf. [accessed 9 February 2016].

John, G. (2014) 'The RSA Supplementary Schools Investigation'. *Prof. Gus John*. Available at: www.gusjohn.com/2014/11/the-rsa-supplementary-schools-investigation/ [accessed 9 February 2016].

Jones, C. (2001) 'Black Women in Ivory Towers'. In: Anderson, P. and Williams, J. (eds), *Identity and Difference in Higher Education: 'Outsiders Within'*. Aldershot: Ashgate, pp. 147–61.

Kingston, P.W. (2001) 'The Unfulfilled Promise of Cultural Capital Theory', *Sociology of Education*, 74 (extra issue), pp. 88–99.

Kintrea, K., St Clair, R. and Houston, M. (2011) *The Influence of Parents, Places and Poverty on Educational Attitudes and Aspirations*. Joseph Rowntree Foundation. Available at: www.jrf.org.uk/sites/files/jrf/young-people-education-attitudes-full.pdf [accessed 9 February 2016].

Kirk, D.H. and Goon, S. (1975) 'Desegregation and the Cultural Deficit Model: An Examination of the Literature', *Review of Educational Research*, 45 (4), pp. 599–611.

Kushnick, L. (1993) '"We're Here Because You Were There": Britain's Black Population', *Trotter Review*, 7 (2), pp. 17–19.

Majors, R. (ed.) (2001) *Educating Our Black Children: New Directions and Radical Approaches*. London: Routledge.

Margolis, E. and Romero, M. (1998) '"The Department Is Very Male, Very White, Very Old, and Very Conservative": The Functioning of the Hidden Curriculum in Graduate Sociology Departments', *Harvard Educational Review*, 68 (1), pp. 1–32.

Mayor of London (2013) *The London Annual Education Report 2013*. Available at: www.london.gov.uk/what-we-do/education-and-youth/education-and-youth-publications/london-annual-education-report-2013 [accessed 11 February 2016].

Mirza, H.S. and Reay, D. (2000) 'Spaces and Places of Black Educational Desire: Rethinking Black Supplementary Schools as a New Social Movement', *Sociology*, 34 (3), pp. 521–44.

Morley, L. (1997) 'Change and Equity in Higher Education', *British Journal of Sociology of Education*, 18 (2), pp. 231–42.

Mountford-Zimdars, A., Sabri, D., Moore, J., Sanders, J., Jones, S. and Higham, L. (2015) 'Causes of Differences in Student Outcomes'. Higher Education Funding Council for England (HEFCE). Available at: www.hefce.ac.uk/media/HEFCE,2014/Content/Pubs/Independentresearch/2015/Causes,of,differences,in,student,outcomes/HEFCE2015_diffout.pdf [accessed 9 February 2016].

NUS (National Union of Students) (2011) *Race for Equality: A Report on the experiences of black students in further and higher education*. Available at: www.nus.org.uk/PageFiles/12350/NUS_Race_for_Equality_web.pdf [accessed 9 February 2016].

Oakeshott, M. (2004) 'The Idea of a University', *Academic Questions*, 17 (1), pp. 23–30.

Roscigno, V.J. and Ainsworth-Darnell, J.W. (1999) 'Race, Cultural Capital, and Educational Resources: Persistent Inequalities and Achievement Returns', *Sociology of Education*, 72 (3), pp. 158–78.

Runnymede Trust (2015) *The 2015 budget: effects on black and minority ethnic people*. Available at: http://socialwelfare.bl.uk/subject-areas/services-client-groups/minority-groups/runnymedetrust/budget15.aspx [accessed 11 February 2016].

Searle, J.R. (1993) 'Is There a Crisis in American Higher Education?', *Bulletin of the American Academy of Arts and Sciences*, 46 (4), pp. 24–47.

Snowdon, G. (2012) 'Graduates: Is a 2:1 the Best Qualification for Landing a Job?', *Guardian*, 10 February. Available at: www.theguardian.com/money/2012/feb/10/graduates-best-qualification-landing-job [accessed 9 February 2016].

Solorzano, D.G. (1992) 'An Exploratory Analysis of the Effects of Race, Class, and Gender on Student and Parent Mobility Aspirations', *Journal of Negro Education*, 61 (1), pp. 30–44.

Spafford, M. (2013) 'How Michael Gove Is Dumbing Down the History Curriculum', *Schools History Project*. Available at: www.schoolshistoryproject.org.uk/blog/2013/03/how-michael-gove-is-dumbing-down-the-history-curriculum/ [accessed 9 February 2016].

Strand, S. (2011) 'The Limits of Social Class in Explaining Ethnic Gaps in Educational Attainment', *British Educational Research Journal*, 37 (2), pp. 197–229.

Strand, S. (2012) 'The White British–Black Caribbean Achievement Gap: Tests, Tiers and Teacher Expectations', *British Educational Research Journal*, 38 (1), pp. 75–101.

Strand, S. (2014) 'Ethnicity, Gender, Social Class and Achievement Gaps at Age 16: Intersectionality and "Getting It" for the White Working Class', *Research Papers in Education*, 29 (2), pp. 131–71.

Strand, S., Malmberg, L. and Hall, J. (2015) *English as an Additional Language (EAL) and Educational Achievement in England: An Analysis of the National Pupil Database*. Department of Education, University of Oxford. Available at: https://educationendowmentfoundation.org.uk/uploads/pdf/EAL_and_educational_achievement2.pdf[accessed 9 February 2016].

Thomas, L. (2002) 'Student Retention in Higher Education: The Role of Institutional Habitus', *Journal of Education Policy*, 17 (4), pp. 423–42.

United States Department of Labor, Office of Policy Planning and Research (1965) *The Negro Family: The Case for National Action*.

Warmington, P. (2014) *Black British Intellectuals and Education: Multiculturalism's Hidden History*. London: Routledge.

Wright, C., Standen, P.J. and Patel, T. (2010) *Black Youth Matters: Transitions from School to Success*. Abingdon: Routledge.

Yosso, T.J. (2005) 'Whose Culture Has Capital? A Critical Race Theory Discussion of Community Cultural Wealth', *Race Ethnicity and Education*, 8 (1), pp. 69–91.

Part II
Conjunctures

7 Exclusion through citizenship and the geopolitics of austerity

Manuela Boatcă

For a long time, citizenship has been viewed as a mechanism meant to counter-balance social inequalities.[1] Western sociologists, working mostly with a nation-state frame of analysis, usually interpreted the institutionalization of citizenship as part of a sequence of social change characterizing modern, democratic societies, in which all citizens are equal before the law and in which particularities of birth such as ethnicity, status or regional origin no longer stand in the way of an individual's social mobility. Drawing instead on recent scholarship that addresses the link between inequalities and citizenship at the global level, this chapter focuses on how membership in the political community of citizens has ensured the relative social and political inclusion of the populations of Western European nation-states, while at the same time accounting for the selective exclusion of the colonized and/or non-European populations from the same social and political rights throughout history and up to this day.

As we shall see, recent developments with regard to citizenship allocation illustrate this enduring double standard: wealthy investors from certain non-Western regions are actively encouraged to purchase European citizenship rights in an unprecedented wave of commodification of residence and citizenship requirements across Europe, while financially strained states and non-Western labour migrants face mounting criminalization, sanctions and austerity measures when attempting to access the same rights. Taken together, these mutually rein-forcing dimensions of increasing global inequalities testify to the *longue durée* of colonially charged racial and ethnic exclusions in the history of modernity more generally, and to the coloniality of citizenship in particular.

Inclusion through citizenship: nation-state perspectives

Time and again, canonical – that is, Western, white, male – sociology has presented and analysed citizenship as a counterbalance of social inequalities. From Max Weber through T.H. Marshall and Talcott Parsons and up to Bryan Turner, the institutionalization of citizenship was seen as part of a sequence of social change characteristic of the West, which entailed progress from bondage to freedom and from ascribed to achieved positions in the inequality structure, ultimately defining the alleged transition from tradition to modernity.

For the German lawyer, national economist and sociologist Max Weber, the rise of citizenship as an institutionalized association of an autonomous status group (Stand) of individual burghers subject to the same law could be traced back to the ancient Greek *polis* and the medieval Occidental city. In his view, the revolutionary innovation differentiating the central and northern European cities from all others had been the principle that 'city air makes man free' (Weber, 1978: 1238), according to which slaves or serfs employed for wages in the city soon became free from obligations to their master as well as legally free. Consequently, in time, status differences between free and unfree city-dwellers gave way to the equality of individual citizens before the law. According to Weber, this possibility not only intensified the economic effort of unfree petty burghers, thus spurring capital accumulation through rational operation in trade or industry, but also constituted a preliminary stage in the achievement of political equality (Weber, 1978). This idea would later become central to the work of British sociologist T.H. Marshall, who proposed the extension of citizenship rights as the principal political means for resolving, or at least containing, the contradictions between formal political equality and the persistence of social and economic inequality (Marshall, 1977).

Drawing on both Weber's and Marshall's analyses, US sociologist Talcott Parsons (1965, 1966) referred to the institutionalization of the basic rights of citizenship as an egalitarian tendency of modern societies, in which universalistic norms gradually replace earlier particularistic solidarities of ethnicity, religion and regional origin. For Parsons, this tendency stood for a shift from societies based on ascriptive criteria to societies based on achievement criteria; the decisive thrust for its implementation had come from the French Revolution, which had 'demanded a community that included all Frenchmen and abrogated the special status of the privilegiés' and whose 'central concept was citizenship, the claim of the whole population to inclusion' (Parsons, 1971: 79). Parsons therefore took Marshall's sequence of citizenship rights to reflect not only a rough temporal series, but also a type of hierarchy of institutional steps towards the main aim of the French Revolution, the equality of membership status. In a thoroughly Occidentalist genealogy of the extension of rights, he viewed the French Revolution as having furthered civil rights, many of which had already been institutionalized in English and American law, as well as political rights, which he, like Weber, dated back to the ancient Greek *polis* (Parsons, 1971).

As late as the 1990s, Western scholars such as the British sociologist Bryan Turner still espoused and further reinforced a Weberian 'West vs. Rest' model of the emergence and development of citizenship, arguing that citizenship is an essentially modern institution that 'evolves through the establishment of autonomous cities, develops through the emergence of the nation-state in the eighteenth and the nineteenth centuries, and finds its full blossoming in the welfare states of the twentieth century' (Turner, 1996: np).

Apart from endorsing an Occidentalist and teleological view of the rise of the institution of citizenship, all these analyses were, in Bryan Turner's own words, 'internalist accounts', that is, taking the nation-state as a unit of analysis (Turner,

1996: np) and seeing it as separate from the empire. As such, they concentrated on the way the allotment of citizenship levels ethnic differences and appeases social conflict within nation-states, yet remained unconcerned with the way it affected colonial subjects and non-Western populations of the same states. Thus, in Parsons' conceptualization, the emergence of modern citizenship was traceable to a single historical event, the French Revolution, and it was limited – both in its context of emergence and its scope – to continental France and its (white, male) population, not the French colonies and their inhabitants in the Caribbean or French India. While ethnic and racial allegiance were treated as traditional ascriptive criteria for social cohesion in national contexts, the role of race and ethnicity in the development of citizenship at the global level was entirely missing from the analysis, as was gender. Feminist scholars accordingly pointed to the fact that citizenship constructs 'a public status and identity – long presumed to be male – that rests in ambiguous ways on the private support world of family, home and women' (Pettman, 1999: 207). They described the exclusion of women from citizenship as 'an intrinsic feature of their naturalization as embodiments of the private, the familial and the emotional' and as such 'essential to the construction of the public sphere as masculine, rational, responsible and respectable' (Werbner and Yuval-Davis, 1999: 6; for further critique, see Boatcă, 2015; Boatcă and Roth, 2016).

Exclusion through citizenship: global perspectives

One of the earliest contributions to an understanding of the double function of citizenship in relation to inequality patterns came from US sociologist Rogers Brubaker in his 1992 *Citizenship and Nationhood in France and Germany*. Emphasizing a 'global perspective', he stated that 'citizenship is a powerful instrument of social closure, shielding prosperous states from the migrant poor' (1992: x). He moreover pointed to the apparent paradox that citizenship is 'internally inclusive' – that is, it extends rights to all those defined as citizens – at the same time that it is 'externally exclusive' – that is, it restricts the access of non-citizens to the same rights. This double function, Brubaker argued, had been present ever since the French Revolution, which had created both the nation-state and its logical corollary, nationalism, in the same breath:

> A nation-state is a nation's state, the state of and for a particular, bounded, sovereign nation to which foreigners, by definition, do not belong. [...] By inventing the national citizen and the legally homogeneous national citizenry, the Revolution simultaneously invented the foreigner. Henceforth citizen and foreigner would be correlative, mutually exclusive, exhaustive categories.
>
> (Brubaker, 1992: 46)

The subsequent generalization of the principle of citizenship allocation in the modern world had meant that every person ought to have the citizenship of at least one state. Yet, as Brubaker pointed out, this development stands in sharp contrast to the institution of citizenship in both the ancient Greek *polis* and European medieval towns, where the possession of citizenship was not a given, but a privilege, while lacking citizenship was no anomaly. By contrast, every state today ascribes citizenship to certain persons at birth through either right of blood (*jus sanguinis*) or right of soil (*jus soli*) arrangements, or a combination of both. This mechanism, as Brubaker noted, was both 'a striking exception to the secular trend away from ascribed statuses' that Western sociologists had repeatedly associated with modern societies and proved that 'the state is not and cannot be a voluntary association. For the great majority of persons, citizenship cannot be but an imposed, ascribed status' (Brubaker, 1992: 32). Naturalization of foreign nationals is not only anomalous and infrequent in most countries, but also mostly limited to legal immigrants to the territory, such that 'by restricting immigration, states indirectly restrict access to naturalization' (Brubaker, 1992: 34). Despite marked differences in their immigration policies, all states remain 'relatively closed and self-perpetuating communities, reproducing their membership in a largely endogenous fashion, open only at the margins to the exogenous recruitment of new members' (Brubaker, 1992: 34).

Brubaker's notion of citizenship as social closure broke with previous approaches to the study of citizenship in several important respects. On the one hand, the focus on the idea of citizenship as membership ascribed at birth prompted the unfamiliar view of the modern state as structurally different from a voluntary association, and of both as different from the institution of citizenship in ancient Greece and feudal Europe. Thus, his analysis explicitly emphasized the discontinuities, rather than the continuities in the historical trajectory of citizenship in the West. On the other hand, his historical and comparative analysis of the German case illustrated that the institution of citizenship was not essentially democratic. Instead, finding that German legislation had first proclaimed equality of all before the law, yet had codified membership of the Stände and their corresponding inequalities, Brubaker denounced the 'pre-national, pre-democratic quality' (1992: 51) of the development of citizenship in Germany. In his view, Max Weber's plea against the 'Polonization' of the Prussian East, which Brubaker quoted as an instance of nationalist conservative attitudes to immigration, was an integral part of the German politics of ethnocultural nationality in the twentieth century (see also Boatcă, 2013).

More recently, analyses of global inequalities have focused on how birthright citizenship, whether under the *jus soli* or the *jus sanguinis* principles, functions as a kind of inherited property that restricts membership in well-off polities to a small part of the world population. Drawing in part on Brubaker's notion of citizenship as social closure, Israeli-Canadian legal scholar Ayelet Shachar (2009) focused on how the intergenerational transfer of citizenship ascribed at birth resembles the intergenerational transfer of property at a global scale. Both inherited property and birthright citizenship grant legitimate title bearers the unconditional right of entry and both restrict access to scarce resources (for example land in the case of property, a welfare system in the case of citizenship): 'Just as fiercely as it externally excludes nonmembers, citizenship can also act as an internal leveller of opportunity by providing the basic enabling conditions for members to fulfill their potential' (Shachar, 2009: 35). More importantly, Shachar notes, both inherited property and birthright citizenship are automatically transferred from one generation to the next. Although widely criticized in relation to both institutions, the hereditary transmission of privilege has been largely dismissed as feudal and inequitable only with regard to property, but has been maintained and even reinforced with regard to citizenship:

> Inherited entitlement to citizenship not only remains with us today; it is by far the most important avenue through which individuals are sorted into different political communities. Birthright principles strictly regulate the entail of political membership for the vast majority of the global population. Membership attributed through accident of birth secures the transmission of membership entitlement for a limited group of beneficiaries, either on the basis of bloodline or birthplace. These beneficiaries, in turn, gain the right to pass the benefit along to the next generation by inheritance.
>
> (Shachar, 2009: 41)

Citizenship is thus shown to function very similarly to the feudal entail, a legal means of restricting future succession of property to the descendants of a designated estate-owner practised in medieval England and elsewhere in Europe. The entail of property offered a tool to preserve land in the hands of dynastic families by entrenching birthright succession and forbidding future generations to alter the estate inherited from their predecessors (Simpson, 1986). By analogy, the entail of citizenship helps preserve wealth in the hands of designated heirs of membership titles – the state's citizens – by allocating political membership at birth in dramatically different opportunity structures (Shachar, 2009: 38–42). In Shachar's gripping comparison, for a girl born in 2001 in Mali, one of the poorest countries in the world, the chances of surviving to age five, having access to clean water or getting an education were incomparably lower than for a baby born at the same time in the United States, where chances for boys and girls on all these counts are nearly identically high. Contrary to an entire Occidentalist tradition of citizenship theory from Weber through Marshall and up to Turner, citizenship and gender, the most decisive factors accounting for these extreme inequalities between individuals in poor and rich countries in the twenty-first century, are both statuses ascribed at birth.

Although she eventually opts for another solution for global redistribution,[2] Shachar views international migration as a 'lifeline' for individuals without birthright privilege in an affluent democracy; migration offers 'a possible way to attain the precious and globally scarce good of citizenship in a stable and well-off polity' (Shachar, 2009: 83). At the same time, empirical analyses of the global income distribution have provided solid evidence for the fact that national citizenship represents the best indicator of an individual's position within the world's inequality structure. On the basis of the Gini coefficients of 96 countries,

Korzeniewicz and Moran (2009) have shown that national inequality patterns can be grouped into two distinct and relatively stable clusters, characterized by high or low levels of inequality, respectively. The high inequality cluster (above a Gini of 0.5), containing the bulk of Latin America, the Caribbean and Africa, has been characterized by systematic exclusion on the basis of ascriptive criteria such as race, ethnicity and gender in order to limit access to economic, social and political opportunity. In turn, the low inequality cluster (below a Gini of 0.3), which encompasses Australia, Japan, Canada, the whole of Western Europe and parts of Eastern Europe, has involved widespread relative inclusion through the extension of property and political rights increasingly derived from achieved (rather than ascribed) characteristics, such as one's education level, and the development of welfare states – which, in turn, have buttressed patterns of democratic inclusion.

Korzeniewicz and Moran find that membership in both clusters can be traced back in time to the eighteenth century, which prompts them to coin the term 'inequality equilibria' for both cases. At the same time, they clearly trace the origins of the institutional arrangements typical of the high inequality equilibrium back to colonial slavery (Korzeniewicz and Moran, 2009: 31). Using country income deciles, they furthermore show that the entire population of Western European countries, the United States, Canada and Australia is located within the two wealthiest global income deciles (with an average per capita income of US$7,898 or higher), while 70–80 per cent of the population of poor countries such as Gambia, Ethiopia, Zambia and Zimbabwe are located within the bottom global decile (with an average of US$266 or lower) (Korzeniewicz and Moran, 2009: 92). Despite the limited explanatory power of average income levels, the exercise convincingly demonstrates that both the middle classes and the working classes of rich countries are located in the wealthiest global deciles, mostly above the income level of the well-to-do 'national elites' of poor countries. Thus, the average income of the poorest decile in Norway is still higher than that of the wealthiest decile in Russia, Hungary, Brazil or Malaysia. Even within Europe, differences can be as stark as to have the poorest decile of Luxembourg (that is, Luxembourg's lower working class) rank on average just above the richest decile of Croatia (that is, Croatia's upper class), although both countries are located within the top income decile at the world level (with an average of US$28,570 or higher).

Canonical sociology usually views the low levels of inequality in wealthy regions as structured around achieved characteristics such as one's level of education or professional position, or the economic growth of the country or region itself. However, as Korzeniewicz and Moran argue, the long-term stability of low inequality levels has been safeguarded by restricting physical access to these regions on the basis of ascribed categories, especially national identity and citizenship, through the control of immigration flows. When taking the nation-state as a unit of analysis, countries with low inequality seem to represent a pattern of relative inclusion of the population through redistributive state policies, democratic participation and widespread access to education. Once the analytical frame shifts to the world economy, this pattern is thus revealed to entail the selective exclusion from the same rights of large sectors of the population located outside national borders (Korzeniewicz and Moran, 2009: 78). Once again, an ascribed characteristic of the type usually associated with the stratification order of feudal societies becomes the main principle of global stratification of modernity.

The above data set not only empirically backs the authors' thesis that national citizenship represents the single most important variable for predicting a person's position within global stratification; it also invites the more radical view that international migration, which entails gaining access to at least the average income of the lower country deciles of a much richer nation-state in its country of destination, becomes the 'single most immediate and effective means of global social mobility for populations in most countries of the world' (Korzeniewicz and Moran, 2009: 107). Thus, migration not only represents a strategy of upward mobility for populations of ex-colonial countries possessing metropolitan citizenship, but also a means of eluding the ascribed position derived from the national citizenship of a poor state for populations able and willing to risk illegal, undocumented or non-citizen status in a rich state.

Using the inequality data for six countries interlinked through considerable migration flows, Korzeniewicz and Moran are able to show how anyone in the poorest seven to eight deciles of Bolivia or Guatemala can move up several global income deciles by migrating to Argentina or Mexico, respectively, and gaining access to the average income of the second poorest decile there – even without gaining the citizenship of the new country of residence. Even more strikingly, anyone but people in the wealthiest decile in both Argentina and Mexico is able to skip several global income deciles by entering Spain or the United States' second-poorest decile through migration (Korzeniewicz and Moran, 2009: 108ff.). In all these cases, the upward mobility of migrant populations is considerably higher than either the average individual educational attainment within the country or the economic growth of one's country of origin would have allowed during a lifetime (judging by the most successful examples of economic growth, such as South Korea in the 1980s or China today).

Approaches explicitly linking the analysis of global inequalities with the issue of citizenship thus operate important changes in our understanding of both phenomena. Shachar's notion of citizenship as inherited property runs counter both to Weber's view that citizenship represents a counterbalance to inequalities of property and to Marshall's claim that citizenship and a capitalist class system are opposing principles (Marshall, 1977; Weber, 1994). It does not, however, relinquish the underlying Occidentalist assumption that citizenship as developed in the West through the legal (and physical) exclusion of non-European, non-white and/or non-Western populations from civic, political, social and cultural rights is a modern, progressive institution. In turn, the claim advanced in Korzeniewicz and Moran's world-historical perspective on inequality is that, since the emergence of Western European nation-states in the nineteenth century, national identity, institutionalized as citizenship, has been the main mechanism ensuring the maintenance of high inequality between the core and the periphery. As such, national identity and citizenship successfully replaced older criteria for global stratification, such as the religious idea of divine rights and the racial principle of white supremacy, to the extent that, in analogy to them, it has been naturalized – that is, it has come to be seen as a natural instead of a socially constructed form of identity and category of social differentiation (Korzeniewicz and Moran, 2009: 100).

This world-systemic reconceptualization sheds new light on the functions of modern citizenship from its very emergence in the context of the French Revolution: on the one hand, the gradual extension of citizenship rights from propertied white males to all white males and to white women (although to a large extent restricted until well into the twentieth century) accounted for the development of low inequality within continental France starting in the eighteenth century. On the other hand, the categorical exclusion of Saint-Domingue's black and mulatto population from French citizenship, irrespective of their property status, ensured the maintenance of high inequality between France and Saint-Domingue/Haiti, as well as between other Western colonial powers and their colonial possessions more generally.[3] It thus becomes clear that the entail of property, which for Shachar is analogous to the entail of citizenship, was a colonial entail that for several centuries helped preserve inherited property – be it in the form of material goods proper or rights to such goods, or in the form of state support, social services and infrastructure – in the hands of the (racially, ethnically and geopolitically) designated heirs to the Western colonial enterprise.

The possession of the citizenship of the former metropole remains to this day a crucial factor deciding the timing and the destination of ex-colonial subjects' emigration, just as it is a factor that may erode support for independence in the remaining colonial possessions. This has been documented for the postcolonial migration flows between several Western European countries and their former colonies or current overseas departments, as well as for the US and its 'protectorates': thus, fear of losing Dutch citizenship has led to an unparalleled increase in Surinamese emigration to the Netherlands in the years preceding Surinam's independence from the 'motherland' (1974–75) and is the main reason behind the lack of political pressure for independence in the Dutch Antilles and Aruba in recent times (van Amersfoort and van Niekerk, 2006). Likewise, the extension of United States citizenship rights to the populations of all Caribbean colonies after the Second World War triggered a massive transfer of labour migrants from the Caribbean to the US.

If citizenship and gender are the most decisive factors accounting for extreme inequalities between individuals in poor and rich countries in the twenty-first century, their systematic racialization and ethnicization additionally mirrors the colonial hierarchies of power established in the wake of the European colonial expansion, enslavement and forced labour regimes put in place since the sixteenth century. All of these hierarchies entailed the total or partial exclusion of non-white, non-Western, colonized and enslaved populations from the social, political and civil rights derived from European rule and, later, citizenship.

Aníbal Quijano's notion of 'coloniality of power' captures this logic by conceiving of coloniality as a set of political, economic and sociocultural hierarchies between colonizers and colonized. Emerging with the conquest of the 'New World' in the sixteenth century, and thus concomitant with modernity and interconnected with it, coloniality is however distinct from previous forms of colonial rule in that it translates administrative hierarchies into a racial/ethnic division of labour; and it is also more encompassing than modern European colonialism alone, in that it transfers both the racial/ethnic hierarchies – that is, the 'colonial difference' – and the international division of labour produced during the time of direct or indirect colonial rule into post-independence times (Mignolo, 2000; Quijano, 2000). Drawing on Quijano's concept of coloniality and Mignolo's corresponding notion of modernity/coloniality, I therefore propose to address the historical continuities that characterize the exclusionary logic of rights allocation in the modern/colonial world-system as a particular instance of coloniality and at the same time a pivotal instrument of rule, which I call the coloniality of citizenship.

The entail of colonial property: citizenship by investment

As shown above, global perspectives reveal the ascribed characteristic of citizenship to be as important for worldwide stratification as class, and hence a crucial driver of international migration and worldwide social mobility. Yet (upper) class membership comes with the significant benefit of being able to sidestep both ascription and the actual migration. Resorting to market mechanisms in order to elude the ascription of citizenship is therefore an increasingly visible, yet rare, option available only to the wealthy few, whose mobility however is seldom described as migration. They are instead referred to as 'global investors', 'expats', or 'foreign residents for tax purposes', while their migration process is more often referred to as 'relocation' or qualified as 'business migration'. The growing commodification of citizenship rights across the world in recent years, that is, the possibility of literally purchasing residence and citizenship in certain countries, not only makes the similarity between citizenship and the entail of property particularly salient. It also prompts the realization that the ascription of citizenship represents no exception to a modern trend away from ascriptive mechanisms, as both Brubaker and Shachar surmised, but a core principle of global stratification in the capitalist world economy.

Conferring citizenship to investors provided they take up residence in a country's territory has been common practice in a number of states, including the UK, the US, Canada, Belgium and Australia. A less common but recently growing practice consists of extending citizenship status to investors without a residence requirement, that is, they neither have to move to the country of their new citizenship nor reside there for a given amount of time. Firmly implemented in Saint Kitts and Nevis and the Commonwealth of Dominica since 1984 and 1993 respectively, such so-called citizenship by investment (or 'economic citizenship') programmes have recently proliferated throughout Southern and Eastern Europe (for a recent overview see Carrera, 2014; Dzankic, 2015).

As one type of naturalization procedure, citizenship by investment programmes have a clearly economic rationale and stand in close connection to the logic of coloniality. On the one hand, states employ them as an alternative development strategy or as a means of managing the global financial crisis. For their very first promoters, the programmes were meant to bridge the transition from the export mono-culture of the colonial economy to more diversified production after independence: Saint Kitts and Nevis, a federation of two islands in the Caribbean, established its programme one year after the islands gained independence from the United Kingdom in 1983. Initially, investment required to obtain citizenship was limited to a real estate option of US$400,000. After the islands' sugar industry was closed under pressures from the European Union and the World Trade Organization, a second option was introduced in the form of a donation to the Sugar Industry Diversification Foundation (SIDF), a charity aimed at conducting research into the development of alternative industries to replace the sugar industry (Dzankic, 2012). Under the headline 'Passports ... for a Price', Reuters pithily summarized the colonial logic behind the move towards investment citizenship by noting: 'For decades, the two-island nation of Saint Kitts and Nevis exported sugarcane to keep its economy afloat. When sugar prices fell, Saint Kitts began to sell an even sweeter commodity: its citizenship' (Abrahamian, 2012).

Similarly, the Commonwealth of Dominica, which gained independence from the United Kingdom in 1978, has established an investor citizenship programme after adverse weather conditions and the decrease in the world prices of bananas, the country's primary crop, had seriously damaged its economy (Dzankic, 2012). On the other hand, for the targeted investors, the economic rationale resides in the fact that, because of their conditions of former British colonies, both Saint Kitts and Nevis and Dominica are part of the Commonwealth of Nations. Their citizens can travel without a visa to more than half of the world's countries, including Canada and all of Europe. They pay no personal income taxes and can take up residence in any of the Caricom member countries at any time and indefinitely.

Within Southern and Eastern Europe, citizenship and residency programmes have taken hold especially as a result of the 2008 financial crisis and the austerity measures imposed by the EU, the European Central Bank and the International Monetary Fund (IMF). The programmes' economic rationale has therefore largely lain in providing a type of austerity management by refinancing debt through the sale of their otherwise inherited property – citizenship. Hungary adopted an amendment to the immigration law introducing an investment citizenship option in December 2012, shortly after the implementation of further austerity measures had been demanded by the EU and the IMF and approved by the government. Under the new law, foreigners who buy at least €250,000 in special government residency bonds with a five-year maturity date are offered preferential immigration treatment and a fast track to Hungarian citizenship with no residence requirement or real estate purchase (Varga, 2012). In 2014 alone, Hungary granted 1,800 investor visas (Hecking, 2015). While Hungary, alongside Latvia, boasts one of the lowest amounts required of investors in Europe, a real estate investment of up to €650,000 also buys foreigners residency rights and in some cases full European citizenship in Ireland, Spain, Portugal, Greece, Cyprus, Macedonia, Bulgaria and Malta, whose investment programmes have all been implemented since 2012 in the context of tightening austerity measures (Harrison, 2013; Peter, 2013). Visa-free travel to core countries, citizenship of a Schengen zone state or even the right to work in the EU thereby become available to the (moderately or very) wealthy. This time around, access to citizenship is restricted 'only' by income, apparently breaking the historical logic of ascribing citizenship at birth. Some authors have therefore introduced the term '*jus pecuniae*', or the right of money, as a new type of criterion for the allotment of citizenship alongside *jus soli* and *jus sanguinis* (Stern, 2011; Dzankic, 2012). However, the commodification of citizenship that *jus pecuniae* involves neither follows an alternative, non-ascriptive logic – since investors already possess an ascribed citizenship, and the newly acquired one can be passed on to future generations by descent; nor does it represent a viable option for most of the world's population. Instead, it is either an option purposely designed for a very select few or – more frequently – is scandalized, stigmatized and, ultimately, criminalized when it threatens to become available to a wider number of people.

In most cases, the declared goal of economic citizenship programmes is to attract wealthy investors, especially from China, but also, and increasingly, from Russia and the Middle East. Both the Hungarian and the Greek governments actively promoted the launch of their investment citizenship programmes in China. Cyprus, interested in preserving financial relations with Russia, initially tried to cut down the amount required for investment citizenship in order to compensate for the losses of the Russian business community in the recent Cypriot bank crisis (Focus Online, 2013). In the meantime, resident Cypriot citizens faced restrictions on the use of debit and credit cards, cheque-cashing and daily withdrawals from their bank accounts, as well as a ban on premature termination and compulsory renewal of all-time saving deposits. Similar austerity measures were imposed on resident Greek citizens during the ongoing debt crisis and bailout negotiations. Although closed banks and cash-strapped ATMs made any form of payment difficult in Greece, money transfer and cash withdrawal restrictions did not apply to investor citizens and Western nationals.

For wealthy individuals of non-Western countries, investment citizenship clearly represents a means of global social mobility that eludes both ascription and migration, and at the same time trumps race. In this regard, it is a globalized instance of what, in the context of racial inequalities in Brazil, has been referred to as 'whitening with money' (Hasenbalg, 2005) – a capital-facilitated symbolic move up the racial ladder. As such, it belies the experience of the great majority of transnational labour migrants, for whom border-crossing awarding upward economic mobility simultaneously entails the risk of downward racial mobility through reclassification as non-white. The fact that such racial reclassification poses very different degrees of difficulty depending on the colonial and imperial history of the context where one's racial identity is being negotiated only reinforces the hierarchies underlying the constructed racial continuum.

At the same time, sharp criticism of economic citizenship programmes as 'an abuse of European Union membership' (*Daily Mail*, 2012) in the case of Hungary or, in the case of Malta, as 'cheapening citizenship' (Passino, 2013; Shachar, 2014) has been instrumental in reasserting EU core countries' leverage on semiperipheral ones. The austerity measures and other sanctions imposed on Cyprus and Malta, which had already implemented their investment citizenship programmes, and Montenegro, which was planning to do so, are illustrative in this regard. Thus, in the context of the debate on the EU bailout of Cyprus's banks, the head of the German Christian Social Union (CSU) in the EU Parliament asked for a reform of Cyprus's citizenship law that would ensure that 'not everyone who has a lot of money receives a Cypriot passport' (Gammelin and Hulverscheidt, 2013). It was also the German CSU which announced that it might request the reinstatement of visas for the citizens of Montenegro if its government implemented a citizenship by investment programme in the country, implying that this decision might affect the previous 'progress' Montenegro had made 'in the area of border management and immigration control' (Vijesti, 12/08/2010, quoted in Dzankic, 2012). In the wake of such reactions, the Montenegrin government has put the implementation of its citizenship by investment programme on hold. In turn, Malta's brand-new citizenship scheme, with an initial investment threshold of €650,000, has been heavily disputed on a number of counts, including the European Commission's concerns that it would naturalize persons born and residing abroad without 'genuine links to the country' (Milmo, 2014). As a result, the Maltese government has amended the scheme to include a more severe residence requirement and further investment in real estate and government bonds, raising the contribution to a total of €1,150,000. It thereby hopes to raise up to €1 billion annually, around one-eighth of Malta's GNP – or the equivalent of 600 investor citizenships (Hecking, 2015).

Despite many of the arguments exchanged by critics and promoters alike, at stake in such debates, however, is not the abstract worth of citizenship, nor the amount of cultural and social ties of members with the national community. Instead, financially strained semiperipheral states are interested in how the commodification of citizenship facilitates the management of austerity, while wealthy core states are concerned about the consequences of the commodification of citizenship for migration to and the rights of potential migrants in core regions of the world economy. From different directions, both are trying to capitalize on the very coloniality that makes the citizenship of certain states a highly valuable commodity.

It is therefore important to note that, while any state's citizenship could theoretically be commodified by becoming the object of investor programmes, it is only the citizenship of few states that lends itself to being commodified by virtue of being a scarce good awarding (relatively) rare benefits. From this point of view, states whose citizenship include the advantage of the above-mentioned visa-free travel to core countries or even the right to legal employment in them, offer what could be referred to as 'premium citizenship' that is attractive to investors. States that are not part of the core, may, as in the case of Saint Kitts and Nevis, use the residual benefits of having been a British colony and today being a member of the Commonwealth of Nations and its visa-free travel area. This, however, hardly compares with the rights accruing from EU citizenship, which include free movement, residence and non-discrimination within the EU, the right to vote for and stand as a candidate in European Parliament and municipal elections, diplomatic protection outside the EU, and so on.[4] Citizenship for sale is not only unavailable to the majority of the world's population, but would not prove a viable economic strategy in any but 'premium citizenship' states, among which European Union member states rank highest.

Thus, according to Henley & Partners, a private British consultancy that has coined the term 'citizenship and residence planning', the EU is home to eight out of the ten countries worldwide whose citizens enjoy the most freedom of visa-free travel (Johansen, 2013). At the same time, the EU is the historic heir to Western colonial states whose possessions covered almost half of the inhabited surface of the non-European world as late as the 1930s and which today control 28 out of the remaining 58 colonial possessions (Böröcz and Sarkar, 2005; Worldatlas, 2013).

The Henley & Partners Visa Restriction Index, produced in cooperation with the trade association for the world's airlines, IATA, ranks Finland, Germany, Sweden, the United States and the United Kingdom number one on account of a total score of 174 countries to which their citizens can travel visa-free (out of a maximum score of 219). Canada and Denmark share second place with visa-free access to 173 countries, followed by Belgium, France, Italy, Luxembourg, Spain, Portugal and the Netherlands at 172 (Henley & Partners, 2014a). Most passport holders in Africa, the Middle East and South Asia have scores below 40, while mainland China has a barely slightly higher score of 45 – equal to that of Jordan, and right below that of Algeria, Cameroon and Rwanda. This explains why EU residence permits are extremely attractive to Chinese investors, and much more so than for Hong Kong investors, who have access to 156 countries on account of holding a 'Special Administrative Region of China' passport – another reminder of residual colonial advantage. Tellingly, the fine print to the index lists all other overseas territories and colonial dependencies of the world in order to clarify that territories 'dependent' on the United Kingdom, Australia, New Zealand, the USA, the Netherlands and France are not considered separate nationalities, but 'destinations' (Henley & Partners, 2014a) and thus do not get their own scores. The colonial entail of property thereby helps perpetuate the colonial entail of premium citizenship for Western states.

Additionally, non-state actors massively cash in on the colonial entail of citizenship by acting as intermediators in the conflict between the interests of states and those of very wealthy individuals. Henley & Partners, which has set up Saint Kitts and Nevis's as well as Antigua and Barbuda's investment citizenship scheme and is now administering Malta's, is located in the British Crown dependency of Jersey, in turn one of the leading offshore financial centres. The consultancy, which stands to make at least €60 million euros from its role as designer and principal contractor of Malta's revised citizenship scheme (Milmo,

2014), hosts an annual Global Residence and Citizenship conference (with an additional forum held in Malta in 2014) advertising the latest options available to wealthy investors in search of dual or 'alternative' citizenships (Henley & Partners, 2014b). Among the benefits, it stresses that alternative citizenship is 'an effective tool for international tax planning' – if one's state of origin imposes stricter tax rules – as well as for 'more privacy in banking and investment'. The highest worth, however, is attached to the insurance feature of citizenship:

> a passport from a small, peaceful country can even save your life when travelling and in times of political unrest, civil war, terrorism or other delicate situations. For good reasons, many international business people and important persons who are active worldwide consider an alternative passport as the best life insurance money can buy.
>
> (Henley & Partners, 2014b)

Not only do state bureaucracies as administrators of investor citizenship lose importance in this context, but the state whose citizenship is being traded no longer is the primary site of wealth-preservation.

Back doors and friendly gateways: the double standard of subversive practices

As investment citizenship and residence programmes open 'global mobility corridors for the ultra-rich' (Bărbulescu, 2014), strategies that provide low-income migrants with far more limited paths to mobility 'from below' are singled out as illegitimate and criminalized. This double standard runs through the global logic of closure and subversion. While both strategies, the one from above as well as the one from below, aim for access to premium citizenship, the criminalization and racial profiling of migrants to core regions – most prominently, the EU and the US – only targets so-called 'poverty migration'. Yet, as visa requirements for the majority of the world's migrants become more restricted, investor citizenships and visas proliferate. The CEO of Arton Capital, a global financial advisory firm, summarized the investors' view of this transformation with the words: 'It's a new world movement – global citizenship is not something you inherit at birth, it's something you have to work towards and invest in. This is the reason investment immigration is growing in popularity' (Ran et al., 2014). Advertising for the UK's newly revised 'tier 1' investor visas, which largely benefit Russian and Chinese millionaires, the head of a British law firm explained that wealthy individuals see London as an 'expat friendly gateway to Europe' (Warwick-Ching, 2012). For labour migrants, on the other hand, inherited citizenship and lengthy naturalization procedures are legally (re)inforced as the only legitimate options. In this context, most European states today scandalize non-European, non-Western or non-white migrants' claims to citizenship, denounce or block illegalized migrant paths to residence and, increasingly, restrict the rights and the duration of refugees' presence on their territory. In all of these cases, there are no friendly gateways waiting. Rather, the accusation is that of entering the world of wealth through the back door.

Thus, according to the French EU Affairs Minister Pierre Lellouche, one of the reasons France spoke out against Romanian efforts to join the EU's passport-free Schengen zone in 2010 was concern about 'the distribution of Romanian passports' to Moldovans. The territory of Moldova was part of the Romanian Principality of Moldavia from the mid-fourteenth through the mid-nineteenth century and part of Greater Romania 1918–40 and 1941–45.[5] Since many Moldovans are ethnically and linguistically Romanian and almost 95 per cent Romanian Orthodox Christians, Bucharest adopted a law granting foreign nationals of Romanian descent the right to become citizens of the country as soon as Moldova gained its independence from the Soviet Union. Since then, Romania has processed an estimated 225,000 citizenship applications from Moldovans (Iordachi, 2012).

The widely read, highbrow German magazine *Der Spiegel* illustrated the typical threat scenario mobilized in anti-immigration arguments with the words:

> [T]he EU, which is already suffering from enlargement fatigue, is stealthily being expanded from the east – without a referendum or any agreements from Brussels, Berlin or Paris. The Moldovans are voting with their feet and marching into the EU's economic paradise – through the back door.
>
> (Bidder, 2010)

As illicit intermediaries can even generate proof of Romanian ancestry where none exists, thereby spurring illegal trade in Romanian passports, EU fears of 'creeping expansion from the East' have fed on exaggerated prognoses of the 'stream of Moldovan migration' into Western Europe. Evidence has, however, shown that Romania's naturalization programme has created proportionately fewer EU citizens than similar efforts in France and the UK (Călugăreanu and Mogoş, 2012) and that Western European states grant far more new citizenships per 1,000 residents than states in any other part of Europe (Milmo, 2014). Nevertheless, France's concern with Moldovan migrants was the first in a line of Western European states' arguments against Romania and Bulgaria joining the Schengen zone. In 2013, the then German minister of the interior, Hans-Peter Friedrich, announced that 'the attempt [to join] will fail because of a German veto' if Romania and Bulgaria insisted on a decision, and he urged both countries to take further steps 'to prevent migrants abusing the system' (*The Economist*, 2013). At the same time, leading EU officials have repeatedly expressed concern that the expansion of the Schengen zone to Romania and Bulgaria would trigger an influx of North African refugees from Greece, which currently has no land connection to the rest of the Schengen space (Brady, 2012). As a result, Romania and Bulgaria's access to the Schengen zone is currently postponed indefinitely, and the countries consequently rank lowest among all EU countries in Henley & Partners' visa restriction index.

The increase in the commodification of European citizenship in the context of tightening austerity regimes not only reflects, but also reinforces, the ongoing widening of the worldwide inequality gap. According to Oxfam reports, the richest 85 people on the planet owned as much as the poorest 50 per cent – or 3.5 billion people – in 2014, down from 388 in 2010. Against this background, the emergence of investor citizenship programmes and the increasing migration and refugee flows into Europe can both be understood as strategies of eluding the ascription of citizenship and the unequal transfer of property underlying it – yet the availability of such strategies across social strata is as unequal as the worldwide distribution of wealth. While regulations and sanctions from supra-state and financial institutions ensure that investor visas remain unaffordable for most or are not introduced at all in financially strained states, austerity measures turn more state assets into commodities benefitting Western banks, creditors and core states: having agreed (but failed) to privatize around €50 billion in property and infrastructure as a way of raising money for its creditors in 2010, Greece now faces the prospect of having to auction off its islands, nature preserves or even ancient ruins under the terms of the most recent bailout in 2015 – a possibility interpreted as a 'selling of history' by advisers to the Greek Ministry of Labour, Social Security and Social Solidarity (Shuster, 2015). Also as part of the bailout deal, strategic state assets such as dozens of Greek airports are to be transferred to the property of a single private company whose major stakeholder is the German state (n-tv, 2015). At the same time, the racial and ethnic policing of non-Western migrants and refugees underlines the immutability of the ascription of citizenship for the wider population, and ultimately the denial of equal opportunities for upward social mobility at the global level.

Citizenship is thus not only a core mechanism for the maintenance of global inequalities in a world capitalist system, but also one on the basis of which their reproduction in the postcolonial present, that is, their coloniality, is being enacted. It is in the context of global capitalism and its corresponding logic of colonial accumulation that the institution of citizenship emerged; the economic and political interests of the Western European colonial powers that pioneered it were essential in defining its central features, and are decisive in maintaining premium citizenships restricted today.

Notes

1 Parts of this chapter summarize arguments previously published in chapters 2 and 6 of *Global Inequalities Beyond Occidentalism*, Ashgate 2015 (see Boatcă, 2015).
2 Shachar's solution, however, tends to reinforce, rather than question, the role of nation-states as bounded communities in guaranteeing such rights: by further analogy to the workings of inherited property, Shachar suggests introducing a 'citizenship tax', a levy on the privilege of birthright entitlement to the citizenship of wealthy states, as a type of 'infrastructure for reducing inequalities' (Shachar, 2009: 138). As one of the added benefits of this global redistributive scheme and as proof of the fact that the effects of citizenship laws are borne both by the beneficiaries and by the excluded, she mentions compensations to formerly colonized countries for 'unjust enrichment' during colonization or occupation:

[...] those with stronger historical ties (through colonialism or conquest, for example) have a stronger claim to gain a say in [...] tackling the unjust fallouts of these cross-border coercive effects. [...] Certain countries which share tighter historical, economic, linguistic, or geopolitical ties may negotiate extended exchange or tax-substitution programs to reflect their contextual interrelationships [...] and interdependence.

(Shachar, 2009: 138; see also Boatcă, 2012)

3 For the history of racial (self-)identification as 'black' and 'mulatto' in the context of the Haitian revolution and its aftermath, in which the category 'mulatto' mostly referred to free landowners, merchants and intellectuals, as opposed to the large masses of enslaved blacks, see Dubois (2004) and Fischer (2004). To this day, the term 'mulatto' is used in the Haitian context to designate high social status, while it is used throughout the Caribbean either as a self-affirmative or pejorative designation. I thank Alanna Lockward for help with the disambiguation of the term in the Caribbean context.
4 In this context, Jelena Dzankic (2014) has recently pointed out that the Cypriot and Maltese programmes are more attractive for investors than those of the Caribbean islands for two reasons.

[...] the naturalised investor will be granted visa-free travel to 151 (Cyprus) or 163 (Malta) states. This is considerably more than they would have by virtue of possessing the best-ranked Caribbean passport, that of Saint Kitts and Nevis which allows visa-free entry to 131 countries. Second, and more importantly, since in the EU the regulation of citizenship is decided by each Member State for herself, an individual may now obtain EU citizenship for roughly the price of a Porsche 918 Spyder [...]. This raises the question of whether it is proportionate and just that access to this array of rights is exchanged for the price of a sports car.

(Dzankic, 2014: 18)

At the same time, Dzankic's differentiation goes against her own earlier claim that *jus pecuniae* has become a third option for the acquisition of citizenship alongside *jus soli* and *jus sanguinis*.
5 Formerly known as Bessarabia, the region was annexed by the Soviet Union during the Second World War and became an independent republic in 1991. According to Romanian officials, many Moldovans regard the Romanian passport as the key to the EU and try to acquire Romanian citizenship as fast as possible using both official and unofficial channels (Călugăreanu and Mogoş, 2012).

Bibliography

Abrahamian, A.A. (2012) 'Passports ... for a Price', *Reuters*, 13 February. Available at: www.reuters.com/article/2012/02/13/us-passport-idUSTRE81B05A20120213 [accessed 18 February 2016].

Bărbulescu, R. (2014) 'Global Mobility Corridors for the Ultra-Rich. The Neoliberal Transformation of Citizenship'. In: Shachar, A. and Bauböck, R. (eds), *Should Citizenship be for Sale?* European University Institute Working Papers, RSCAS, 2014/01, pp. 15–16.

Bidder, B. (2010) 'Romanian Passports for Moldovans. Entering the EU through the Back Door', *Der Spiegel*, 13 July. Available at: www.spiegel.de/international/europe/romanian-passports-for-moldovansentering-the-eu-through-the-back-door-a-706338.html [accessed 11 April 2015].

Boatcă, M. (2012) 'Review: Ayelet Shachar: The Birthright Lottery. Citizenship and Global Inequality', *Critical Reviews on Latin American Research*, 1 (1), pp. 1–4.

Boatcă, M. (2013) 'The Many Non-Wests. Marx's Global Modernity and the Coloniality of Labor', *Deutsche Zeitschrift für Philosophie*, 34 (special volume), pp. 209–25.

Boatcă, M. (2015) *Global Inequalities Beyond Occidentalism*. Farnham: Ashgate.

Boatcă, M., and Roth, J. (2016) 'Unequal and Gendered: Notes on the Coloniality of Citizenship', *Current Sociology*, 64 (2), pp. 191–213.

Böröcz, J. and Sarkar, M. (2005) 'What is the EU?', *International Sociology*, 20 (2), pp. 153–73.

Brady, H. (2012) *Saving Schengen: How to Protect Passport-Free Travel in Europe*. London: Centre for European Reform.

Brubaker, R. (1992) *Citizenship and Nationhood in France and Germany*. Cambridge, MA: Harvard University Press.

Călugăreanu, V. and Mogoş, A. (2012) 'How to Buy an EU Citizenship', *Jurnalul National*, 12 September. Available at: www.jurnalul.ro/anchete/how-to-buy-an-eu-citizenship-623530.htm [accessed 17 May 2013].

Carrera, Sergio (2014) 'How Much Does EU Citizenship Cost? The Maltese Citizenship-For-Sale Affair: A Breakthrough for Sincere Cooperation in Citizenship of the Union?' Center for European Policy Studies. *Papers in Liberty and Security in Europe*, No. 64, pp. 1–51.

Daily Mail (2012) 'Hungary "sells EU passports" in return for bailout funds'. 31 October. Available at: www.highbeam.com/doc/1G1-306917234.html [accessed 31 October 2015].

Dubois, L. (2004) *Avengers of the New World. The Story of the Haitian Revolution*. Cambridge, MA: Harvard University Press.

Dzankic, J. (2012) 'The Pros and Cons of Ius Pecuniae: Investor Citizenship in Comparative Perspective'. European University Institute Working Papers, RSCAS, 2012/14. Fiesole: European University Institute, pp. 1–18.

Dzankic, J. (2014) 'The Maltese Falcon, or: My Porsche for a Passport!' In: Shachar, A. and Bauböck, R. (eds), *Should Citizenship be for Sale?* European University Institute Working Papers RSCAS, 2014/01, pp. 17–18.

Dzankic, J. (2015) 'Investment-Based Citizenship and Residence Programmes in the EU', European University Institute Working Papers, RSCAS, 2015/08. Fiesole: European University Institute, pp. 1–33.

Feere, J. (2010) 'Birthright Citizenship in the United States. A Global Comparison'. Center for Immigration Studies: Backgrounder, August, pp. 1–20. Available at: www.cis.org/sites/cis.org/files/articles/2010/birthright.pdf [accessed 2 May 2014].

Fischer, S. (2004) *Modernity Disavowed. Haiti and the Cultures of Slavery in the Age of Revolution*. Durham and London: Duke University Press.

Focus Online (2013) 'Eintrittskarte in die EU: Zypern lockt Reiche mit Staatsbürgerschaft', 15 April. Available at: www.focus.de/politik/ausland/eintrittskarte-in-die-eu-zypern-lockt-reiche-mit-staatsbuergerschaft_aid_960645.html [accessed 2 April 2014].

Gammelin, C. and Hulverscheidt, C. (2013) 'SPD sträubt sich gegen Rettungspaket'.

Harrison, V. (2013) 'Europe's Golden Visas Lure Rich Chinese', *CNN Money*, 26 November. Available at: http://money.cnn.com/2013/11/26/news/europe-golden-visas/ [accessed 18 February 2016].

Hasenbalg, C. (2005) *Discriminação e desigualdades raciais no Brasil*. Rio de Janeiro: Graal.

Hecking, C. (2015) 'Pässe für Millionen', *Die Zeit*, 13 May. Available at: www.zeit.de/2015/18/staatsbuergerschaft-kaufen-fluechtlinge-europa [accessed 10 July 2015].

Henley & Partners (2014a) 'Global Visa Restriction Index 2014'. Available at: www. henleyglobal.com/files/download/hvri/HP%20Visa%20Restrictions%20Index%20 141101.pdf [accessed 18 February 2016].

Henley & Partners (2014b) 'Why You Need Alternative Citizenship'. Available at: www. henleyglobal.com/why-alternative-citizenship/ [accessed 18 February 2016].

Iordachi, C. (ed.) (2012) *Reacquiring the Romanian Citizenship: Historical, Comparative, and Applied Perspectives*. Bucharest: Curtea Veche.

Johansen, M. (2013) 'The Best Passports to have for Unrestricted Travel around the World', *International Business Times*, 10 November. Available at: www.ibtimes.com/best-passports-have-unrestricted-travel-around-world-1422038, [accessed 18 February 2016].

Korzeniewicz, R.P. and Moran, T.P. (2009) *Unveiling Inequality. A World-Historical Perspective*. New York: Russell Sage Foundation.

Lacey, M. (2011) 'Birthright Citizenship Looms as Next Immigration Battle', *New York Times*, 4 January. Available at: www.nytimes.com/2011/01/05/us/politics/05babies. html?pagewanted=all&_r=0 [accessed 5 May 2014].

Marshall, T.H. (1977) *Class, Citizenship and Social Development: Essays*. Chicago: University of Chicago Press.

Mignolo, W. (2000) *Local Histories/Global Designs. Coloniality, Subaltern Knowledges, and Border Thinking*. Princeton: Princeton University Press.

Milmo, C. (2014) 'Passports for Profit: British company to make "disgusting amounts of money" from controversial EU passport sale', *Independent*, 30 January. Available at: www.independent.co.uk/news/uk/home-news/passports-for-profit-british-company-to-make-disgusting-amounts-of-money-from-controversial-eu-9094251.html [accessed 18 February 2016].

n-tv, 2015, 'Athen will Flughäfen versilbern. Fraport prüft neues Airport-Angebot', 9 August. Available at: www.n-tv.de/wirtschaft/Fraport-prueft-neues-Airport-Angebot-article15684476.html [accessed 18 February 2016].

Oxfam (2014) *Even It Up. Time to End Extreme Inequality*. Available at: www.oxfam. org/even-it-up [accessed 18 February 2016].

Parsons, T. (1965) *Theories of Society: Foundations of Modern Sociological Theory*. New York: The Free Press.

Parsons, T. (1966) *Societies; Evolutionary and Comparative Perspectives*. Englewood Cliffs, NJ: Prentice-Hall.

Parsons, T. (1971) *The System of Modern Societies*. Englewood Cliffs, NJ: Prentice Hall.

Passino, C. (2013) 'Malta Launches Controversial Citizenship Scheme', *Forbes*, 14 November. Available at: www.forbes.com/sites/carlapassino/2013/11/14/malta-launches-controversial-citizenship-by-investment-scheme/ [accessed 18 February 2016].

Peter, L. (2013) 'EU Shrugs off European Race to Woo Rich Foreigners', *BBC News*, 18 November. Available at: www.bbc.com/nws/world-europe-24940012 [accessed 18 February 2016].

Pettman, J.J. (1999) 'Globalisation and the Gendered Politics of Citizenship'. In: Yuval-Davis, N. and Werbner, P. (eds), *Women, Citizenship and Difference*. London and New York: Zed Books.

Pew Research Center (2013) 'Unauthorized Immigrants: How Pew Research Counts Them and What We Know About Them', 17 April. Available at: www.pewresearch. org/2013/04/17/unauthorized-immigrants-how-pew-research-counts-them-and-what-we-know-about-them/ [accessed 6 May 2014].

Quijano, A. (2000) 'Coloniality of Power, Eurocentrism, and Latin America', *Nepantla: Views from South*, 1 (3), pp. 533–74.

Ran, Y., Jia, C. and Chunyan, Z. (2014) 'Migrants Find a Home for Capital in Pursuit of Foreign Residence', *China Daily*, 23 January. Available at: http://usa.chinadaily.com.cn/epaper/2014-01/23/content_17254104.htm [accessed 18 February 2016].

Shachar, A. (2009) *The Birthright Lottery. Citizenship and Global Inequality*. Cambridge, MA: Harvard University Press.

Shachar, A. (2014) 'Dangerous Liaisons: Money and Citizenship'. In: Shachar, A. and Bauböck, R. (eds), *Should Citizenship be for Sale?* European University Institute Working Papers, RSCAS, 2014/01, pp. 3–8.

Shachar, A. and Bauböck, R. (eds) (2014) *Should Citizenship be for Sale?* European University Institute Working Papers, RSCAS, 2014/01. Fiesole: European University Institute.

Shachar, A. and Hirschl, R. (2007) 'Citizenship as Inherited Property', *Political Theory*, 35 (3), pp. 253–87.

Shuster, S. (2015) 'Greece may have to sell islands and ruins under its bailout deal', *Time*, 13 July. Available at: http://time.com/3956017/greece-bailout-selloff/ [accessed 18 February 2016].

Simpson, A.W.B. (1986) *A History of the Land Law*, 2nd edition, Oxford: Clarendon Press.

Stern, J. (2011) 'Ius Pecuniae – Staatsbürgerschaft zwischen ausreichendem Lebensunterhalt, Mindestsicherung und Menschenwürde'. In: Dahlvik, J., Fassmann, H. and Sievers, W. (eds), *Migration und Integration – wissenschaftliche Perspektiven aus Österreich*, Jahrbuch 1. Wien and Göttingen: V&R Unipress.

Süddeutsche Zeitung, 9 January. Available at: http://sz.de/1.1568342 [accessed 18 February 2016].

The Economist (2013) 'Romania and the EU: Not Ready for Schengen', 17 March. Available at: www.economist.com/blogs/easternapproaches/2013/03/romania-and-eu [accessed 2 July 2014].

Turner, B.S. (1996) 'Introduction: Marx and Nietzsche'. In: Turner, B.S. (ed.), *For Weber. Essays on the Sociology of Fate*. London: Sage.

van Amersfoort, H. and van Niekerk, M. (2006) 'Immigration as a Colonial Inheritance. Post-Colonial Immigrants in the Netherlands, 1945–2002', *Journal of Ethnic and Migration Studies*, 32, pp. 323–46.

Varga, J.T. (2012) 'Hungary Provides €250.000 Fast Track into Europe. VJT & Partners highlights the importance of the new Hungarian investment immigration law'. In: PRWEB. December 12. Available at: www.prweb.com/releases/2012/12/prweb10227642.htm [accessed 31 March 2014].

Warwick-Ching, L. (2012) 'Moscow's rich buy £1m entry into UK', *Financial Times*, 30 November. Available at: www.ft.com/cms/s/0/a0d6be06-3aff-11e2-b3f0-00144feabdc0.html#axzz40cDtm3Co [accessed 18 February 2016].

Weber, M. (1978) *Economy and Society. An Outline of Interpretive Sociology*, Vol. 1. Berkeley and Los Angeles: University of California Press.

Werbner, P. and Yuval-Davis, N. (1999) 'Introduction: Women and the New Discourse of Citizenship'. In: Yuval-Davis, N. and Werbner, P. (eds) *Women, Citizenship and Difference*. London: Zed Books, pp. 1–38.

Worldatlas (2013) 'Dependencies and Territories of the World, 2013', Worldatlas.com, January 2013. Available at: www.worldatlas.com/dependtr.htm [accessed 18 February 2016].

Yuval-Davis, N. and Werbner, P. (eds) (1999) *Women, Citizenship and Difference*. London: Zed Books, pp. 207–20.

8 Refugee Keynesianism?

EU migration crises in times of fiscal austerity

Peo Hansen

As I write this in the winter of 2016[1] the European Union is beset with crises: financial, monetary, growth, deflation, unemployment, Grexit, Brexit, Ukraine, to name some of the major ones. For the moment, though, the one topping the headlines is the so-called refugee crisis, including all that has followed in its wake of intergovernmental vitriol, border controls between EU members and collapsing Dublin and Schengen systems. But the current refugee crisis is just one amongst many in the big family of migration-related EU crises. Another impending crisis of course concerns the future of free movement for EU citizens, or 'EU migration', which is intimately, but far from exclusively, linked to the current Brexit crunch. To this we should add the fast-ageing EU's ballooning 'demographic deficit', a crisis calling for millions upon millions of new labour migrants that seem out of reach; or as an *Irish Times* (2013) headline captured it: 'Is Europe on the verge of demographic collapse?' We could mention too the emigration crises that are plaguing many EU member states and which in some places have generated demographic collapses that are past the on-the-verge stage (e.g. Juska and Woolfson, 2015).

In this chapter I want to deal with this, what we may call, big picture of EU migration crises. Too often EU migration crises and EU migration policy areas are treated separately, even as unrelated or distinct, both in the public debate and in scholarship. In the public debate we tend to deal with what politicians whine the loudest about at the moment, be it benefit tourism, Roma beggars, illegal immigration or portentous floods of asylum-seekers. In scholarship we have the general tendency of compartmentalized research, where some study asylum policy, others examine third-country labour migration, yet others delve into the legal details of EU citizens' free movement; and rarely do they meet. The former tendency testifies to the sorry state of large parts of the news media. Whereas sports journalists readily help us spot a footballer pretending to be fouled, news reporting has a much harder time calling the bluff when a prime minister wants to moan us into believing that 2,000 refugees on the opposite side of Dover pose an existential threat to Britain.

As for the latter tendency within research, although specialization and demarcation are often necessary and unavoidable, we could make use of more attempts at comprehensive and synthetic accounts that ask if there are dots to connect between the various migration policy areas and the recurrent crises. In what follows I obviously cannot account for all of the abovementioned crisis and policy areas. Instead, I will limit myself to the big enough conundrum of how we may understand the EU's dual and seemingly contradictory objectives of less migration, the mantra of the refugee crisis, and more migration, the mantra of the demographic crisis. Would it not seem natural to expect that the refugees be greeted as a first, albeit modest, step towards reducing the EU's gigantic demographic deficit? As one report in the *Financial Times* (2016a) had it, commenting on the draconian efforts by some EU members to keep refuges out: 'Poor demographics suggest they should welcome an influx of fresh workers. Finland is, for example, the most rapidly ageing country in the world behind Japan.' Or may a joint analysis of these 'less-and-more' objectives, at least from the Brussels perspective, actually give at hand that the EU rather perceives of them as somehow logically harmonious?

In my effort to suggest answers to these and other questions I will touch on the importance of historical perspectives on EU migration policy, if only to acknowledge that the current situation is contingent on migration policy choices made by the EU in the recent past, something that tends to go missing in the often highly presentist accounts on EU migration policy. In line with this volume's thematic I will also engage with the concept of austerity. As a starting point, I take that in the world of politics, migration and migrants constitute austere categories, denoting a paucity of the social embeddedness that citizenship offers, or what a path to citizenship through permanent residence offers.

I will begin by briefly commenting on the refugee crisis and the rather unambiguous EU response of scrambling to stem the tide, which will then spill over into the equally unambiguous, yet less well-known, EU response to the Union's alleged demographic emergency of scrambling to hugely increase the intake of third-country labour migrants. From there I go on to attend to the question as to why Brussels and member states do not see refugees as the answer to the EU's dire demography. I suggest that the answer to this question rests with an austere calculus, which, for both fiscal and racial reasons, effectively thwarts the type of expansive public investment and citizenship regime that would be required to, so to speak, allow the EU's demographic deficit to be perceived as congruent with the global refugee surplus. Here I will focus on Germany and Sweden, two countries that initially *did* take some steps in the direction of such congruity, but which since have recoiled. In the chapter's final part I shall thus suggest some explanations for this sudden change.

Minimalist refugee migration

While in the midst of the EU's escalating and clamorous refugee *cum* political responsibility crisis it is easy to fall for the seemingly ultra-obvious notion that the EU wants to minimize migration in all its forms. Said Martin Wolf (2015) of the *Financial Times*: 'Europeans just want to be left alone. But the EU lives in a world of chaos. It needs to find a way to cope, other than by becoming a fortress that lets the desperate perish on its defences.' To be sure, the EU's asylum policy is replete with physical, virtual and legal fortifications aiming to keep refugees out, which also explains the tens of thousands of people who have died in the Mediterranean in recent decades while fleeing war, poverty and persecution. Donald Tusk, the head of the European Council, is thus as amateurishly deceptive about the past as he is candid about the end goal of it all when he stated the following at the end of September 2015: 'It is clear the greatest tide of refugees and migrants is yet to come. So we need to correct our policy of open doors and windows. Now the focus should be on proper protection of our external borders' (quoted in *Daily Telegraph*, 2015a). True, borders between Turkey and Greece and then onwards through Balkan non-EU members were initially forced open thanks to the exceptional refugee situations in Syria and Turkey. But this is not EU policy as such; rather it is seen by the EU as a mammoth policy failure and hence the enormous efforts on the part of the EU, starting in the late summer of 2015, to negotiate a refugee blocking settlement with Ankara.

Since EU cooperation on asylum policy began in the late-1980s, the EU's objective has been quite unequivocal about not wanting asylum-seekers on its territory. It is thus important to remember that while there were refugees coming to the EU in the early 1990s too, hardly anyone had to perish in the Mediterranean (Guild *et al.*, 2015: 4). But since then there has been a steady increase in casualties, and it has gone in tandem with an EU harmonization primarily bent on devising policies, systems, legal instruments and third-country cooperation for the purpose of denying asylum-seekers entry into the EU.[2] The EU's common visa policy and carrier sanctions legislation have been particularly culpable in precluding legal and thus safe access to the EU for asylum-seekers (Guild *et al.*, 2015). As mentioned, due mainly to the Syrian war, the number of refugees who have entered the EU in the past couple of years is clearly unprecedented by EU standards; but much of the response follows a historical pattern. Just recall the virtual panic that broke out in the EU during the winter of 1998 – triggering a succession of crisis meetings in Brussels and elsewhere – following the disembarkation of slightly more than 1,200 Kurdish refugees in Italy. Here the then German Interior Minister Manfred Kanther declared that '[i]n view of this threatening situation, Western Europe must view itself as a security community' (quoted in *International Herald Tribune*, 1998a). Kanther also referred to the Kurdish refugees as representing a 'criminal wave of migration' (quoted in *International Herald Tribune*, 1998b).

Another poignant example in recent history would be the 2005 tragedies in and around the Spanish North African colonial 'enclaves', Melilla and Ceuta (which are situated on the Moroccan Mediterranean coast). Since Melilla and Ceuta are fully incorporated into metropolitan Spain, they are also fully integrated into the EU (see Gold, 2000). From the time when Spain became an EU member in 1986, Ceuta and Melilla have increasingly been made to serve as key hubs in Spain's and the European Union's escalating fight against so-called illegal immigration. In the 1990s, and aided by EU funding, the enclaves, and thus the EU's borders in Africa, were gradually transformed into outright fortifications, walled in by miles and miles of parallel fences, hedged off by barbed wire entanglements, and equipped with electronic sensors and thermo-cameras. To these fortifications large numbers of people from various African countries have gone for decades now in the hope of crossing into the EU to find work or seek asylum. Often they live under deplorable conditions in makeshift shanties on the Moroccan side.

In September and October 2005, developments took a new and serious turn when a few hundred of the shanty dwellers attempted to break through by storm-ing the fences surrounding Ceuta. The Spanish-Moroccan guard responded by opening fire, possibly killing as many as five people, while many were seriously wounded in the stampede. A week later a similar breakthrough attempt took place at the EU border to Melilla, with the guard acknowledging that it had shot and killed at least six people (Mead, 2005; Davies, 2010). In the ensuing Spanish debate, attention was mostly focused on the need to reinforce the borders around the enclaves and on means to increase the deportation of 'illegals' from the areas in and around Ceuta and Melilla. The new socialist government in Madrid promptly announced that it intended to seek assistance from the army in the fight against illegal immigration (Mead, 2005). The European Commission's reaction was in line with Madrid's and consisted, initially, of dispatching a group of border control experts to the area and of an offer to the Moroccan government of €40 million for border control reinforcement. Subsequently, the Commission also called on the Moroccan government to sign a (still pending) readmission agreement with the EU (ECRE, 2005).

Given the intense fire that the Hungarian government came under in the summer of 2015 for building a fence on its border with Serbia, it was interesting to note that the overwhelming majority of the criticism made it sound as if the Hungarian action was somehow unprecedented. Even the European Commission joined the choir for a while, when this seemed the opportune thing to do, and wanted to make it sound as if border fences and the reality – which the Commis-sion has worked so hard to realize – that asylum-seekers have no regular ways to enter the EU somehow are contrary to the EU's so-called 'European values'. As the Migration, Home Affairs and Citizenship Commissioner Dimitris Avramo-polous (2015) stated in August when asked about the Hungarian fence:

> We have only recently taken down walls in Europe: we should not be putting them up again. [...] The Commission does not promote the use of fences and encourages member states to use alternative measures. We are here to take down walls not to erect.' Subsequently, upon news leaking out about Austrian plans for a fence with Slovenia, the Commission reiterated that 'fences have no place in Europe.
>
> (Quoted in Maurice, 2015)

Nothing could of course be further from the truth. Yet the fact that it could be uttered in the first place speaks volumes about the meagre public awareness of the EU's 30-year record on asylum policy harmonization.

A few months later, however, complaints and moral grandstanding over the erection of walls and border controls had all faded into the background. As a *Financial Times* report had it in late November 2015: 'What Hungary's Viktor Orban was pilloried for initiating is almost becoming best practice.' Indeed, as I write this, many member states, and maybe the Commission too, are seriously considering assisting Macedonia, a non-EU member, to close its border with Greece in order to block refugees heading north. As part of this, with Greece being accused of failing to control 'irregular migration', the Commission is also threatening to expel Greece from Schengen (*Financial Times*, 2016b; 2016c).

Maximalist labour migration

But if Fortress Europe – as another way of expressing the objective of minimizing 'inflows' – has its merits when it comes to asylum policy, it fits poorly in other areas of EU migration engagements. For if the refugee crisis calls for minimizing inflows, the EU's demographic crisis calls for maximizing inflows. In its 2005 'Policy Plan on Legal Migration', the European Commission (2005: 4) warned that unless the EU manages to drastically increase labour immigration, the EU's working-age population is expected to contract by some 52 million by 2050. Furthermore, as is underscored in the Commission's '2012 Ageing Report',[3] looking only to 2020 the EU would need a net migration of 25 million in order to keep the working-age population stable at current level. This means that the Union would have to net an additional 11 million migrants to the already projected 14 million (EC [European Commission], 2012: 51–6). According to the '2015 Ageing Report', moreover,

> the age structure of the EU population is projected to change dramatically in the coming decades (EC, 2015a: 20). Indeed, the old-age dependency ratio is projected to take a huge turn for the worse over the period 2013–60, the Union moving 'from having four working-age people for every person aged over 65 years to only two working-age persons.
>
> (EC, 2015a: 22)

This provided, economic growth and migration growth have become two sides of the same coin in the EU's economic and political ambitions. This was made clear already in the Lisbon Strategy (2000–10) and now constitutes one of the cornerstones of 'Europe 2020', the EU's current ten-year plan for growth (EC, 2010a: 18; EC, 2011a: 4). From the perspective of the Commission, a large-scale increase in labour migration has become so urgent that the then Home Affairs Commissioner referred to it as a matter of 'our economic survival' (Malmström, 2010).

Before saying anything further about the more contemporary developments, however, it is important to take note of the relatively recent nature of the Commission's current position as a strong advocate of external labour migration (ELM), which thus differs from the quite consistent and continuous policy approach that the Commission, since at least the early 1980s, has taken to the other major areas of migration policy, that is, asylum, border security, 'illegal migration' and free movement for EU citizens. From the early 1970s to the late 1990s, and in sharp contrast to today, the Commission instead championed an official line of policy that advised against labour migration to the EU from non-OECD countries. In its 'comprehensive approach' to migration, presented in 1994 (and originally drafted in 1991), the Commission advocated a three-pronged strategy, calling for: (1) 'Taking action on migration pressure'; (2) 'Controlling migration flows'; and (3) 'Strengthening integration policies for the benefit of legal immigrants' (EC, 1994: 11).

Deemed the only 'realistic' option at the time, this (what is now referred to as) 'zero migration' policy also served as an important public relations tool from the mid-1980s onwards, promising EU citizens that the transformations brought about by the Single Market would not lead to an increase in external migration (Hansen and Hager, 2012). In an information booklet from 1996, for instance, addressing the 'European citizen', Brussels took care to note that many 'are concerned about immigration [...], thinking that this could increase once internal border controls have been fully swept away'. The question that many EU citizens were asking, according to the Commission, could thus be phrased as follows: 'Will the eventual dismantling of all internal borders lead to an increase in levels of immigration to my country, both from inside and outside the Community?' To this the Commission could give a reassuring answer: 'No, it should not. The fundamental point about dismantling the Community's internal borders is that this process must be accompanied by the synchronized tightening of all external borders' (EC, 1996: 13–15).

By the turn of the millennium this, by now, habitual policy picture was to be significantly revised. To be sure, the revision did not affect the pursuit of border security, which would continue unabated. But it did involve a remarkable reversal of the EU's stance on ELM. All of a sudden, Brussels would start issuing statements such as the following: 'The Commission considers that the zero immigration mentioned in past Community discussion of immigration was never realistic and never really justified'; and

> it is clear from an analysis of the economic and demographic context of the Union and of the countries of origin, that there is a growing recognition that the 'zero' immigration policies of the past 30 years are no longer appropriate.
>
> (EC, 1999: 2; 2000: 3)

That said, it is of course crucial to make clear that the 1980s and 1990s by no means were characterized by 'zero' labour immigration to the EU. On the contrary, several million new labour migrants from around the world arrived during these decades. Most of these new arrivals, however, were not legal or regular labour migrants. They were irregular, undocumented or 'illegal'. An important enabling factor for this development is to be found in the liberalization of the EU economy that got under way in the 1980s. Weakened labour unions and labour laws, pressure for low-skilled production and low-wage and temporary employment, in conjunction with a fast-growing service sector and informal labour market of outsourced and sweated labour were factors fuelling the EU's growing demand for irregular labour migrants – that is, the type of labour often most suited for such economic and labour market conditions (see, e.g. Schierup, Hansen and Castles, 2006).

In the early 1990s research started to attend to this development and was able to demonstrate that many EU governments that claimed to be fighting illegal immigration in actuality were quite content with the fact that their economies were profiting from the cheap labour performed by irregular migrants (Over-beek, 1995; Castles, 2004: 223, 214). For instance, as was uncovered by the *Guardian*, in 2002 Spanish authorities rounded up African migrants on the Canary Islands and flew them to the mainland, where they were simply dumped off in areas where the agribusiness needed labour (Lawrence, 2011). In most cases, of course, this procedure works in indirect ways, foremost through a more or less deliberate eschewal of systematic controls of employers and workplaces. In dodging the demand side, this obviously checks the efficiency of ever so extensive migration barriers erected for the purpose of tackling the supply side of irregular migration. For all the firm commitments made by successive British governments to clamp down on 'illegal immigration', for instance, the country's independent Migration Advisory Committee, as Martin Ruhs points out, has revealed that, statistically speaking, firms employing irregular migrants currently run the risk of being subjected to a tax authority inspection 'once in every 250 years' and 'to be prosecuted once in a million years' (Ruhs, 2015: 19).

In the official rhetoric, Brussels and EU governments refrain from acknowledging that they, in fact, have been advancing policies that are conducive to 'illegal immigration'. The conversion that took place around the turn of the millennium only acknowledged the EU's great demand for 'legal' labour migrants.

Nonetheless, the new policy also contained a certain measure of candour when it was first launched. Thus, when the Commission presented its new official approach to labour immigration it was fairly obvious that the Commission recognized its breach of promise to the EU citizens, and that it, as a consequence, had been saddled with a tough public relations challenge. Brussels thus appeared to be apprehensive that EU citizens would respond negatively to the official abrogation of 'zero immigration', possibly interpreting it as portending less restriction and an uncontrolled inflow of immigrants. After all, the EU had gone from an official policy firmly resolved to uphold 'zero' labour immigration from non-OECD countries to a policy forecasting the entry of millions of new migrants almost overnight. In order to obviate a possible public disapproval of this abrupt shift, the Commission soon came up with a series of public relations measures to be adopted by elite actors. 'A shift to a proactive immigration policy', the Commission asserted, will 'require strong political leadership to help shape public opinion' (EC, 2000: 22). In its detailed opinion on the Commission's new approach to migration, the EU's consultative body, the European

Economic and Social Committee (2001: 111), voiced similar concerns: 'It will not be easy to persuade public opinion to take a favourable view of the more open immigration policy now being proposed, but far-reaching work to this end is now urgently required.'

In the face of the dropped pledge to uphold zero immigration, the EU immediately made a new pledge to EU citizens to implement even harsher measures against 'illegal' migration. Early on, for instance, the Commission (2002: 8) pointed to the merits of 'the forced return of illegal residents', arguing that this could 'help to ensure public acceptance for more openness towards new legal immigrants against the background of more open admission policies particularly for labour migrants.'

Refugees as a demographic growth boost?

As already seen, medium and long-term demographic projections constitute the foundation for the Commission's outlook on external labour migration in the coming decades. They have been used consistently throughout as justification of Brussels' stance and to drive home the point that external labour migration (ELM) is above all structurally determined and, as such, should not be allowed to be compromised by immediate business cycle and unemployment concerns, but rather needs to be seen as an increasingly urgent necessity in order to sustain growth, competitiveness and social welfare in the EU. Instead of the member states going it alone, devising between themselves inconsistent responses (or few responses at all) at odds with the overall functioning of the EU, the Commission approaches these demographically induced migration challenges as calling for common, coordinated and increasingly harmonized policies.

From the demographic projections, giving at hand a rapidly ageing Union, the Commission then derives in more detail the short-, medium- and long-term labour demand with regard to skills required, sectoral assessments and overall structural changes in the labour market. Important to keep in mind is that the Commission does not foresee ELM as the sole solution to the demographic deficit. However, what is interesting is that the Commission has come to lean more and more in this direction. For some time, as reflected in the Commission's (2005: 5) 'Policy Plan on Legal Migration' from 2005, the official view was that '[i]mmigration does not provide in itself a long-term solution to falling birth rates and an ageing population, but it is one of the available tools within a broader policy mix.' Since then, however, and as seen in numerous statements and documents, not least in the Commission's earlier cited '2012 Ageing Report', ELM is more and more deemed as, if not the only remedy, certainly *the* most important one, equipped with fairly detailed estimates of the required volumes of migrants and the serious consequences from failure to act in accordance.

This tendency is reflected too in Brussels' increasingly alarmist and frustrated calls for member state cooperation on ELM, or as put by the then Home Affairs Commissioner Cecilia Malmström:

When I meet ministers responsible for labour policies, they almost all speak of the need for immigrant workers – and it's true, we need hundreds of thousands, millions in the long term. But when the ministers go and speak in front of their national publics, this message is not to be heard at all.

(Quoted in Barber, 2011)

When subsequently referring to the necessity of stimulating labour migration, Malmström sounded an even more pessimistic tone: 'But it is politically impossible to attain in today's Europe' (quoted in Larsson, 2013; see further Hansen, 2016).

This provided, we are now all set to turn to the puzzle, spelled out initially, about the seemingly contradictory goals of less migration as a resolution to the refugee crisis, on the one side, and more migration as a resolution to the demographic crisis, on the other. If the Commission mourns the political impossibility of launching large-scale labour migration to the EU, we must ask, why does it not celebrate the current large-scale refugee migration as a compensatory gift from heaven? In other words, why does it seem politically impossible for the Commission to make up on the swings what it loses on the roundabouts? If the objective is to increase the labour pool, refugees should come in very handy given that the large majority are young and working-age. Certainly, the number of refugees is nowhere near satisfying the Commission's labour migration demand projections. But still, should not the refugees be seen as a crucial first step in the right direction?

So far, however, no such synergetic reasoning is to be found on Brussels' agenda. Instead of seizing the moment to try and convince the member states to perceive of the refugee arrivals not as a crisis but rather as a demographic and economic growth opportunity, the Commission has gone ahead and spent its energies on devising new measures to make it harder for refugees to enter the EU. These measures include a further militarization of the Mediterranean for the stated purpose of intercepting smugglers – applying military force if necessary – in the business of taking refugees across the Mediterranean, which is practically the only means that refugees are left with since the EU has plugged all regular (or 'legal') and safe routes to enter the EU. This scheme goes under the names 'Operation Sophia' and 'European Union military operation in the Southern Central Mediterranean', or EUNAVFOR MED, and was readily agreed and swiftly launched in June 2015 (Council EU, 2015). According to the European Union External Action Service, which is headed by the EU's High Representative of the Union for Foreign Affairs and Security Policy and Vice-President of the European Commission, Federica Mogherini, '[t]he aim of this military operation is to undertake systematic efforts to identify, capture and dispose of vessels as well as enabling assets used or suspected of being used by migrant smugglers or traffickers' (European Union External Action, 2015). The terminology of 'migrant smugglers or traffickers' is of course very consciously applied in order to divert attention from refugees and asylum-seekers as well as the obvious fact that these vilified 'smugglers' are the sole reason why there are *refugees* in the EU in the first place.

Another even more important pursuit at the time of writing is of course a much coveted and criticized refugee deal with Turkey to have Ankara agree to seal the border to the EU (agreed in part on 29 November 2015). But since EU leverage vis-à-vis Turkey has dwindled in recent years, this has proved to be a difficult task; and with the EU's hasty cash offer to Turkey to tighten the refugee spigot, initially of €1 billion but then quickly raised to €3 billion, no one could fail to notice Brussels' desperation. This desperation was also fuelled by high-ranking EU officials' impression that Turkish President Tayyip Erdogan has been purposefully funnelling refugees to the EU in exchange for a sweet deal. 'Europe's most ardent courtship of a Turkish leader in the post-Ottoman era' was how *Financial Times*' Alex Barker described the spectacle (2015). Doing his part, Commission president Jean-Claude Juncker was up front about the fact that in order to come to a swift agreement with Ankara, the EU would have no problem compromising human rights and democratic freedoms and liberties. This meant that the Commission also made sure to delay until after the Turkish elections the publication of its annual Progress Report on Turkey's compliance with human rights and democracy, as well as to soften the report's language. As Juncker put it before the European Parliament on 27 October:

> We face two possibilities and these are the options. We can say that EU and the European institutions have outstanding issues with Turkey on human rights, press freedoms and so on. We can harp on about that but where is that going to take us in our discussions with Turkey?

In clarifying further, he went on to say: 'We know that there are shortcomings but we need to involve Turkey in our initiatives. We want to ensure that no more refugees come from Turkey into the European Union' (quoted in *Daily Telegraph*, 2015b). In addition, as Barker (2015) also notes, Brussels and Berlin wilfully contributed their bits in boosting Erdogan's election prospects with high-level meetings in Brussels and Merkel visiting Erdogan in Istanbul.

In relation to this, we should mention two other major recent initiatives taken by the Commission to prevent refugees from reaching and staying in the EU. The first concerns the proposal (issued in September 2015) for a regulation 'establishing an EU common list of safe countries of origin' (EC, 2015b), so as to facilitate an accelerated return of people (from 'safe countries') seeking asylum in the EU. The initiative is intimately linked to the ongoing refugee negotiations with Turkey, since it proposes to have Turkey included in the list of safe countries, and as such it is also intimately linked to the EU's ongoing trading of human rights concerns for refugee expediency. As Human Rights Watch's senior Turkey researcher, Emma Sinclair-Webb (2015), comments:

> It is scandalous and short-sighted that the EU is willing to ignore the huge crackdown under way in Turkey in its attempt to secure a deal to keep out refugees. [...] [T]he European Commission has proposed a regulation to designate Turkey a safe country of origin. This means that Turkish citizens,

such as journalists and Kurds fleeing state abuse, would presumptively be assumed *not* to face persecution if they apply for asylum in the EU. This, despite a 23 percent approval rate for asylum applications from Turkish nationals in the EU in 2014.

Finally, we should also mention Brussels' recharged push for a massive increase in returns of failed asylum-seekers and irregular migrants, which was launched with the 'EU Action Plan on Return', also in September 2015 (EC, 2015c). The Plan is adamant that the return curve turns sharply upwards from today's general rate of 40 per cent, and it proposes a whole battery of new measures and ways to strengthen old ones. It speaks in terms of the 'returnable', of the EU's surroundings in terms of an 'Eastern flank' and a 'Southern side', of the enterprise to 'muster adequate leverage' vis-à-vis countries in North- and Sub-Saharan Africa, of 'brisk action', 'swift legal procedures', 'forced return' and that 'removal should not be undermined by a premature ending of detention' (EC, 2015c). The Commission does not hide its frustration with tardy member states and thus anticipates '*infringement procedures* against Member States that do not fully comply with all its provisions including the obligation to issue and enforce return decisions' (EC, 2015c: 4–5, italics in original). This also goes for third countries that drag their feet in signing readmission agreements with the EU, these agreements being held up as one of *the* chief instruments in significantly increasing the number of returns.[4] In this context, and '[w]hile the EU's Eastern flank is now well covered through readmission agreements', it is the task of getting North and Sub-Saharan African countries to sign that appear in the limelight. Among the priority countries to be added to the list of signatories are Morocco, Egypt, Ethiopia and Afghanistan (EC, 2015c: 12), all in line, we must assume, with today's EU standards of human rights, the rule of law, democracy, refugee rights and overall state stability.

As if this was not enough, the Plan also takes us down the whole Freudian slippery slope when it states that the reason for having an asylum system in the first place is to ensure an efficient return policy: 'An effective return policy requires the existence of a *functioning asylum system*, to ensure that unfounded asylum claims lead to swift removal of the person from the European territory' (EC, 2015c: 5, italics in original). Asylum policy has thus been turned on its head, now to primarily serve as a handmaiden to return policy. The Plan does not waste any time in promoting this precise transformation, instructing, for instance, that

> [a]sylum-seekers need to be informed of the possibility of assisted voluntary return early on and at all stages of the asylum procedure, to provide a sound alternative to rejected asylum-seekers and to those who wish to discontinue their claim to return to their countries in dignity.

Described in this fashion it should be obvious that we are no longer dealing with an asylum system; what we rather have is a return system. Being marked by a bellicosity probably not seen since Franco Frattini's days as Home Affairs Commissioner (2004–08), the 'EU Action Plan on Return' is therefore also a highly revealing document. As such it should be obligatory reading to those who persist in the fantasy that 'more Europe' somehow offers an antidote to the termination of the asylum institution that practically all member states currently champion.

Labour replacement through circular migration, rather than through paths to citizenship

Having answered conclusively the question whether or not Brussels could appreciate and promote refugees – the overwhelming majority of whom are working age or soon to become – as a positive rejuvenation of the greying Union, we still need to explain this seeming contradiction. I should also say that the initial question concerning such a refugee dividend is not a contrived one but a claim that figured prominently in Germany and Sweden during the early stages of the crisis. As Germany's Interior Minister Thomas de Maizière insisted in defence of admitting refugees: 'We are a country of immigration. We need people. We need young people. We need immigrants.' He added: 'All of you know that, because we have too few children' (quoted in *Independent*, 2015). 'A country with a decreasing population is a stagnating country', said Sweden's minister of justice and migration, Morgan Johansson, when maintaining that asylum-seekers needed to be seen as 'an investment for our country' (*Sveriges radio*, 2015). Commenting on Sweden's high number of asylum admissions, the Swedish prime minister, Stefan Löfven, put it similarly at an EU meeting in Brussels in June 2015. While the undertaking was not frictionless, it was also 'an asset': 'We must recognise that if we do not do this now, we are going to have a gigantic problem in a few years' (*Guardian*, 2015).

But in order to understand why the seeming contradiction, as far as the European Commission is concerned, does not at all constitute a contradiction we need to know something more about the system or regime within which Brussels anticipated large-scale labour migration is to be managed. The key terms here are circular migration and security, with circular migration defined as 'migrants coming to the EU for short periods and going back to a third country after the end of the contract' (EC, 2014a; see also EC, 2007; 2011b).[5] That is to say, the Commission's policy on new external labour migration to the EU builds, first, on the conception that the largest part of it should be of a temporary nature, lacking any guarantees (or visions) of paths to citizenship; second, it should be strictly demand-driven from a labour market perspective; and third, it is set up to be jam-packed with control mechanisms so as to guarantee security and avoid any forms of 'unwanted migration'. Already here we can spot the obvious mismatch between external labour migration (ELM) and the current entry of refugees, given that refugee protection and the asylum system have a penchant for long-term stay and permanent residence provisions, or, at least, make people less deportable. In addition, the asylum process is seen as slow and costly due to a heavy legal apparatus and rarely present fast-tracks to the labour market.

Contrary to what many had anticipated when the Commission reversed its stance on ELM some 15 years ago, Brussels' advocacy of multi-million labour migration, and the ostensibly smooth circulatory system forming part of it, has not occasioned a relaxation of the EU's fixation with migration security. Quite the contrary, and with the current refugee situation deemed totally at odds with security, refugees are apparently also seen as being totally at odds with ELM management.

To get a better sense of this logic we could take a look at the 'overarching framework' within which ELM is set to operate (EC, 2011b: 5), entitled the Global Approach to Migration and Mobility (GAMM), which was first adopted in 2005. Here, 'all relevant aspects of migration' are accounted for and brought together into a 'comprehensive' and 'balanced' framework for the purpose of managing migration and mobility (EC, 2011b; 2014b). The most recent Valletta Summit on Migration (European Council, 2015) between the EU and African states, in November 2015, as well as the European Agenda on Migration (EC, 2015d), presented in May 2015, both testify to the EU's ambition to further consolidate this 'comprehensive' framework (see Carrera *et al.*, 2015). Alongside measures to create cooperation with third countries on 'illegal' immigration, border security, return and refugee reception, much effort is thus also devoted to make these compatible with the opening of new and development-enhancing channels for 'legal' labour migration to the EU. Since the upheavals in North Africa, the war in Libya and the ongoing Mediterranean refugee and migration crisis, EU migration policy activity targeting North Africa has grown exponentially (EC, 2013b). According to the Commission, these crises have accentuated the need for improved migration management in the Mediterranean area, so as to facilitate labour migration for North Africans in need of work and to help the EU meet key labour demands and amend its demographic problems. The focus here is to promote circular labour migration to the EU, built on 'real' and 'clearly identified labour demands' that will 'help to meet the need for highly skilled workers in the expanding sectors of the EU's economy but also help fill many jobs requiring a mix of lower skills' (EC, 2011c: 7, 9; European Council, 2015).

Yet, when speaking of compatibility between policies on 'illegal' immigration, border security and return, on the one side, and labour migration, on the other, this should not be understood as a symmetric relationship; rather, it is a highly asymmetrical one where the latter is to be made compatible with the former. Security, then, overdetermines ELM in all its forms, although it is less emphasized in migration policy involving high-skilled labour.[6] As the Commission (2011a: 7) has emphasized on numerous occasions in recent years, the EU must 'ensure that the need for enhanced mobility does not undermine the security of the Union's external borders'. In its contribution to the UN High-level Dialogue on International Migration and Development in 2013, moreover, the Commission (2013a: 4) maintained crucially that '[i]n the absence of effective governance, the costs of migration may be significant, and can include social tensions with host populations – often exploited by populist forces – and pressure on scarce resources. Uncontrolled migration may also aggravate security threats.' Finally, as stated in the Valletta Summit on Migration's Action Plan (European Council, 2015: 16):

> We are determined to strengthen the fight against irregular migration in line with existing agreements and obligations under international law, as well as mutually agreed arrangements on return and readmission. [...] We will improve cooperation on return and sustainable reintegration which can only enhance migration and mobility policy and make it more effective and comprehensive.

In keeping with the ways in which EU asylum policy more and more is set to serve as a handmaiden to return policy, it seems as if ELM not only is set to serve EU labour demands; it should also serve as leverage to obtain security guarantees from sending countries.

To illustrate a bit further we could take a brief look at the EU's Seasonal Workers Directive (Dir. 2014/36/EU),[7] which was adopted in February 2014. The directive specifies the terms of entry, stay and rights of third-country nationals who apply to be employed as seasonal labour – e.g. in tourism, agriculture and horticulture – in the EU for a maximum stay of between five and nine months within a 12-month period. As a partial solution to the problem of high unemployment in North African countries and elsewhere, the Commission has, within the framework of GAMM (as discussed above), made repeated calls for better migration management in the Mediterranean and for more legal migration channels to the EU. The directive fits with this objective by being the first one to be promoted in terms of circular migration and by being specifically designed to support development and prevent 'illegal immigration'. As part of this, the directive puts much emphasis on 'safeguards to prevent overstaying or temporary stay from becoming permanent'. Accordingly, the directive's catalogue of rights is meagre and does not provide for intra-EU mobility, family reunification and it limits equal treatment in a number of areas (see, e.g. Joint NGO Statement, 2011; Hansen, 2016). In addition, and since we are dealing with seasonal and circular migration, there is no mention of migrant 'integration' in this directive. But this may also be contingent on the fact that the migrant labourers addressed in this directive are said to enter highly segregated labour markets that, as the Commission has underscored time and again, face a permanent and growing 'structural need for low-skilled and low-qualified workers' that cannot be satisfied by 'EU national workers, primarily owing to the fact that these workers consider seasonal work unattractive' (EC, 2010b: 2–3).

This should provide enough clarity as to why refugees, in the eyes of the European Commission, cannot be welcomed as a much-needed demographic labour boost. They simply do not live up to the criteria set for how labour migration should be managed. These criteria apply exclusively to the austere category of the temporary and circular migrant. The one, that is, who is admitted to the Union for immediate work, and whose prospects for permanent stay, and hence substantial rights and paths to citizenship, range between perchance and pathetic.

Although much work is now being devoted to gouge the asylum institute, as seen above, asylum law and policy are still largely incompatible with Brussels' favoured labour migration regime. The same applies to the relationship between the circular labour migrant and the admitted asylum-seeker.

The labour migration regime propagated by Brussels is synonymous with an austere rights regime. As such, it tallies with the overall austerity regime imposed by governments and EU institutions within the union as such. In this picture, the catalogue of rights inherent to the asylum institute appears as utterly anachronistic. The same, we could add, applies to the catalogue of rights inherent to free movement and EU citizenship, which explains why many member states are eager to gouge this institute as well. It should also provide a clue as to why EU citizens who utilize free movement have been reassigned to the austere category of (EU) migrants. Stripping migrants of rights, rather than citizens, obviously makes for an easier task.

In all, the European Commission wants millions of migrants as replacement labour, but it wants it in the austere or, to speak Polanyian, fictitious commodity form of circular labour, *not* in the embedded, capacious form of refugees put on paths to citizenship.

Refugees welcome, Tschüss austerity

If this summarizes my explanation of the current austerity regime's role in preventing Brussels from accepting refugees as a positive contribution to the EU's demographic deficit, let me conclude this chapter with some unfinished business. Recall my earlier reference to the then Home Affairs Commissioner Cecilia Malmström's pessimistic tone regarding the prospects of getting the member states to understand the necessity of a massive increase of labour migration to the EU. She went as far as saying that such an undertaking is 'politically impossible to attain in today's Europe'. Yet, in the autumn of 2015 a window of opportunity seemed to have opened for this exact undertaking, with the two main receivers of asylum-seekers, Germany and Sweden, invoking what I have coined as the 'refugee dividend' to defend and explain why their large admission was not only justifiable from a humanitarian standpoint, but why it was also economically rational. The dismal demographic outlook, they claimed, simply spoke for itself. It was done, as one Leader in *The Economist* (2015) put it at the time, 'not just for moral reasons but for selfish ones, too', adding:

> Europe's labour force is ageing and will soon begin to shrink. [...] Immigrants, including asylum-seekers, are typically young and eager to work. So they can help ease this problem: caring for the elderly [...]. African and Arabs are young. Europe can borrow some of their vitality'.

In the business press and parts of the corporate world a buzz was created around the refugee dividend and the seeming ease with which it could be realized. Daimler CEO Dieter Zetsche spoke of young and skilled refugees as 'just the sort of people we're looking for' (*Financial Times*, 2015b). Or as one columnist in the *Los Angeles Times* (2015) phrased it: 'helping to alleviate Europe's refugee crisis could help defuse Germany's demographic one.' A triple win was in clear sight: labour for business, demographic relief for states and protection for refugees. Researchers chimed in too, some claiming that the business community was leading the way in showing governments the upside posed by refugee migration, hailing humanitarian efforts extended by corporate giants such as Google, Norwegian, Federal Express, Facebook, American Express and JP Morgan Chase. Such charitable contributions walked hand in hand with 'a business opportunity, as new arrivals offer their talents and knowledge to forward-thinking firms'. In this way, Koser (2015) and others argued, corporations were doing what 'politicians in fear of (or in thrall to) xenophobic currents have struggled to accomplish', namely to 'make the case for the bright side of the refugee influx: it can help close Europe's demographic deficit, plug gaps in the labour market, and supply a cohort of young workers and taxpayers for the future.'

Yet, what is overlooked here is that this was precisely the message that the *governments* of Germany and Sweden kept repeating … until they stopped repeating it. In September 2015 the sentiment was that 'Germany's generosity towards the refugees shows no sign of abating' (Godin, 2015). Come December, and we had gotten used to a different beat, with Angela Merkel imparting that 'we took on board the concerns of the people, who are worried about the future, and this means we want to reduce, we want to drastically decrease the number of people coming to us' (*Reuters*, 2015a). Come January and German finance minister Wolfgang Schäuble decides to go public with some measured vindication of Viktor Orban: 'To be honest, we have to admit that not everything Hungary has done has been wrong' (*Süddeutsche Zeitung*, 2016). And come February, Germany's deputy finance minister, Jens Spahn (2016), had this to say: 'If we do not manage to reduce the numbers coming in significantly, and soon, the refugee crisis has the potential to tear German society apart, politically and culturally.'

This U-turn just makes the initial governmental responses in Germany and Sweden seem even more remarkable and un-European. They stood in glaring contrast to the spiteful rhetoric and policies – or the plain indifference – exhibited by most other EU members. For the first time, arguably, in the 30-year history of EU asylum policy cooperation, it looked as if two members were about to break ranks, parting with the EU's established policy of refugee prevention to instead advocate a policy of refugee admission. In other words, the EU's refugee austerity was finally challenged by a bid for refugee expansion. Or so it seemed for a few short months in the summer and autumn of 2015.

I have already explained why Brussels was not swayed by Germany and Sweden's invocation of a refugee dividend. But why, then, did they stop invoking it? To begin with, the sudden policy shift in Germany and Sweden is not satisfactorily explained with reference to a simple caving in to racial austerity à la Denmark or Hungary. To be sure, Berlin and Stockholm do act out of 'fear of

[...] xenophobic currents', as Koser put it above. That is, in seeking to fend off the challenge from the extreme right and, increasingly, the traditional right, they are indeed adapting to their policies, and, to some extent, to their rhetoric, as for instance seen in Jens Spahn's statement.

Still though, this only goes so far in explaining the abrupt shift from a policy of 'welcome' to one of rejection, from a policy designating refugees as a demographic-economic necessity to one branding refugees as a societal peril. In moving towards a deeper and more complex explanation we need to say something more about austerity, thus adding the alleged financial peril posed by refugees. Or to state what ought to be quite obvious; that is, in order to challenge refugee austerity in today's EU this necessarily also implies challenging the EU's master regime of fiscal austerity. Otherwise the first will only go as far as the latter allows. Berlin and Stockholm's initial responses were thus not naïve in the sense of failing to anticipate, as the prevailing opinion has it, that there were both material and public tolerance limits as to how many refugees could be admitted. Rather, what they failed to anticipate was that saying welcome to refugees inevitably would have required saying goodbye to austerity writ large. What was truly naïve, then, was the failure to reckon with the fact that the refugee reception would require huge public investments and huge public planning efforts. And they had plenty of time to prepare, since relatively large numbers of refugees had started arriving long before the summer and autumn of 2015. In addition, it would have required a strong, determined and skilled political leadership and mobilization, none of which, save for the lone figure of Angela Merkel, was forthcoming. What did emerge, of course, was an astounding popular engagement, substantial parts of which is still active and indispensable in making up for shortcomings of state and local agencies, although this work is flying under the media's radar. Governments readily exploited this effort when that seemed opportune, just to discard it when the refugee dividend was rearticulated as an ominous fiscal burden.

Already in the early autumn of 2015 finance ministries were starting to grumble: 'The unexpected cost of looking after a record influx of refugees in Germany could scupper Finance Minister Wolfgang Schaeuble's cherished goal of achieving a balanced budget for the next five years, coalition sources said on Thursday' (*Reuters*, 2015b). Since then the grumble has grown into a roar, with finance ministries' warnings going in tandem with media images of refugees illustrating ill-boding headlines about 'Ballooning Refugee Costs' and 'Asylum Costs: Germany's Budgetary Burden'. Underneath the latter headline in *Handelsblatt* the introduction read: 'A surging population of refuges in Germany could burst its balanced budget with billions of euro in added outlays' (*Handelsblatt*, 2016). The fact that Germany simultaneously could report a record budget surplus of some €20 billion has done nothing to temper the crisis mode over refugee costs. On the contrary, Schäuble has just become even more adamant that the country's fiscal health hinges on a drastic reduction in refugee numbers, his deputy, Spahn, adding that '[m]oney for other things that we might want is simply not there' (*Irish Times*, 2016).

This message, that spending is reserved for unwanted refugees, whose numbers need to be drastically cut so as to not sabotage the budget any further, has antagonized the social democratic coalition partner, which, in February 2016, instead proposed a 'new solidarity project' that would allow for a general increase of necessary social welfare spending. Sigmar Gabriel, the SPD leader and vice chancellor, warned that the singling out of refugees as the only spending item ran the risk of being divisive. That is, by maintaining that a budgetary surplus takes priority over social cohesion, the CDU, Gabriel claimed, becomes complicit in the current right wing radicalization. Whereas Merkel's response reiterated the importance of sticking with a balanced budget, Schäuble's was implacable, denouncing Gabriel's intervention as 'pitiful' (*Die Zeit*, 2016).

Interestingly enough, the Swedish finance ministry has adopted a similar outlook, reaffirming its commitment to a budget surplus and a budget ceiling while at the same time underscoring that today, as stressed by the finance minister Magdalena Andersson, 'the margins under the ceiling are way too thin' and that '[t]his is due to Sweden having admitted an exceptionally large number of asylum seekers'. Precisely because of these high refugee costs, Andersson goes on, and in order to honour the budget ceiling, the government is obliged to cut projected spending in a number of areas, while also making necessary adjustments to decrease the number of asylum-seekers and keeping refugee costs in check (Andersson, 2015). In addition, the government, just like its German counterpart, has been very vocal about ensuring the return of huge numbers of rejected asylum-seekers and 'economic migrants'.

The actions of both Germany and Sweden demonstrate to the full the power of austerity and its disciplinary force. Berlin and Stockholm fear that the refugee admission will jeopardize balanced budgets and spending limits – the EU's supreme political economy – and so they act in accordance. While there are differences between Brussels' avoidance of the demographic refugee dividend, on the one side, and Germany and Sweden's eventual reversal, on the other, they nonetheless coalesce around the same basic austere outlook. The Commission's model for labour migration cannot, by definition, accommodate refugees-*cum*-labour on a path to permanent residence or citizenship. This obviously contrasts with Germany and Sweden's asylum systems and thus also explains why these systems now are being both externally ring-fenced and internally squeezed of social allowances, permanent residence and family reunification. These drastic adjustments demonstrate how the commitment to fiscal austerity trumps the efforts to avoid what are alleged to be pending demographic disasters. Of course, one could argue that all the politicians' talk about the refugee dividend was mere talk, a tactic to buy time when choices were few and the situation somewhat overwhelming. Given the initial popular outbursts in favour of refugee reception, governments might also have judged it wise to keep their tight-fisted budget officers in the background for the time being.

However this may be, it does not take away one bit from the fact that a crucial aspect of the refugee dividend indeed was put into practice. Making room for refugees, saying they were needed and that they should be allowed to stay, unequivocally meant providing enough room in the budget. For a brief period, then, Germany and Sweden decided it was proper to open their purses and start the public spending spree, one that they have yet to contain and for which Angela Merkel is paying a high price at the moment, as seen in the frequent attacks from within her own party and cabinet. In this sense we can speak of a very real *acting on* the refugee dividend, and with this action, this lapse into fiscal expansion, the 'refugee crisis' also made for a rare Keynesian laboratory environment. The results have not been long in coming and they have not been surprising either, with economic growth gains from refugee spending being detectable already at the end of 2015 (OECD, 2015). In September 2015, Thomas Piketty (2015) took note of the opportunity: 'The plight of the refugees is an opportunity for Europe to jump-start the continent's economy. Germany's attitude is a model to follow.'

Since then numerous reports corroborate this picture, with the refugee-related spending impacting positively on economic growth in the EU in general, and with a more significant mid- and long-term impact predicted for those countries (i.e., Germany, Sweden and Austria) that have admitted the brunt of the refugee population (see, e.g. IMF, 2016; Statistics Sweden, 2016). 'Refugee wave behind Sweden's GDP growth', ran the headline in Sweden's major business paper following the release of the exceptionally strong fourth quarter growth figures, showing a 4.5 per cent gain compared with 2014, whereas the growth figure for 2015 stood at 4.1 per cent (*Dagens industri*, 2016). As reported by the *Financial Times* (2016d), '[e]conomists credited the refugee crisis for helping boost growth as a record number of asylum seekers [...] led to an increase in consumption and government spending'.

These developments, in combination with a mounting criticism of fiscal austerity in general coming from a number of high places (e.g. OECD, 2016), are of course vindication for the Keynesian outlook. In contrast to the rosy hopes pinned on the private sector to lead the way – mirroring the hopes currently driving monetary policies of low to negative interest rates and quantitative easing – it has been public spending and government action that have actually done the job. But as I have already shown, with this impact out in the open, Germany and Sweden seem dead set on going back to basics, terminating what could only be an interlude of public spending. In the eyes of fiscal hardliners, the growth accrued is obviously the wrong, 'artificial' type of growth. By the same token, and in line with Brussels' policy, refugees are now seen in both Sweden and Germany as the wrong type of migrants. Refugee migration is not circular, but often permanent and in any case difficult and expensive to dispose of, the latter explaining all the efforts that currently are going into new return policies. In addition, it encompasses rights and social welfare provisions, which both Germany and Sweden are working hard to trim at the moment. Moreover, as noted in the preceding, refugees are not easily matched with labour markets, this requiring strong support structures. This latter issue has of course been high on the agenda since the outset, counting as perhaps the most crucial one by scores of stakeholders. The IMF, for one, argues that '[t]he sooner the refugees gain employment, the more they will help public finances. Their successful labour market integration will also counter some of the adverse fiscal effects of population ageing' (IMF, 2016: 5).

Indeed, there is basically unanimous agreement concerning the imperative task of ensuring refugees' swift labour market integration. This being one of the most crucial problems, a failure to resolve it will obviously have serious consequences. This is what makes Berlin and Stockholm's decision to retreat back under the budget ceiling even more startling. Because even if they should succeed in reducing the asylum admissions significantly, a significant increase in public spending and investment is still going to be needed, unless, that is, we relapse into wishful thinking about a trailblazing private sector coming to the rescue. As Anke Hassel argues, many of those areas which are key to successful refugee integration, including education, active labour market programmes, childcare and housing, are precisely those most severely affected by Germany's prolonged period of meagre public investment and spending cuts. Skills training, for instance, was cut by more than 40 per cent between 1995 and 2012 (Hassel, 2015: 3). Regardless of its economic powerhouse standing, then, Hassel (2015: 2) shows that Germany actually 'is less prepared for the mammoth task of integration than many others in the OECD'. Hence, 'Germany will only be able to turn the refugee crisis into an opportunity if the federal government ups its game with regard to public investment in general, and educational programmes in particular' (Hassel, 2015: 3). Yet, for the time being, such an approach has been thoroughly ruled out by both Germany and Sweden.

Writing in the midst of these events unfolding (in early March 2016) and with dramatic changes and new developments seemingly occurring every day, even speculating about what the *near* future may hold can feel daunting. Yet this should not keep us from pointing to the obvious risks involved in Germany and Sweden's decision to recommit to rigid budget discipline at a time when public investment, planning and intervention in the labour market are urgently needed. It makes for a negative spiral to take hold, with further calls for budget tightening going in tandem with further calls for refugee tightening: preventing entries and increasing returns, on the one side, and blocking social welfare provisions, paths to citizenship and family reunification, on the other. In doing so, in claiming that refugees are a fiscal burden that can only be eased through border enforcements and scrimping on those already here, is not only making a mockery of any calls for integration into society and labour market. It is also a vindication to those who claimed that refugees were a bad idea in the first place. A vindication, that is, for those forces who are advocating various kinds of racial austerity, mostly in the form of anti-Muslim hostility. In order, therefore, to stem the tide of racial austerity in the EU it is necessary, although not sufficient, to break with fiscal austerity. For a little while, it seemed as if there was a small window of opportunity for this. Not because Germany and Sweden intended such a break – not at all. But since they aspired for a responsible refugee policy they were also compelled to be fiscally responsible and make room for necessary spending increases. Since then fiscal irresponsibility has taken hold once more and, with it, we are faced with a familiar, irresponsible EU asylum policy dynamic, where refugees-not-welcome has, once more, become the only game in town.

It is often said that the refugee crisis has become even more serious than the euro crisis. Much less thought has gone into how we might connect them. What I have argued here is that two countries' initial handling of the former inadvertently provided a recipe for how – if prescribed to the EU as a whole – the dire socioeconomic consequences of the latter could be mitigated. Let's call it refugee Keynesianism. And the 'refugee' part is key in this recipe, since Keynesianism is usually thought of as applying to citizens, the broad strata thereof. The irony is therefore so much greater, because a common claim amongst those, including some on the Left, who want to stop or limit refugee admission is that the state's primary responsibility lies with its citizens. Hence, the argument goes, it is wrong to have citizens foot the refugee bill against their will, particularly, as some on the Left would add, in a situation of growing poverty and working-class hardship. Apparently, years of extreme austerity across the EU, hammering citizens, in general, and working-class citizens, in particular, have failed to put such fantasies to rest. As if the neoliberal austerity state could act responsible towards citizens in the first place; and as if the removal of refugees would be the thing ushering in such responsibility. Rather, and through a fluke of luck, it took a refugee 'crisis' and a refugee 'burden' to impart a glimpse of how a socioeconomic crisis could be alleviated and how citizens could be relieved of the burden of austerity. A responsible resolution of the refugee crisis, then, requires a responsible economic policy in the EU; and, vice versa, a responsible economic policy in the EU would enable a responsible handling of the refugee crisis. In a nutshell: 'Wir schaffen das.' Too bad this was not a Freudian slip, signalling the sensible realism the EU so desperately needs, or ...?

Notes

1 This chapter was finalised in March 2016.
2 The literature corroborating this point is extensive and I thus chose not to cite any one in particular.
3 Jointly prepared with the EU's Economic Policy Committee.
4 As of today (2015) 17 countries have signed readmission agreements with the EU, including notorious human rights abusers such as Pakistan, Turkey and Sri Lanka (EC, 2015c).
5 For in-depth accounts on circular migration as it relates to EU policy, see the contributions in Triandafyllidou (2013); Venturini (2008); Feldman (2012); Carrera and Hernández i Sagrera (2009).
6 As indicated in the EU's 'Key messages' to the UN High Level Dialogue on International Migration and Development: 'All states should review existing barriers to human mobility, with a view to remove barriers which are not justified from a security point of view and are unnecessarily hindering economic competitiveness and regional integration' (EC, 2013a: 11).
7 Directive 2014/36/EU of the European Parliament and of the Council of 26 February 2014 on the conditions of entry and stay of third-country nationals for the purpose of employment as seasonal workers. The UK, Ireland and Denmark do not take part in this directive.

Bibliography

Andersson, M. (2015) 'Så klarar vi utgiftstaket 2016', *Dagens industri*, 18 December.

Avramopolous, D. (2015) Press Conference, published 20 August. Available at: www.youtube.com/watch?v=vQtZQr1aZX0 [accessed 5 March 2016].

Barber, T. (2011) 'A line to hold', *Financial Times*, 15 June.

Barker, A. (2015) 'EU bows deeply to Erdogan in bid to relieve migrant crisis', *Financial Times*, 23 November.

Carrera, S. and Hernández i Sagrera, R. (2009) 'The Externalization of the EU's Labour Immigration Policy', *CEPS Working Document*, 321, Brussels: Centre for European Policy Studies.

Carrera, S., Blockmans, S., Gros, D. and Guild, E. (2015) 'The EU's Response to the Refugee Crisis: Taking Stock and Setting Policy Priorities', *CEPS Essay*, No. 20, 16 December, Brussels: Centre for European Policy Studies.

Castles, S. (2004) 'Why migration policies fail', *Ethnic and Racial Studies*, 27 (2), pp. 205–27.

Council EU (2015) 'Council Decision (CFSP) 2015/972 launching the European Union military operation in the southern Central Mediterranean (EUNAVFOR MED)', *Official Journal of the European Union*, L 157/51, 23. 6.

Dagens industri (2016) 'Flyktingvågen ligger bakom Sveriges BNP-tillväxt', 29 February. Available at: www.di.se/artiklar/2016/2/29/flyktingvagen-ligger-bakom-sveriges-bnp-tillvaxt/ [accessed 5 March 2016].

Daily Telegraph (2015a) 'EU chief: Close the doors and windows as millions more migrants are coming', 24 September. Available at: www.telegraph.co.uk/news/worldnews/europe/11887091/EU-chief-Close-the-doors-and-windows-as-millions-more-migrants-are-coming.html [accessed 5 March 2016].

Daily Telegraph (2015b) 'EU should not "harp on" at Turkey about human rights, says Jean-Claude Juncker', 27 October. Available at: www.telegraph.co.uk/news/worldnews/europe/turkey/11957432/EU-should-not-harp-on-at-Turkey-about-human-rights-says-Jean-Claude-Juncker.html [accessed 5 March 2016].

Davies, N. (2010) 'Melilla: Europe's dirty secret', *Guardian*, 17 April.

Die Zeit (2016) 'Schäuble wirft Gabriel "erbarmungswürdige Politik" vor', 27 February. Available at: www.zeit.de/politik/deutschland/2016-02/sozialpaket-wolfgang-schauuble-sigmar-gabriel-fluechtlingskrise-kritik [accessed 5 March 2016].

EC (European Commission) (1994) 'On immigration and asylum policies', COM(94) 23 final, Brussels, 23. 2.

EC (1996) *Europe ... questions and answers: The European Union – What's in it for me?* Luxembourg: Office for Official Publications of the EC.

EC (1999) 'Proposal for a Council Directive on the right to family reunification', COM(1999) 638 final, Brussels, 1. 12.

EC (2000) 'On a Community Immigration Policy', COM(2000) 757 final, Brussels, 22. 11.

EC (2002) 'Green Paper on a Community Return Policy on Illegal Residents', COM(2002) 175 final, Brussels, 10. 4.

EC (2005) 'Policy Plan on Legal Migration', COM(2005) 669 final, Brussels 21. 12.

EC (2007) 'On circular migration and mobility partnerships between the European Union and third countries', COM(2007) 248 final, Brussels, 16. 5.

EC (2010a) 'EUROPE 2020: A strategy for smart, sustainable and inclusive growth', COM(2010) 2020 final, Brussels, 3. 3.

EC (2010b) 'Proposal for a directive [...] on the conditions of entry and residence of third-country nationals for the purpose of seasonal employment', COM(2010) 379 final, Brussels, 13. 7.

EC (2011a) 'Communication on migration', COM(2011) 248 final, Brussels, 4. 5.

EC (2011b) 'The Global Approach to Migration and Mobility', COM(2011) 743 final, Brussels, 18. 11.

EC (2011c) 'A dialogue for migration, mobility and security with the southern Mediterranean countries', COM(2011) 292 final, Brussels, 24. 5.

EC (2012) 'The 2012 Ageing Report: Economic and budgetary projections for the 27 EU Member States (2010–2060)', European Economy 2/2012, DG Economic and Financial Affairs.

EC (2013a) 'Maximising the Development Impact of Migration: The EU contribution for the UN High-level Dialogue', COM(2013) 292 final, Brussels, 21. 5.

EC (2013b) 'On the work of the Task Force Mediterranean', COM(2013) 869 final, Brussels, 4. 12.

EC (2014a) '5th Annual Report on Immigration and Asylum (2013)', COM(2014) 288 final, Brussels, 22. 5.

EC (2014b) 'Report on the Implementation of the Global Approach to Migration and Mobility 2012–2013', COM(2014) 96 final, Brussels, 21. 2.

EC (2015a) 'The 2015 Ageing Report: Economic and budgetary projections for the 28 EU Member States (2013–2060)', European Economy 3/2015, DG Economic and Financial Affairs.

EC (2015b) 'Proposal for a Regulation [...] establishing an EU common list of safe countries of origin for the purposes of Directive 2013/32/EU [...] on common procedures for granting and withdrawing international protection, and amending Directive 2013/32/EU', COM(2015) 452 final 2015/0211 (COD), Brussels, 9. 9.

EC (2015c) 'EU Action Plan on return', COM(2015) 453 final, Brussels, 9. 9.

EC (2015d) 'A European Agenda on Migration', COM(2015) 240 final, Brussels, 13. 5.

Economic and Social Committee (2001) 'Opinion [...] on the "Communication from the Commission to the Council and the European Parliament on a Community immigration policy"', *Official Journal of the European Communities*, No C 260 (2001/C 260/19), 17. 9.

ECRE (European Council on Refugees and Exiles) (2005) 'Justice and Home Affairs Council 12–13 October', AD2/10/2005/ EXT/RW, Brussels, 10 October.

European Council (2015) Valletta Summit on Migration, 11–12 November. Available at: www.consilium.europa.eu/en/meetings/international-summit/2015/11/11-12/ [accessed 5 February 2016].

European Union External Action (2015) 'European Union Naval Force – Mediterranean Operation Sophia', Update November 2015, EU Naval Force Med Media and Public Information Office.

Feldman, G. (2012) *The Migration Apparatus: Security, Labour, and Policymaking in the European Union*. Stanford: Stanford University Press.

Financial Times (2015a) 'Europe heads for a jam over loss of passport-free travel', 27 November.

Financial Times (2015b) 'War victims feel warmth of "Generation Merkel"', 10 September.

Financial Times (2016a) 'Pressure on welfare model spawns fears Nordics are tuning nasty', 5 February.

Financial Times (2016b) 'EU weighs ringfencing Greece to stop migrant flow', 23/24 January.

Financial Times (2016c) 'Athens faces ejection from borderless EU zone over migrant processing errors', 28 January.

Financial Times (2016d) 'Surging Swedish economy raises questions over negative rates', 29 February. Available at: www.ft.com/intl/cms/s/0/c9e63df6-decd-11e5-b7fd-0dfe89910bd6.html#axzz41qXXIwAI [accessed 5 March 2016].

Godin, R. (2015) 'Why Angela Merkel is so generous to the refugees', *EurActiv*, 9 September. Available at: www.euractiv.com/section/justice-home-affairs/news/why-angela-merkel-is-so-generous-to-the-refugees/ [accessed 5 March 2016].

Gold, P. (2000) *Europe or Africa? A Contemporary Study of the Spanish North African Enclaves of Ceuta and Melilla.* Liverpool: Liverpool University Press.

Guardian (2015) 'Europe needs many more babies to avert a population disaster', 23 August. Available at: www.theguardian.com/world/2015/aug/23/baby-crisis-europe-brink-depopulation-disaster [accessed 5 March 2016].

Guild, E., Costello, C., Garlick, M., Moreno-Lax, V. and Carrera, S. (2015) 'Enhancing the Common European Asylum System and Alternative to Dublin', *CEPS Paper in Liberty and Security in Europe*, No. 83, September, Brussels: Centre for European Policy Studies.

Handelsblatt (2016) 'Asylum Costs: Germany's Budgetary Burden' 19 February. Available at: https://global.handelsblatt.com/edition/372/ressort/politics/article/germanys-budgetary-burden [accessed 5 March 2016].

Hansen, P. (2016) 'The European Union's External Labour Migration Policy: Rationale, Objectives, Approaches and Results, 1999–2014', *OECD Social, Employment and Migration Working Papers*, No. 185, Paris: OECD Publishing.

Hansen, P. and Hager, S.B. (2012) *The Politics of European Citizenship: Deepening Contradictions in Social Rights and Migration Policy.* New York: Berghahn Books.

Hassel, A. (2015) 'Germany needs to up its game if it wants to integrate a million refugees', Hertie School Research Blog, 18 December. Available at: www.hertie-school.org/blog/refugee-crisis-germany-risks-and-opportunities/ [accessed 5 March 2016].

IMF (2016) 'The Refugee Surge in Europe: Economic Challenges', IMF Staff Discussion Note, January, SDN/16/02.

Independent (2015) 'Refugee crisis: The map that shows why some European countries love asylum seekers', 16 September. Available at: www.independent.co.uk/news/world/europe/refugee-crisis-the-map-that-shows-why-some-european-countries-love-asylum-seekers-10492642.html [accessed 5 March 2016].

International Herald Tribune (1998a) 'Bonn Lists Steps to Close Europe's Borders to Kurds', 6 January.

International Herald Tribune (1998b) 'Bonn Hails 8-Nation European Pact to Slow Flood of Kurdish Refugees', 10–11 January.

Irish Times (2013) 'Is Europe on the verge of demographic collapse?', 6 June. Available at: www.irishtimes.com/news/science/is-europe-on-the-verge-of-demographic-collapse-1.1417948 [accessed 5 March 2016].

Irish Times (2016) 'Wolfgang Schäuble warns German budget surplus must go to refugees', 25 February. Available at: www.irishtimes.com/news/world/europe/wolfgang-schäuble-warns-german-budget-surplus-must-go-to-refugees-1.2548386 [accessed 5 March 2016].

Joint NGO Statement (2011) 'EU Seasonal Migrant Workers' Directive: Full Respect of Equal Treatment Necessary', 20 April, http://lastradainternational.org/lsidocs/joint%20ngo%20statement.pdf [accessed 5 March 2016].

Juska, A. and Woolfson, C. (2015) 'Austerity, labour market segmentation and emigration: the case of Lithuania', *Industrial Relations Journal*, 46 (3): pp. 236–53.

Koser, K. (2015) 'A Migration Agenda for the Private Sector', Project Syndicate, 27 October. Available at: https://www.project-syndicate.org/commentary/europe-private-sector-response-to-refugees-by-khalid-koser-2015-10?barrier=true [accessed 5 March 2016].

Larsson, E. (2013) 'Om du har ett jobb borde du få komma in i EU' (Interview with Cecilia Malmström), *Arbetet*, 15 March. Available at: http://arbetet.se/2013/03/15/om-du-har-ett-jobb-borde-du-fa-komma-in-i-eu/ (accessed 23 August 2014) [accessed 5 March 2016].

Lawrence, F. (2011) 'Spain's salad growers are modern-day slaves, say charities', *Guardian*, 7 February.

Los Angeles Times (2015) 'For Germany, refugees are a demographic blessing as well as a burden', 10 September. Available at: www.latimes.com/world/europe/la-fg-germany-refugees-demographics-20150910-story.html [accessed 5 March 2016].

Malmström, C. (2010) 'Malmström proposes EU coordination of labour migration', 13 July. Available at: http://ec.europa.eu/commission_2010-2014/malmstrom/news/archives_2010_en.htm [accessed 5 March 2016].

Maurice, E. (2015) 'Austria says won't close border, still plans small fence', *euobserver*, 29 October. Available at: https://euobserver.com/migration/130878 [accessed 6 March 2016].

Mead, N. 2005. 'Melilla: bloodbath on the African-Europe frontier', *openDemocracy*, 10 October. Available at: www.opendemocracy.net/people-migrationeurope/melilla_2905.jsp, [accessed 5 March 2016].

OECD (2015) *Migration Policy Debates*, No. 8, November.

OECD (2016) *Interim Economic Outlook*, 18 February.

Overbeek, H. (1995) 'Towards a new international migration regime'. In: Miles, R. and Thränhardt, D. (eds), *Migration and European Integration: The Dynamics of Inclusion and Exclusion*. London: Pinter.

Piketty, T. (2015) 'For an open Europe', *Fusion*, 10 September. Available at: http://fusion.net/story/195478/for-an-open-europe/ [accessed 5 March 2016].

Reuters (2015a) 'Angela Merkel wants to "drastically reduce" reduce refugee arrivals in Germany', 14 December.

Reuters (2015b) 'Ballooning refugee costs threaten Germany's cherished budget goals', 17 September. Available at: www.reuters.com/article/us-europe-migrants-germany-budget-idUSKCN0RH22320150917 [accessed 5 March 2016].

Ruhs, M. (2015) 'Is unrestricted immigration compatible with inclusive welfare states? The (un)sustainability of EU exceptionalism', Centre on Migration, Policy and Society, Working Paper No. 125, University of Oxford.

Schierup, C.-U., Hansen, P. and Castles, S. (2006) *Migration, Citizenship, and the European Welfare State: A European Dilemma*. Oxford: Oxford University Press.

Sinclair-Webb, E. (2015) 'No, EU, Turkey is not safe for everyone', *openDemocracy*, 23 October. Available at: www.opendemocracy.net/emma-sinclair-webb/no-eu-turkey-is-not-safe-for-everyone [accessed 5 March 2016].

Spahn, J. (2016) 'Germany needs cool heads and a swift cut in migrant numbers', *Financial Times*, 17 February.

Statistics Sweden (Statistiska centralbyrån) (2016) *Sveriges ekonomi*, No. 1.

Süddeutsche Zeitung (2016) 'Rückkehr sollte der Normalfall sein', 16/17 January.

Sveriges radio (2015) 'Regeringen lovar satsning på ensamkommande', 20 August. Available at: http://sverigesradio.se/sida/artikel.aspx?programid=3993&artikel=62366 52 [accessed 5 March 2016].

The Economist (2015) 'Let them in and let them earn', 29 August.

Triandafyllidou, A. (ed.) (2013) *Circular Migration between Europe and its Neighbourhood: Choice or Necessity?* Oxford: Oxford University Press.

Venturini, A. (2008) 'Circular Migration as an Employment Strategy for Mediterranean Countries', *CARIM Analytic and Synthetic Notes*, 2008/39, Florence: European University Institute.

Wolf, M. (2015) 'A refugee crisis that Europe cannot escape', *Financial Times*, 22 September. Available at: www.ft.com/intl/cms/s/2/3967804c-604b-11e5-a28b-50226830d644.html#axzz40YDZ2moc [accessed 5 March 2016].

9 Restrained equality

A sexualized and gendered colour line

Nacira Guénif-Souilamas

Current austerity programmes in Europe and beyond implement a policy of restrained equality that has become part of the state apparatus since the continental growth slowdown in the 1970s. Through a range of measures – from laws slowly dismantling the former welfare state to policies aiming to restrict immigration, securitize the population and back the fight against terror at the expense of racialized citizens and migrants' fundamental rights and freedom of circulation – Europe at large is gradually betraying its democratic ideals, as if they never were meant to be fulfilled. As I will argue in this chapter, and demonstrate through a number of examples drawn mainly, but not only, from contemporary France, this paradigmatic shift in policy-making lays bare a hidden agenda and exposes a deep foundational principle of the European polity that has never been properly acknowledged: to secure enduring inequalities within an increasingly heterogeneous European population by fending off the egalitarian and multicultural trend that is inherent to democratization. As we shall see, this agenda and principle is today translated into internal and external wars, waged both against new European citizens and against former colonized peoples of Africa and the Middle East.

If equality is not to be achieved in the multiracial, postcolonial and post-migration societies that characterize our multicultural times, democracy itself will remain incomplete. In addition, it may also mean that democracy will never extirpate itself from the matrix that gave birth to it in Ancient Greece as well as in European empires built on conquest, exploitation, enslavement and indigenization. Both the ancient Athenian model and the European imperial model relied on racial, gender and human hierarchies that disqualified strangers, typically excluded as barbaric, along with children, elders, disabled, women and slaves. These marginalized segments of the population, whose exclusion was a necessary prerequisite of the 'democratic' constituency, and who thus reveal that democratic equality was but a restrained equality, appear in today's Europe as migrants, refugees and Roma, and they add up with the Jews, Arabs and blacks, and more recently with the Muslims, all of whom are inhabitants and most of whom are citizens of the 'old continent'.

Restrained equality regime and its colour line: mapping a structural divide

The regime of restrained equality affects European and extra-European citizens alike, but in opposite ways. Racialized and sexualized groups subjected to this regime are typically put under a minority rule and are retained beyond colour lines that proliferate across spaces, institutions and minds. Theories of the so-called 'sexual contract' (Pateman, 1988) and its blind spot, women of colour (Combahee River Collective Statement, 1977) on the one hand, and 'the racial contract' (Mills, 1997) on the other hand, agree on the reasons why women of colour and people of colour face restrictions and evictions in their ability to access supposedly common rights and freedoms tied to equality and citizenship. Contesting the widespread claim that liberty provides the preliminary means to achieve equality, I will rather argue that unequal access to rights translates into an unequal access to freedom. What the hidden agenda (Shohamy, 2006) of restrained equality allows and sustains in contemporary European societies is precisely the numerous practices that make racialized and gendered migrants and minorities ineligible for liberty. The effectiveness of this agenda relies on its wide diffusion and remoteness: while there may be loud and vocal demands for expulsion of both groups by means of deportation or exclusion, they are in fact already subjected to an unuttered politics through which they are denied basic and civil rights and de facto put in a subaltern and illegitimate position.

If the regime of restrained equality is as old as European world dominance itself, it has come to play a particular role in our era when, after the slowdown of economic growth that began in the 1970s and the arrival of late financial capitalism, it comes to operate in a situation marked by recursive 'crises', nationalist depression and populism, processes that are all triggered by Europe's de-imperialization and provincialization. The loss of leadership, whether political or economic, resonates with the loss of might as a superior conveyor of civilization. Until recently, the consequences of this double loss often went unnoticed: the cultural and collective memories of postcolonial subjects, migrants and minorities were shut down as illegitimate and amnesia was the rule. Still today, history continues to be voiced and phrased by the world's former conquerors (Subrahmanyam, 1997), yet it seems that their sovereignty has shrunk, as they are pressed to surrender to their new master: financial capitalism. Hence, a tarnished Europe survives its losses partly by fuelling a renewed mode of governmentality based on the racialization of populations (Foucault, 2004: pp. 111–12). Again, these populations face Europe's racist demons.

A third perspective allows me to refine the map of a democratic 'climate change' that has brought 'austere histories' as well as its twin phenomenon, the regime of restrained equality, to dominance in contemporary European culture. I am thinking of the general transformation of European and Western societies toward a politics of fear and surveillance that monitors individual and collective motility and freedom of expression. This massive and often discreet, if not secret, move of European governments from a state of rights towards a 'state of security'[1] or even a 'state of terror'[2] (Loraux, 2002) calls for an investigation of austere narratives of national ethnic homogeneity that justify the retention of migrants in camps, centres or at borders, as well as the symbolic, political and social containment of postcolonial minorities. Moreover, the same transformation also sheds light on repressive state policies aimed at autochthonous populations in case they protest against or resist being governed by the combined agenda of security and restrained equality. In times such as ours, when drawing the colour line between those who are entitled to belong and those who are not has become a patriot/ic act, the blurring of this line by activists and citizens who are ready to un-white themselves and denounce the double standards of citizenship is viewed as a betrayal that calls for narrow surveillance and intimate control, if not repression (Invisible Committee, 2009). Public intimidations, admonitions against 'political correctness', vilifications of 'naïve' solidarities, support for allegedly 'disloyal' minorities who are fomenting internal and external chaos – these are some of the rhetorical techniques and ideological cover-ups for the ongoing destruction of social welfare and political bonds across European societies. These techniques are particularly appreciated when mastered by migrant and minority representatives, and especially so if they are female or citizens of colonial descent who dismiss the idea of colonial repentance and deny or minimize the impact of the present colonial, racist and sexist rule under which they live. They thus make up the exceptions to the general standard of exception, and they benefit from exemptions that enable them to gain access to supposed equal rights. They are rewarded with titles, appointments and compensations, which amount to far less than what they resign: their political and human sovereignty. They stand on the colour line at the very point where the regime of restrained equality operates unhindered, sanctioning its fearsome implementation since it is not publicized as such but rather translated into various policies that disperse the task of restraining equality across the whole spectrum of public policies and social relations. Beyond the space they spectacularly mark, lie scattered multitudes of individuals who are bound in their dismissal and unaware of their disgrace in the eyes of whoever is entitled to select those who will – and will not – benefit from the generosity of their masters and mistresses.

Another remarkable point that narrowly ties austerity policies to the hidden agenda of restrained equality, thus showing how both rely on racialized and sexualized 'austere histories' in which colonial memories are silenced, is the way they mimic one another. Austerity policy is all about expanding the regime of restrained equality beyond the boundaries of race and gender, so as to subject all citizens claiming access to labour, social security, housing (Desmond, 2016), healthcare, retirement and lifelong education under its rule. Conditionality has become the new standard of universal welfare, as criteria and restrictions have been introduced that make it increasingly difficult for a vast range of individuals and sectors in European societies to access welfare benefits. What austerity policies are largely about, then, is to turn universal rights (and the benefits that may follow) into restricted ones, transforming them into privileges. This major shift in public policies gradually reduces the segment of the population that will enjoy a wide range of rights, and it increases the number of those who will lose benefits they once were able to access.

The regime of restrained equality thus draws its powerful effectiveness from the fact that its mode of action is at once widely spread and unnoticeable: each and every one may potentially be subjected to eviction, reservation, expulsion or retention. No one remains outside of the web in which equality can be denied through the operations of the racialized and gendered colour line.

As we see, then, the regime of restrained equality causes a multi-layered uncertainty that triggers the implementation of plans that cut and reduce, limit and divide, equality as a fundamental right. Full and plain equality is no longer on the agenda. If equality was indeed a beacon for Western European democracies after the Second World War, it was never achieved, in part because of the colonial rule that still today stretches its shadow over such countries as Germany, the UK, the Netherlands, Italy, Denmark, France and others. At present, it divides local populations between those who can and those who cannot claim equal rights as regards citizenship, education, work, housing, social welfare and family status. This divide once ran along a colour and gender line, and it still serves the same purpose: to restrain equality by turning fundamental rights and opportunities into a scarce good, thus removing them from the realm of common goods. Thus, one can only experience equality in segmented and narrowly controlled fields, and for limited periods of time. If this restrained equality is one of the trademarks and objectives of the current austerity plans imposed in various countries, it is rarely acknowledged as such. Consequently, segments, bits, remainders of equality may be granted under conditions of eligibility by state governments and their subsidiary agencies, such as the EU or privatized agencies of welfare. What today enacts these rules and distinctions of inequality, by which colonial powers formerly extended their hegemony, are social networks, rhizomatic bioeconomies and biopolitical instruments of selection.

Randomization and upgrading are the key modes of an unequal distribution of equality based on the social effect (and affect) of gender and race, intuitively anticipated and produced in cultural encounters, various social fields and across class relations. Arbitrary choice and unpredictable selection shape the ordinary lives of those depicted as socially unfit and harmful. The consequences of this denial of equality do not remain intimate or private, but they extend into the public space and burst into riots, occupations and confrontations, and ultimately, at the global level, into asymmetric and imperial conflicts and wars. Far from being merely the result of a postmodern turn, such states of mind and means of government are rooted in material and institutional remnants of the colonial order.

The pattern I have discussed shows close similarities with regulations aimed at populations associated with migration, integration and naturalization. In their case, general policies concerning education, health, housing or employment are qualified by numerous criteria that restrain their application to aliens and strangers who cannot prove a full right to access them. On the other hand, immigration, integration and naturalization policies are increasingly implemented according to specific political goals and objectives: to limit the presence and the imprint of aliens, who are likely to become integral to the country they live in, and then also to control their impact on the population once they intend to become citizens. One may thus consider these latter policies as the explicit expressions of the regime of restrained equality. And one may consequently understand why their implementation is a matter of urgency all across Europe: they have the biopolitical objective to define the complexion of its present and future population. The racialization and sexualization entrenched in the restrained equality regime derives from its task to perpetuate structural inequalities by drawing a colour line that justifies why certain rights are denied to certain groups or individuals. The skin colour fiction, the sexual deviance of Arab youths, or the gendering of the 'other' religion, are objectifications of normative rules that limit the social possibilities of equal rights. In such instances, social life is defined as a realm of equality because it is always-already racially indexed. It is race as a system that sustains equality as the property of people who share whiteness or any colour equated to it. Or put simply, since equality cannot be extended indefinitely to all sectors of social life and all kinds of populations, it is racially and sexually limited by a restrained equality regime that operates through the colour line. It all boils down to the assumption that equality is scarce; hence the need for a regime that confines equality within a gendered and racial colour line.

Here we must ask under what circumstances the regime of restrained equality, geared towards alien and foreign populations, also start to apply to the native people in countries that used to draw the line between the two. Or should we rather ask whether the universal principle, claimed to be the model of European welfare state exceptionalism, was actually always an illusion, which could be upheld only for as long as prosperity reigned and economic growth made it possible to extend welfare to unprivileged parts of the native population? Ageing, poor qualification, low income, uselessness, weak health, are again becoming criteria that disqualify more and more humans from gaining equality in their own countries of citizenship. They are henceforth lumped together with the usual suspects, who are denied access to rights either because of their demeanours (displaying an illegitimate mobility, being undocumented, travelling alone, being moneyless and lacking a home), or because of their essentialized features (being illiterate, speaking the local language with an accent, having unadjusted habits, being young, strong, coloured and male, practising a 'different' religion, or wearing a veil).

A public realm infused by the restrained equality colour line

Far from being an oxymoron, unequal democracy is thus the pattern of action and government of today's nation-states. In France for instance such a pattern returns us to a pre-revolutionary state of mind, which ensures that rights are again viewed as privileges (Elias, 1939, 2012; Guénif-Souilamas, 2006b). In such a matrix, in which inequalities are repackaged as restrained equality, any right is potentially a privilege. If a right is reserved for some but not granted to all, it becomes a privilege. Inequalities that were supposed to be erased or at least addressed thus remain untouched, or they are merely tackled at the margin by providing specific rights to certain selected groups while at the same time denying the very same rights to other groups. In that respect, the right to circulate and to mobility is recognized for those who can afford it, the tourist, for example, or to those whose purpose authorizes mobility, for example businessmen, 'expats', NGO employees, academics, reporters and journalists, or documented skilled or unskilled labour migrants who fulfil the economic, professional and legal requirements for border crossing.

This pattern does not convey direct exclusion. Instead, there are a multitude of ways to be evinced, disqualified, ineligible and finally declared useless. But even this final uselessness should not be taken literally, as even useless people contribute at their own expense to the upgrading of those rights that they are denied. Restrained equality is the dispersed and at the same time rhizomatic way of waging low-intensity wars and consolidating rights in the hands of a white majority that views itself as a racial minority under siege.

Contemporary public discourse entertains a dangerous oscillation between the denunciation of migrants and/or refugees, who are supposedly spreading insecurity by their mere presence, and the designation of Arab and black Muslim minorities, who are presumably bound to become terrorists, by underlining that both groups may find allies in white citizens, who in turn are recast as accomplices by a police state which is prone to criminalize leftist, ecologist and anticapitalist activism. European states intentionally tie various segments of the population to the war against terrorism, finding its latest phrasing after the Paris attacks of January and November 2015 by a French socialist president, oddly mimicking a former US leader's martial posture and warlike statements uttered some 15 years ago. Security and surveillance, or any other responses to the so-called State of Terror, have become major assets of austere economic policies, which find increasing support in versions of national and European histories characterized by colonial aphasia and amnesia (Stoler, 2013). Race and gender are more than adjustable variables in such instances; they are rather major tools of inequality regimes implemented through individual and collective constraints. The rule of restrained equality thus relies more and more on assigned identities of migrants, descendants of migrants, labelled minority groups and/or individuals, appearance and behaviour, skin colour and dress code, gender conformation and sexual orientation, including homonormativity. Any combination of these features produces lines of division that act in favour of a government of bodies and lives that strips certain groups or constellations of individuals from their means of existence and their access to a long-claimed but always elusive and differentiated equality. Yet as we have seen, with or without economic exploitation, the subtle oppression pattern always encompasses a symbolic understated dimension that makes it arduous for people on each side of the colour line to locate, isolate and measure its mode and consequences.

Two contrasting examples illustrate this point: on the one hand, so-called 'search-and-rescue operations', on the other so-called 'stop-and-search' routines. The equivocal tendency of European states to simultaneously practise both games illustrates their need to present themselves as being both compassionate and strong, practising, for example, a humane deportation policy while at the same time firmly discouraging any attempt to cross the Channel or the Mediterranean. In this way, they deter criticism that their hardening policies betray Europe's self-image as the birth continent of human rights and universal humanism. In that respect, the case of the Calais 'jungle' in northern France highlights how a local problem of shelter and mobility – never addressed because its inhabitants are mainly young, non-white, male 'illegal' migrants, and hence not entitled to food, hygiene and mobility – has become a major stumbling block in the negotiations for the UK to remain a member of the EU (Migreurop, 2015; Gisti, 2016; Chrisafis *et al.*, 2016). Yet one should keep in mind that such state negotiations downplay the major political issue of who is entitled to enjoy mobility as a fundamental right. The recurrent scenes of camp dismantling and destruction (Agier, 2013) in Calais or South England, or in the case of the Roma camps in northern Paris, have annihilated imaginative collective protection and solidarity across the colour line. The violence committed by both police and some local inhabitants against undocumented young men underscores the far-reaching spectrum of restrained equality when men of colour are not subjects of rescue actions but rather searched and stopped by all means. Along the same line, the stop-and-search police routines have become a major locus of eviction from basic rights aimed at young non-white men, mainly Arab, black and Muslim, who increasingly fall under suspicion. In the past decade, Muslim veiled women have faced a double standard from the Western soft power: searched and rescued at distant theatres of war on terror, stopped, searched and stigmatized as a potential internal enemy, especially if wearing a face veil. The routinized police harassment of youngsters and young adults highlights internal boundaries along which people of colour are expelled from their national identity, sometimes through murder. Scattered across homelands, deaths at the hands of police officers or racist nationals rarely attract public attention as they are not counted as losses for the nation. Rather, and according to the logics of restrained equality, these violent and precocious deaths may even be viewed as a form of revenge or honour crime by which the former colonial power cleanses the stain of its lost supremacy, a loss of which it is eternally reminded precisely by those all-too-visible young male coloured bodies. As confirmed by recent verdicts, the police officers held responsible for the death of racialized youth are rarely convicted by the juridical system (ACAT, 2016).[3] The case of the two police officers who, in 2005 in the suburban city of Clichy-Sous-Bois, refrained from rescuing three youngsters who sought to escape by sheltering in a high-voltage power installation where two of them ended up being killed, is illustrative of this. The event triggered three long weeks of urban riots. Ten years after the event, the officers were acquitted (*Le Monde*, 2015). In January 2016, a police officer who had shot a fleeing 28-year-old Arab man in

the back was acquitted on the grounds that he had exercised his right of legitimate defence (Robert-Diard, 2016). In the French public eye these lives amount
to nothing. They do not catch the attention of state justice and are rarely
mourned (Butler, 2009). Unable to survive the violence they unwillingly inspire,
these precarious lives are enrolled in a necropolitics that supports the 'virtuous'
racism (Guénif-Soulamas, 2006a) against colonial and migrant minorities as
well as the supremacy of the majority group (Mbembe, 2003). The impunity and
invisibility with which this system can operate as a comprehensive programme
to tame otherness confirm the restrained equality regime: the transformation of
common rights into privileges for selected ones ends up making certain lives
disposable.

Migrant and minority women are in no better position on the transnational
labour market, where they struggle to survive and protect their physical integrity
on journeys that often end up in private households where they become
dependent on educated women who can afford to outsource their care for
parents, children and home. Recurrent stories are told and shared across Europe
about undocumented nail polishers who are being exploited by documented
migrants, or middle-class families ignoring the dire consequences of underpaid
and undeclared housekeeping. Both examples mark out a race and gender divide
that prompts everybody that does not have to serve under such precarious conditions to consider themselves better off. In this way, transnational capitalism,
serviced by national austere policies, shapes entire populations into exploitable
matter and leave to the individuals themselves the dirty task to sort out who will
benefit and who will bear the load of rough exploitation.

The racialization of Arabs and Muslims at a transcontinental scale

More crucial to the argument made here, racist trends such as the Christian anti-
Semitism, which from now on is supposed to be passed, seem to be projected to
the new internal enemy, that is, to the new French or European citizens of
migrant and colonial background, be they Arab, black and/or Muslim. At the
same time, other forms of suspicion are bound to appear as racism also targets
immigrants from the former colonies, a process that eventually morphs into a
prejudice against Muslim refugees that is inseparable from European islamophobia (Hajjat and Mohammed, 2013). Consider what has already been happening
in the past few years, as governments and policymakers, after having tried hard
to look the other way, must somehow address the consequences of the human
mobility from war-torn areas in Africa and the Middle East toward Europe and
the West more generally. If policymakers have for long held onto the belief that
all problems have been at least potentially prevented by the century-long consolidation of the welfare state, this same belief now appears merely as a gloss-over
tactic that frees them from taking responsibility for the ongoing dismantling of
welfare systems and the concomitant installation of austerity measures and
systems for biopolitical surveillance.

Therefore, the main articulation of race is no longer restricted to black or mixed 'Afropeans' but expands to include Arabs, Muslims and Roma. As was previously the case with European anti-Semitism, which construed Jews as the internal other, or as the inferior race to be destroyed, Islam today stands for a monstrous ontology in the sense that it designates an identity that cannot be separated or stripped from its human embodiment. Often viewed as an irreducible and proliferating religion, or as *the* 'paradigmatic' religion (Anidjar, 2003), Islam today stands for more than a religion. Garbed in the fashion of the old colonial empires, Islam again equates race in the sense that it is intrinsic to the humans supposed to embody it and plays a crucial role in the othering of those who can claim neither rights nor shares in the capitalist system of oppression. The European Jews once embodied this intrinsic otherness, living alongside but outside of the Christian majority in prosperous cities, to the point that ghettos were built to separate them from the Christians. Along the same lines of segregation as the ones implemented in camps scattered across colonial spaces, migrants and minorities today experience similar biopolitical methods of dispersion and segregation. Eventually, this leads to the destruction of human lives: another instance of necropower.

Indeed, all people designated as Muslims are here caught in a double bind that is potentially lethal: on the one hand, 'muslimness' cannot be separated from its embodiment; on the other hand, the presumed Muslims, born what they are and expected to remain what they are, must nonetheless at all costs relinquish their possible muslimness. According to this perception Muslims are racialized and this racialization reaches a further stage once it is combined with a sexualized essentialization of their habits, behaviour, dress code and beliefs, all of which are derived from their presumed religiosity and its gender standards. Operating like a reflecting surface, Muslim men are thus supposed to express the same disdain towards their female counterparts that European men for centuries expressed against 'their' women and their colonial subjects but which they, according to the narrative of European modernity, are said to have left behind. For the hegemonic majority, Muslims still inspire awe, hatred and disgust of a kind that runs all the way back to the Orientalism trope and that, in complete oblivion of its colonial roots, imposes the stigma of a backward immigrant culture upon Muslims who supposedly are unable to comply with integration models and civilizing injunctions. I must also mention that superlative Other who combines the identity of the Muslim and the refugee, an identity which for majority Europeans is a contradiction in terms and forecloses identification, unless the candidate is an unveiled woman or a homosexual that demands to be rescued and emancipated. In this sense 'integration' becomes the new proxy for a colonial rule that governs migrants, who have illegitimately made use of the mobility that entitled groups can take for granted and who are pitted against other minorities, whether colonial, migrant, sexual, cultural or racial.

Islamophobia/homophobia as virtuous racism in the colonial present

It thus becomes clear that the coloniality of this racism has less to do with the fact that its immigrant object of policy and discourse comes from the former colonies than with the fact that Europe, in the very same period, has been 'colonized' by financial capitalism, which led to the collapse of national economies in 2008. Therefore, there is no reason to engage with the ongoing questioning about what 'Pakis' do to a diverse Britain and white Brits, or how Moroccan immigrants and their descendants damage the Dutch multicultural model, or again why Turks do not integrate in Germany or France. If the former are ex-natives of the British Empire, and thus dissimilar to the current newcomers in Europe, the latter do not have any obvious colonial ties to the societies where they pause in their odyssey. Rather, the common question for these nation-states, seeing that their identity politics is being translated into a politics of fear, is whether they are able to admit that they are simultaneously colonial and postcolonial: colonial with respect to a continuous governmental logic that transforms the former subjects' descendants into today's illegal migrants or subaltern citizens; postcolonial with regard to the apparently disturbing ability of these subalternized and marginalized citizens and would-be citizens to nevertheless exist in countries that so strongly reject them that they deeply affect their political biotope just by claiming and embodying their belonging.

Among the many answers to this paradox, one is 'Islam'. In times of austerity, the presence of the coloured, visible and repulsive otherness of 'Islam' is a blessing for conservatives, populists and partisans of inequality. It is playing a key role in implementing the hidden agenda of inequality that each country gears towards immigrants and minorities who must be kept outside the private club of equality.

In this context, it is interesting to consider female objects of racism, for they disclose the ways in which sexism predictably pits the group of veiled Muslim women (Guénif-Souilamas, 2014) against secular or 'moderate' Muslims and Arab and black women who can make careers by publicly denouncing Islam as a whole. The heroines of the latter group have entertained prominent roles in Europe. For each country, certain names come to mind. What unites them, beyond the various ways in which they play out their mandatory anti-Islam stance, is that they alternate as tokens and decoys in a public spectacle where their often attractive complexion and their supposedly bold statements serve to distract attention away from the real issues at stake: persistent inequalities that are not bound to be reduced or tackled. In this spectacle, too, it can be seen how the regime of restrained equality functions in the creation of hierarchies that serve to legitimize an unequal democracy. Whether defined by citizenship, whiteness, homo- or heteronormativity, Christianity, secularism, or a mix of any of these, restrained equality operates as a sorter between who is eligible and who is not for various rights and privileges.

The operative criterion, in these cases, is sexuality and its connection to citizenship (Mosse, 1985, 1996). Sexuality is here a sign of propriety or appropriateness and it also serves as proof of a successful domestication. Or, conversely, sexuality functions as a label of inappropriateness and impropriety that leads to public scapegoating of what is perceived as deviant, promiscuous or oppressive habits and attitudes (Trinh, 1986/1987). The 'civilized minorities' who abide by these criteria become the accomplices in the implementation of measures that pretend to rescue and emancipate persons of 'their kind', at the expense of veiled women and bearded men who will remain trapped in backward states of exception.

The common marker of this series is Islam – not so much as a religion, however, but as a floating signifier in the same sense as Stuart Hall (1997) has referred to race: a floating signifier filled with meanings, facts and narratives, activated by and colliding with a specific *esprit du temps* with its typical uncertainties and obsessions, its ideas of order and disorder, its fears of losing substance and might, its passion for security and securitization, just to mention a few – and not forgetting the rescue narratives that come with it. Once one factors in Islam and its associated markers of 'muslimness' that lie scattered in various places and under multiple appearances, what remains is the notion of an otherness within, an internal threat that can only be circumscribed by giving it sense and face. This is, for example, what ongoing counter-terrorist manhunts and search operations aim at fulfilling.

This is also the context in which the discourse on 'Islam' and homosexuality may be situated. For the purpose of restrained equality, segments of this population, namely the gay Arabs and/or Muslims, should be saved from their very nature, not from their nature as gays, or from a gayness constructed as a nature, but from their nature as Muslims, which is seen as an obstacle to their human and sexual emancipation. Hence, since muslimness is racialized, its visibility is perceived as a threat that has to be fought and extirpated by segments who identify with whiteness.

In order to make sense of the ongoing wave of rescue narratives concerning the so-called gays in the French banlieues (what new-wave crusaders call 'Muslimistan') who supposedly would be abandoned, harassed or threatened by their family and group if they come out and affirm their homosexuality, one should recall how this narrative started. It reactivates the Janus figure – at once desirable and despicable – of the Arab boy (Guénif-Souilamas and Macé, 2004). The origins of this European fantasy can be traced back to the colonial era when educated bourgeois men, and to some extent women, set routes to the east and the south and opened an Orientalist move (Said, 1978; Massad, 2007). This narrative endures in the postcolonial situation when men and women from the former colonies, usually known as immigrants, settle in their former mainland and turn it into their homeland.

In the current depiction and description of the Arab boy, the straight perception of his figure as a violent heterosexual is merely a projection of what the straight European and local heterosexism wants to see in this stereotype. Not only is the 'Arab boy' accountable for the vanishing of sameness but also for threatening the sexual and matrimonial market by repeated and close encounters with female and male natives (Guénif-Souilamas, 2006a). On the one hand, he disrupts the heteronormative order that has to do with seducing women, and has become a landmark of French straight republicanism or of a European narrative of egalitarian gender relations, by accessing the white woman market. On the other hand, he weakens this very special French blend of homosociality, by queering the French love and sex scene with uninvited practices such as secret pederasty, unclaimed homoeroticism, crossing borders of sexual markers and stigma by variations on the theme of 'trans'.

If this says something of homophobia, this has to do with the reluctance of straight white French men in charge to relinquish their sexual power over all objects of desire, including young Arab males. It says much less, if anything, of a supposedly Muslim hatred for gays, and lesbians, that would be a product of their intimate story and intrinsic nature. Forgetful of the tastes for same sex that prevail no less in Arab or Muslim societies than in other ones, Muslim expressions of hatred for homosexuality may well be a resistance to a Westernized conception of sex relations and the idea of sexuality as *identity*, imposed during the colonial times, that does not comply with the sexuality episteme coined by Foucault, and all its various versions, homo, hetero and more. Fitting into the order of sexuality, understood as a tool of power that rules bodies and subjects, is central to the conception of sexual freedom and of sexual obedience to a norm, which one may then also choose to disclaim. Such disclaim may then not be homophobia but rather a resistance to the Western frame of sexuality and the normative definition it entails and imposes on individuals, such as giving an account of one's sexuality. Hence, homophobia remains centrally the expression of straight white Christian men, and women, willing to preserve their power, sexual as well as political, by presenting themselves as saviours of any weak sexual subjects who are looking for protection, such as homosexuals who have become the new victims. Yet, one must keep in mind that in order to be saved, they must claim a homosexual identity, thus re-enacting the very norms they may not fit. Interestingly, however, different states across Europe seem to be establishing differing 'sexual nationalisms' in complex responses to the three-fold presence of feminism, gay emancipation and Islam. Rather than a sexual democracy (Fergusson, 1991; Fassin, 2005), France promotes a sexual republic by imposing heterosexist conformity on its racialized subalterns, namely to mimic the French male courtesy as a proof of one's domesticated nature. At the same time, it pressures them to also become gayfriendly, while the Catholic white French majority claims a compulsory heteronormativity and absolves itself from its inability to express a compassionate gesture towards homo-parenthood. The French combination of homophobia and islamophobia stands in stark contrast to the homonationalist Netherlands, which castigates desired Moroccans for being too straight and sets gayfriendliness as a national standard for all.

Whitening, whitewashing and laundering: the magic of moral panic

These narratives are vivid, most effectively playing their part in the criminaliza-tion of the sub/urban racialized and socially marginalized youth across Europe. Yet, they have temporarily been forsaken for another moral panic episode in Cologne in early 2016. Widely reported and hysterically commented, the spec-tacular nightly sexual assault of male mobs against women celebrating the New Year incited wild debates on untamed Arabs, whether migrant, refugees or national minority, who were pointed out as the perpetrators. Many aspects of the debate were triggered by their race, projected onto their supposed skin colour and religion. In this sense, the debate discloses how restrained equality and its colour line are imposed. First, the victimized women became all white and young in the commentators' view, regardless of their actual ethnicity and age. This discursive appropriation of their bodies also shows how they became 'res-cueable' and thus could be reclaimed by their real allies and legitimate partners: the white men. Such rhetoric of course obscures the fact that, on the night of the assaults, the women were saved neither by the police nor by other people in the crowd, with few and mostly unacknowledged exceptions – especially that of a male refugee saving an American student. Arrogantly and out of ignorance, the vast majority in Germany and beyond in Euramerica, reiterated almost exactly Spivak's liminal statement of 'white men saving (protecting) brown women from brown men'. Except that in order to become rescueable, all assaulted women first had to be whitened; or maybe a more correct subtext would show, in that instance, that white women are browned to be rescued, meaning subdued. Either way, the public stance ignored that the crowd of women was actually mul-ticultural, what Germany refuses to be. Such visible facts escaped the would-be saviours, who thus offered their lip service to civilized solidarity instead of making or suggesting any effective effort to prevent structural sexism, which was the main trigger of the assaults. It prevented everyone from identifying the strong patriarchal remnants in Europe that are not imported by refugees.

Yet, there is no exceptionality in what happened in Cologne, it is just another instance of what the end of a patriarchal order produces when it is on the verge of collapse. If white dominant groups gained a major outcome in this episode of moral panic, one of the major collateral damages hurt the ideal enemy as it served to erode public confidence in the courageous German state policy in favour of receiving refugees from the Middle East war zone. Moreover, this belated rescue narrative enabled white straight men, in Germany and elsewhere, to save their privileges and to re-enchant their discredited political world and word by playing the card of a superficial patriarchal anti-sexism. And this to no little extent through a re-orientalist scenery where they were thrilled to experi-ence the oppression of women by coloured men far more closely than they had been able to when watching the crowded squares of the Arab revolutions. It is no coincidence, of course, that the so-called mob assault in Cologne was equated with the overblown violations of women in Tahrir Square in 2011. Indeed, the unexpected event in Cologne almost satisfied the lust for a real confrontation with what is today cast as a Muslim invasion, if not an occupation. It also offered an opportunity to European politicians wanting to rid themselves from accusations for not having acted swiftly and effectively enough in response to 'the refugee crisis' or ordinary sexist oppression. Obviously, then, both these issues may be considered as instances of the racialization and sexualization that is at play in the regime of restrained equality, to the effect that the victim is at once being blamed and denied basic rights. The Cologne event, providing a glimpse of the regime of restrained equality, thus enabled a laundering of the austerity politics and its forthcoming acts of betrayal and silencing, whitening the women so that they can be saved as victims, whitewashing political failures and cowardice stemming from a reactionary move against a multicultural Europe. In this respect, the women in Cologne and the young Arab girl described below are pushed into the same trap by unfriendly men acting out the colour line and the restrained equality it allows.

A re-orientalization tale: the derivative economy of emotion and fear

Straight out of her bubble bath into suicide bomber gear: this is how Hasna Ait Boulahcen was presented as she, allegedly, became the first Arab-French female suicide bomber in the aftermath of the 13 November 2015 Paris attacks. The story of a 'cowgirl' or 'party girl', depending on the medium reporting on how she craved to die in such a fashionable manner, became viral, as did her pictures and Facebook posts. The presentation of the material intended to vilify her as a 'radicalized' girl, once harassed in her family, and eventually, despite her minor, peripheral role in the plot, as a cousin of one of the instigators, sacrificed for the sake of state security. Her fate was sealed a few days after the attacks, when special police forces killed many 'terrorists' in an apartment in a poor neighbourhood north of Paris. However, it then turned out that the pictures were not hers and that she had no suicide belt on, but that she died asphyxiated by the smoke a male terrorist released when he blew his. Before dying, she appeared at a window, tried to reach out to the police and screamed hands up: 'Sir, please, let me out, let me out at least.... He's going to blow someone up! Sir, I'm scared, I'm scared' (for a close report, see Marteau *et al.*, 2015; Suc, 2016).

Regardless of the fact that regular killings take place further east and south at the very same time in theatres of endless imperialist wars, this picturesque side event was highlighted to flesh out in a gendered manner an extreme violence, labelled 'Islamist terrorism', targeting a so-called way of life in Europe. The portrait of the female figure standing out from the male group that plotted the attacks bears all the markers of an orientalist trope. Eroticization, availability, estrangement, a spectacular embodied excess combined with a reckless livelihood are all engrained in the images, reports and comments surrounding the fate of this young Arab-French woman. Furthermore, she rejoins another orientalized male figure, the religious fanatic represented in orientalist painting and literature, most effectively epitomized in the Danish cartoons and the globalized affair that ensued after their release in 2006, first in Denmark, then in France, by *Charlie Hebdo*. As is well known, the result of this controversy on unconditional freedom of speech and blasphemy has been a moral crusade that eventually reached a climax after the January 2015 killings in Paris by spreading a 'Je suis Charlie' world anthem.

Re-enacted in this first female would-be terrorist, a pattern of interpretation reiterates itself, borrowing the same features as the ones put into circulation after the previous attacks in France. All the protagonists are rooted if not trapped in the long-lasting orientalism perspective with a twist that media expansion ('the electronic, postmodern world') allows. Beyond its 'traditional exoticism … in this electronic age, the Orient too has drawn nearer to [the Western citizen] and is now less a myth perhaps than a place crisscrossed by Western, especially American interests' (Said, 1978: 26). The 're-orientalization' under way links up to the classical depiction of the other – 'the oriental' being created as too distant by 'obliterating him as a human being' (Said, 1978: 27) and simultaneously as too close and too similar since s/he is a citizen – by circulating its proliferating images in a viral mode. If Edward Said's *Orientalism* is juxtaposed to Walter Benjamin's essay on 'The Work of Art in the Age of Mechanical Reproduction', we become aware, I suggest, of such a moment of re-orientalization, of a continuum in which orientalism collides with its proliferating iconographic avatars and is thus aggravated and intensified. Past and present iconic representations are now gathered in some sinister genealogy, speaking for the same goal of spreading terror through random death, and a graphic ideology referred to as an Islamist fundamentalism. In that respect, the ongoing re-orientalization testifies to a re-enchantment of the Euramerican world, offering pundits and moral entrepreneurs an opportunity to praise their own values and to put at their forefront a henceforth compulsory gender equality that is intended to justify all the wars that it wages. Be it paradoxical or not, the European re-enchantment stems from the apparent concern about the overwhelming evidence that citizens of migrant and colonial descent, whether from France or Belgium, are involved in a transnational and deterritorialized terrorism. As survivors of the Bataclan theatre attack stated, the murderers looked and spoke just like themselves, they seemed to belong to the same society and to have led the same kind of life. They were not even remotely alien, but homegrown European citizens, whether from Belgium or France, and in this sense not different from the ones behind the 2007 London attacks. *They were alike but not equal.*

The perpetrators' backgrounds make clear that they were not outcasts or disadvantaged: most of them lived in middle-income families. Relying on these facts, some hastily jump to the conclusion that they did not face racism or discrimination and thus had no reason to act out in such a horrendous way. Structural dimensions are thus put aside and focus is put on the 'monstrous personalities', on the beasts within and the so-called 'radicalization processes' of these criminals. Henceforth, presumed Muslims are supposed to vocally disown them (Arab *et al.*, 2015). Yet, the restrained equality that affects those who have been stripped of their humanness may at least explain in part why they may be drawn to an ideology of mass destruction that relies on graphic illustrations of executions supposed to be integral to an essentialized Islam. The purpose here is not to address and exhaust all the complex paths that lead to the 'state of terror' encountered in vast regions of the world, but rather to unearth one of them: the deep and narrow connection between the politics of austerity and the politics of restrained equality, an alliance that is characteristic of times of fear and terror and that supports financial capitalism and its proxy, Euramerican world military and economic supremacy. Let me then finally examine what this combination of the state of terror and the politics of austerity stands for and describe how restrained equality underwrites all phases of its apparently unstoppable expansion. This requires a twofold argument: one that explores the repackaging of terror in post/colonial times and another that describes how restrained equality functions by entertaining a delusional agency.

The 'state of terror' encompasses terrorism but has a larger scope. It includes manipulations of a politics of fear and panic, which always has deep effects on the perception of the other, whether from within or without, whose violent actions aim to disrupt a state order that is considered to be unjust and oppressive. In this situation, both terrorism and its author, whether known or unknown, whether claimed or not, is designated as the enemy, and this very naming precludes any acknowledgement of belonging for anyone who is confused with or suspected to be associated with the culprits. Such 'assemblages', which lead to the othering of broad human segments of the national and global population, become powerful tools for social formations and cultures in search of cohesion, be it through coercion, repression or state violence. In that sense, terrorism also stands for the undesired other who has be/come too close, too familiar, and who is presented by the ruling hegemonic group as likely to exert violence on ordinary people. The sources of fear and terror can thus be displaced to the other, which may lead to the criminalization of everybody who shares the same background or ethnicity. Since terrorism effectively generates distinctions between good citizens and 'evil' ones, thus disrupting social and cultural commonalities, it has become the best ally of austere policies serving late capitalism and the austere histories on which it relies. The narrow connection between these two dynamics erases the internal coloniality that Europe has inherited from the patterns of exploitation and oppression implemented by colonial rule, and it enables a denial of their continued presence in today's polities. This colonial past endures in the present by handing over the most vulnerable and/or undesirable humans to the rules of an unequal economic order, which they, at once, serve and depend on. Integral to this device is a moral economy that operates through a gendered racialization that disqualifies and disowns those who are bound to a harsher and longer economic and symbolic exploitation, namely the migrants, 'illegal' or documented, the minorities of colonial and migrant descent and the internal minorities such as the Roma. All these groups, conceived as being visibly different, are disconnected from their own collective memories and deprived of the capacities and resources that would allow them to articulate their histories. Instead, they are incorporated into another narrative, that of the nation, and its generous integration policy, which they are expected to embrace and embody. In this context, the mechanism of restrained equality plays out as a filter or a decoy that subtends the illusion that certain rights, which are presented as common, are accessible to all, whereas in reality they are always-already upgraded to privileges and removed from the common. The diffused mode of allocation of rights, benefits and protection pertaining to the current economy also fits in with the individualized mode of granting citizens of migrant and colonial descent certificates of domestication and integration, showing their adequacy to the value systems that, allegedly, are inherent to the society they intend to belong to, yet without ever granting them full citizenship and full equality.

Belonging means whitening oneself and thus contributes to the whitewashing of the unequal and racist system one lives in.

Interestingly, the highly unconditional freedom of speech praised early after the 'Je suis Charlie' tag became compulsory turned highly *conditional* under the state of emergency that was proclaimed after the November attacks in France. One step away from the state of exception and two from the state of war, this stage allowed repression even against environmentalist activists demonstrating during the COP21 world gathering in Paris two weeks later. The double standard was glaring: free speech and right to assembly for climate activists and civil society had to be sacrificed in the search for and protection against suspected 'islamists' or 'jihadists' who threatened free speech. It reached a higher level when the police used violence against students and workers protesting a law meant by the socialist government to dismantle labour protections.

In a rhizome-like world, whatever is allocated to the other through gestures of essentialization eventually bounces back to the sender. In that respect Europe is no exception. Or, rather it had created itself as *the* exception but must now resign such exceptional central status and return to its provincialized place in a connected world. If such exception stemmed from its power of expansion through conquest, enslavement and colonization, this process is now proven to be over, not only because of decolonization but more crucially because of the decentring dynamics that weaken Europe's economies and erode its political power.

For decades, migrants have faced unwelcoming policies that have reminded them of their dis/mis/placement and dis/mis/qualification in order to be able to dismiss whatever claims they make. They are made to pay for the disturbance and disorder they introduce by their mere presence. One may understand the strong will to silence them as a way of erasing their past and their memories and of annihilating their ability to fully exist as equals in the various regions of Europe where they live. As these 'masses of aliens', nurtured in independence struggles and histories of migration, and embodying the remnants of a colonial past, have been drawing closer to mainland Europe, they trigger a re-orientalization that designates them as undesired new European citizens of migrant and colonial descent. After decades, during which they were contained as aliens and monitored to remain alien, they have recently become instrumental in replacing the enemy of the Cold War with the enemy of the so-called 'clash of civilizations'. Simultaneously, as formerly colonized peoples move to their former mainland and thus reactivate older colonial encounters, Western countries have revived the orientalism that was entrenched in their now dismantled colonial rule. Hence both coloniality and orientalism sustain the regime of restrained equality; no longer simply by blunt exclusion, but by means of eviction, reservation, retention and contention.

In Western Europe, depicting the racialized youth as unbalanced, violent and disoriented has become routine. The young woman, pulverized by the terrorism moment she became linked to, is no exception to this banal rule. Articulated analyses, of the kind that could demonstrate who are really responsible for the current low-intensity wars, or detect historical patterns of racism and inequality, or analyse the collective dynamics of oppression and resistance, are in today's Europe substituted by narrowly framed psychological portraits and images of poor parenthood, which in turn are seen as the results of cultural deficiencies, social inabilities and weak personalities. All of which cause people to surrender to the discourses of violence and fanatic hatred welled in Islam. Such shortcuts indicate a gendered and racialized component that sustains state policies of fear as well as the politics of identity. Consequently, they help ensure that equality will not happen. For that purpose, race and gender by means of racialization and sexualization are activated as powerful tools for the drawing of a colour line. Such a colour line is stretching across Europe, manifesting itself in a reactionary and populist order that spreads across nations and ignores state borders, so as to better tighten presumed continental and cultural boundaries. Conversely, the colour line runs along internal boundaries, which divide populations that share a past and present marked by colonialism and migrancy, depriving some groups of basic social rights and separating them from citizens who are entitled to such rights. The sexual and gendered colour line remains invisible and its effects are usually denied or simply blamed on some enduring sense of crisis. By thus remaining unnoticed, the colour line repackages the colonial rule. Being apparently dismantled at the state level, coloniality continues to operate on the level of everyday lives that are increasingly shaped by austerity policies.

Such processes of separation and division therefore help to allocate privileges to white dominant groups and selected minorities of the population. They rely on the constant invention and reinvention of religious, racial and ethnic features allotted to gendered and sexualized individuals, who are often presented as a compact mass of aliens. The power of this restrained equality, exerted through eviction, reservation, co-optation and selection, lies in the fact that it understates the colonial pattern. It can thus be activated all the more forcefully in an internal colonization that subordinates, victimizes and exploits minority citizens and coloured aliens, and in an external colonization that is managed by the so-called war on terror and its counter-terrorism apparatus.

All these reorientalized ingredients, mixing sexuality and religion, provide the expanding audience of a state politics of fear with reasons to willingly submit itself to an extended state of emergency and thus relinquish its rights and power to authorities. As Judith Butler (2009) points out, this tendency frames anyone who is resisting the authoritarian transformation as a visible other, bearing signs and stigmas of difference that through yet another metamorphosis may cause him or her to be identified as possible threats or even as the very culprit of the democratic shortfall.

Candles or camps

Are we to conclude, then, that all lives do not bear the same value? Some are bound to be celebrated and mourned with candles and totemic reminders when killed by labelled terrorists. Other lives are disposable and can either be encamped or forgotten and left unmourned when killed by the police. Such routines prove the validity of an observation made by Achille Mbembe (2013). He speaks of the 'becoming negro' of large segments of peoples across the late-capitalist world. When the intrinsic value of the human is stripped from its site of existence, the human body, this body may be subjected to pure exploitation, either as a symbolic scape-goat, a labour force or as a displaceable, disposable and ultimately destroyable asset. Not only does restrained equality rely on the 'becoming negro' of the world, but one may also speak of a 'becoming Palestinian', in respect to a policy of containment operating through checkpoints and internal colonies. Or one may, in view of more recent events, speak of a 'becoming Muslim', especially in countries where they are present as a minority religion and population. These ways of exerting power act as means of reducing entitlements and facilitating the eviction of a wide range of activists and subaltern inhabitants.

We are witnessing the reunification of a transcontinental Euramerica, reorienting its sovereignty towards the region from where, centuries ago, white supremacy expanded worldwide. Its fierce and arrogant defence is its most urgent task vis-à-vis an enemy that it has created for itself across time and space. Through stunning gestures and fascinating stances, Euramerican countries persist in their denial of responsibility for the current state of affairs. If for the time being, the common enemy is conveniently called Islam, this also hints of forthcoming names and designations, which will be combined so as to construct a paradigmatic Other, in whatever form is needed for the sake of an unequal order.

The 'state of terror' has become the best ally and the major asset for late-modern financial capitalism, and, for that matter, also for austerity policies and the austere histories they rely on. If this signifies the opening of a new episteme, one cannot shy away from putting at work from a feminist and anti-racist point of view facts such as the coloniality of power or the reactive wars of white supremacy, and the notions of decoloniality and subalternative agencies as modes of resistance. Axiological neutrality is out of date; the time has come for thorough inquiries into situated knowledge productions that sustain or dismiss restrained equality and its colour line.

Notes

1 In an op-ed released after the French president announced the extension of the state of emergency, Giorgio Agamben (2015) describes a paradigmatic shift from the rule of the state of law to the rule of the state of security. This rule borrows from the politics of fear, terror and internal war, as a means to avoid, obscure or efface the dynamics of democracy and absorb the disorder and instability produced by *stasis*, the ancient Greek state of civil

war or uprising triggered by excessive inequalities between autochthones, known as Eupatrids (well-born) and 'barbaric' aliens. On *stasis*, see further Loraux (2002).
2 The *New York Times* regularly carries articles under a section entitled 'State of Terror', thus showing a significant shift from the war on terror labelled after the 9/11 attacks. This further inoculates in minds the notion that terror is a common fate of the 'Western world' imposed on it without any reason from its outskirts and from remote regions suddenly embodied in its streets and venues by homegrown young 'terrorists'.
3 The CNDS (Commission Nationale de Déontologie de la Sécurité) was appointed for a few years (2006–10) to investigate rights denials and abuses from police officers; it issued a yearly report and publicized cases that illustrated illegitimate violence on behalf of officers in their duty. http://cnds.defenseurdesdroits.fr/rapports/annuels.html [accessed 22 March 2016].

Bibliography

ACAT (2016) www.acatfrance.fr/public/rapport_violences_policieres_acat.pdf [accessed 22 March 2016].

Agamben, G. (2015) 'De l'Etat de droit à l'Etat de sécurité'. *Le Monde*, 23 December. Available at: www.lemonde.fr/idees/article/2015/12/23/de-l-etat-de-droit-a-l-etat-de-securite_4836816_3232.html [accessed 3 March 2016].

Agier, M. (2013) *Campement urbain. Du refuge naît le ghetto*. Paris: Éditions Payot.

Anidjar, G. (2003) *The Jew, the Arab: A History of the Enemy*. Stanford: Stanford University Press.

Arab, C., Boubeker, A., Fadil, N., Guénif-Souilamas, N., Hajjat, A., Mohammed, M., Moujoud, N., Ouali, N., Soumahoro, M. (2015) 'How does it feel to be a problem?' Truthout, 26 January. Available at: www.truth-out.org/speakout/item/28742-how-does-it-feel-to-be-a-problem-a-statement-by-french-social-scientistsof-arab-and-african-origin-following-the-paris-attacks [accessed 24 March 2016].

Benjamin, W. (1936/2010) *The Work of Art in the Age of Mechanical Reproduction*. New York: Prism Key Press.

Butler, J. (2009) *Frames of War: When is Life Grievable?* New York: Verso.

Chrisafis, A., Walker, P. and Quinn, B. (2016) 'Calais "Jungle" camp: clashes as authorities demolish homes', *Guardian*, 1 March. Available at: www.theguardian.com/world/2016/feb/29/french-authorities-begin-clearance-of-part-of-calais-jungle-camp [accessed 4 March 2016].

Combahee River Collective Statement (1977, 1983) *Home Girls: A Black Feminist Anthology*, Barbara Smith (ed.). New York: Kitchen Table, Women of Color Press.

Desmond, M. (2016) *Evicted: Poverty and Profit in the American City*. New York: Crown Publishers.

Elias, N. (1939, 2012) *On the Process of Civilisation*. Dublin: UCD Press.

Fassin, E. (2005) *L'inversion de la question homosexuelle* Paris: Amsterdam.

Fergusson, A. (1991) *Sexual Democracy: Women, Oppression and Revolution*. Boulder, CO: Westview.

Foucault, M. (2004) *La naissance de la biopolitique. Cours au Collège de France (1978–1979)*. Paris: Hautes Etudes, Seuil.

Gisti (2016) 'Calais: Les bulldozers ne font pas une politique !' *Le Gisti* (Groupe d'information et de soutien des immigré·e·s), 22 February. Available at: www.gisti.org/spip.php?article5261 [accessed 4 March 2016].

Guénif-Souilamas, N. (2006a) 'The other French exception: virtuous racism and the war of the sexes in postcolonial France', *French Politics, Culture and Society*, 24 (3), pp. 23–41.

Guénif-Souilamas, N. (ed.) (2006b) *La république mise à nu par son immigration*. Paris: La Fabrique.

Guénif-Souilamas, N. (2014) 'French religions and their renewed embodiments'. In: Cady, L. and Fessenden, T. (eds), *Religion, the Secular, and the Politics of Sexual Difference*. New York: Columbia University Press, pp. 195–207.

Guénif-Souilamas, N. and Macé, E. (2004) *Les féministes et le garçon arabe*. La Tour d'Aigue: Editions de l'Aube.

Hajjat, A. and Mohammed, M. (2013) *Islamophobie*. Paris: La Découverte.

Hall, S. (1997) *Race, the Floating Signifier*. The Media Education Foundation. Available at: www.youtube.com/watch?v=bMo2uiRAf30 [accessed 22 March 2016].

Invisible Committee (2009) *The Coming Insurrection*, Cambridge, MA: The MIT Press.

Le Monde (2015) www.lemonde.fr/police-justice/article/2015/05/19/mort-de-zyed-et-bouna-la-parole-de-deux-policiers-blancs-l-emporte_4635934_1653578.html [accessed 22 March 2016].

Loraux, N. (2002) *The Divided City: On Memory and Forgetting in Ancient Athens*. New York: Zone Books.

Marteau, S., Piel, S. and Seelow, S (2015) 'Assaut de Saint-Denis: confusion et questions', *Le Monde*, 24 December, p. 10.

Massad, J. (2007) *Desiring Arabs*. Chicago: Chicago University Press.

Mbembe, A. (2003) 'Necropolitics', *Public Culture*, 15 (1), pp. 11–40.

Mbembe, A. (2013) *Critique de la raison nègre*. Paris: La Découverte.

Migreurop (2015) 'Calais declaration: we must refuse the encampment of foreign citizens and the closure of borders'. Migreurop. Observatoire des frontières, 18 December.

Mills, C.W. (1997) *The Racial Contract*. Ithaca, NY: Cornell University Press.

Moriarty, D. (2012) *Funding Models for Irish Film Makers*. Dublin: Collins Press.

Mosse, L.G. (1985) *Nationalism and Sexuality: Respectability and Abnormal Sexuality in Modern Europe*. New York: Howard Fertig.

Mosse, L.G. (1996) *The Image of Man: The Creation of Modern Masculinity*. Oxford: Oxford University Press.

Pateman, C. (1988) *The Sexual Contract*. Stanford, CA: Stanford University Press

Robert-Diard, P. (2016) 'A Bobigny, "la police tue et la justice acquitte"', *Le Monde*, 16 January. Available at: www.lemonde.fr/police-justice/article/2016/01/16/a-bobigny-la-police-tue-et-la-justice-acquitte_4848370_1653578.html [accessed 21 March 2016].

Said, E. (1978) *Orientalism*. NewYork: Vintage Books.

Shohamy, E. (2006) *Language Policies: Hidden Agendas and New Approaches*. London and New York: Routledge.

Stoler, A. (ed.) (2013) *Imperial Debris: On Ruins and Ruination*. Durham, NC: Duke University Press.

Subrahmanyam, S. (1997) 'Connected histories: notes towards a Reconfiguration of Early Modern Eurasia', *Modern Asian Studies*, 31 (3), Special Issue: The Eurasian Context of the Early Modern History of Mainland South East Asia, 1400–1800. pp. 735–62.

Suc, M (2016) 'La vérité sur l'assaut du RAID à Saint-Denis', Mediapart, 31 January. Available at: www.mediapart.fr/journal/france/310116/la-verite-sur-l-assaut-du-raid-saint-denis [accessed 4 March 2016].

Trinh, T. Minh-Ha, (1986-1987) 'She, The Inappropriate/d Other'. Discourse No 8, Winter.

10 Writing history for an uncertain future

Concluding remarks

Julia Willén and Stefan Jonsson

At the end of this book we should ask what alternatives there are to the austere historiography and austere tendencies of contemporary European culture that the authors of the previous chapters have discussed.

As we know, the temporal dimensions of past and future never converge; instead they dissolve into the present. As David Scott argues, '[i]t is as though we always-already know the salient shape of the present to be called into question by the intervention of our criticism' (Scott, 2014: 41). In that sense – as we cannot situate ourselves outside of our contemporaneity – this book must also be seen as an intervention into a certain future. The challenge as we see it is to approach history, as well as the present that has been produced by that history, in a way that enables the shattered and divided past to be narrated as a recognized shared experience. What we propose is a history that takes its point of departure in the colonial wound, rather than treating it as something passed, healed and reconciled with.

As several of the contributors to this volume point out, there is a problem in current writing of Europe's past that bears implications for its present – and its future. Europe has been writing itself as modern and liberal, not only as the cradle of philosophy but also as the womb for universal values and human rights. By separating Europe's colonial past from its neoliberal present, Europe enables itself to escape its accountability for the current world order, to fence itself off from migrants coming here to seek refuge, and to discriminate against its postcolonial citizens. A couple of critical questions arise in this dilemma.

The first question has to do with how Europe's colonial history hitherto has been written mostly from the margins. There is certainly no lack of historical scrutiny with regards to European colonialisms. If we restrict ourselves only to the past three or four decades (which excludes major figures such as Frantz Fanon, CLR James, Léopold Sédar Senghor, Aimé Césaire, Cheikh Anta Diop), an impressive body of scholarly work has been dedicated to this field. Here we can go all the way from the elaborations of colonialism's role in Europe's economic history by, for instance, Samir Amin, Fernand Braudel, Immanuel Wallerstein, André Gunder Frank, and others, or from monumental surveys such as those by Eric Wolf, Marc Ferro, Wolfgang Reinhard or Angelo del Boca. We can also mention any number of contributions from within the broad field of postcolonial theory and postcolonial studies, originating in pioneering work by, to mention just a few, Stuart Hall, Edward Said, Ranajit Guha, Gayatri Spivak, Walter Mignolo, Partha Chatterjee, Valentin Mudimbe, Dipesh Chakrabarty, Amina Mama and Enrique Dussel (see further, Chapter 1, p. 15, note).

As impressive as it may be, though, such fundamental contributions of historical scrutiny have not managed to challenge the basic Eurocentrism characterizing mainstream historiography. For one, why is it that the era of colonialism is not recognized as one of the distinct and crucial eras of European modern history? Although colonialism is sometimes presented as an epoch, it is not integrated into the linear construction of history that goes from Antiquity to Modernity, but is rather situated outside of it, as its supplement.

Epochs rarely have the opportunity to name themselves – naming comes after. Maybe the long nineteenth century, which today is often being summed up as the century of progress – industrialization, capitalism and nationalism – is better understood through the overarching name of colonialism. As theorists linked to the Coloniality/Modernity-collective have suggested, perhaps what we today call modernity is better conceived, in the *longue durée*, as the age of Coloniality, starting with the seminal year of 1492 which both marked Columbus's colonization of the 'New World' and the Spanish Reconquista (cf. Dussel, 1993; Quijano, 2000; Mignolo, 2011).[1]

As several contributions in this book make clear, hegemonic history in Europe has indeed been written, and continues to be written, with address to a specific subject: the austere – in the ascetic, minimalist sense of the concept – European. This subject remains exclusive, folded upon its own identity. To read the marginalized histories as if they are of no central concern to this central 'I' of European austerity means, in effect, that the marginalized remains in the margin, and that those who supposedly are at its core remain the subjects of historiography. One conclusion to be drawn from this book is that any historian who is dedicated to the history of Europe needs to consider coloniality as an ever-present context. 'Europe and colonialism' is not a special field within history but part and parcel of the European past – and of the European present. This also implies that we need to shift the weight of our interpretations of different historical accounts. As Gayatri Spivak insists, this demands a reading practice

> for which the first condition and effect is a suspension of the conviction that I am necessarily better, I am necessarily indispensable, I am necessarily the one to right wrongs, I am necessarily the end product for which history happened.
>
> (Spivak, 2004: 532)

To sustain the status quo of historiography becomes increasingly problematic in a multipolar world consisting of many centres, where historical tracing does not always have to go via Europe. New historical grammars and routes emerge that re-create South-to-South lineages and genealogies, South-to-North influences and impacts, and East-to-South entanglements and connected histories (for examples, see Subrahamnyam, 1997; Linebaugh and Rediker, 2000; Hofmeyr, 2004; Shareef, 2005; Nuttall, 2009; and Shilliam, 2015).[2]

The question is thus: how do we break open and mobilize the constituents of the *hegemonic* history that remains more or less unmoved despite four decades of postcolonial critique and a century of anti-colonial activism *inside* Europe? Susan Buck-Morss' reminder, however delayed and overdue it may seem, is here to the point: 'If we have become accustomed to different narratives, ones that place colonial events on the margins of European history, we have been seriously misled' (Buck-Morss, 2009: 39). The postcolonial (and Benjaminian) insistence that universal history remains partial in every instance that it excludes parts of this totality, keeps being ignored.

It was precisely toward this reduction that Hegel, in *The Phenomenology of the Spirit*, hastened (thereby contradicting himself) when he declared that 'the wounds of the spirit heal, and leave no scars behind' (Hegel, 2004: 407). In Rebecca Comay's reading of this passage she points out that this healing amounts to an attempt to leap out of the circle of repetition:

> Like the crumbling ruins of Carthage, the deed vanishes without a trace, the wounds heal without a scar. Erasure, not commemoration, is the last word of the *Phenomenology* – both its iconoclastic promise and its repressive blank. The blankness is ambiguous: it testifies both to the radical openness of the future and to the effacement of the missed opportunities of the past.
>
> (Comay, 2011: 149)

Hegel's history has occluded some of its past conflicts under the ideological blanket of 'harmony' that appear as 'blank pages' (Comay, 2011: 149). But the past is not a finished book; as Walter Benjamin writes in his essay on Eduard Fuchs, history writing needs to be created 'out of the counted group of threads which represent the woof of the past fed into the warp of the present' (Benjamin, 1937: 37). To Benjamin, history as a 'woof' is a 'thoroughly dialectical mode' and he continues: 'For centuries threads can become lost and are picked up by the actual course of history in a disjointed and inconspicuous manner' (Benjamin, 1937: 37). The colonial past that is sweeping through Europe – albeit unacknowledged and actively evaded – is this lost thread, and the return of this repressed nightmare uncovers the wound as still open: time was always out of joint. The dialectical conflict between this past and the hegemonic powers that refuse to acknowledge its existence is taking place here and now.

Austere futurities

The second question is oriented towards the future. What is the horizon of expectation in which we, as scholars of European history and society, find ourselves today? Evidently the future of Europe will be plural. It will be everything that is not 'pure', because that purity never existed. It will be a Europe characterized by religious plurality, lingual plurality and culture as the mesh that make this plurality intelligible and meaningful. Europe is standing at a crossroads – after all, that is what *crisis* implies – where we have to choose what kind of future the history we write is oriented towards. Is it oriented towards a future of a plurality that implies co-existence, or a plurality that is built upon segregation and cultural incompatibilities?

At the same time, it must be recalled that a future-oriented view is precisely what is prohibited by the politics and history of austerity. We are thus situated within an ideological order for which the future itself appears as an impossibility, not only because we appear to have accepted neoliberalism as the end of history, but also because the material conditions for any earthly future are being depleted, ruined and consumed well in advance. Today, not even social democrats are nourished by the ideal of liberated grandchildren; on the contrary, there seems to be a contradictory present guided by the ideal of total nihilism on the one hand (live as if there is no future) and a submission to the ideals of austerity on the other.

What we appear to be witnessing today is a retrogression of a short historical period where civil, political, social and cultural rights were expanding to include more and more human beings. As many contributors to this volume point out, this is something that is taking place semi-covertly, semi-openly.

Several comparisons have been made between our own period and the European 1930s, marked as it was by economic crisis, austere politics and economics, and increasing fascist tendencies that were gradually accepted until they became naturalized as part of the political landscape. The actualization of Walter Benjamin's late writing is symptomatic: we are living in tragic times. The resemblance is conspicuous.

There is, however, one big disparity between our own present and the 1930s, which might be located in the expansion of the European welfare state in the twentieth century and above all among the middle classes that were produced (or constructed) by this development, as large numbers of people gradually detached themselves from their working-class origins. Eighty years ago, the memory of the antagonistic proletariat was still a vivid part of the consciousness of the bourgeoning middle classes. Today, generations marked by conformist middle-class consciousness have obliterated this memory, and what has also disappeared is thus the knowledge that rights, which are now taken for granted, were only won through struggle and may again have to be defended through struggle. By contrast, for those subjects whose citizenship status was always within a grey zone – that is, the imperial subjects, the *indigènes*, the postcolonial citizens, the migrants and the working classes – access to rights was always precarious.

On the other hand, for those European subjects who voluntarily bow to austerity politics in the name of crisis, enduring a period of frugality is a sacrifice made for a larger cause. The stripping down of rights and access to welfare is perceived as a temporary measure within a prevailing ideology that orients crisis-driven effects of hatred and fear towards other precarized groups. The foreclosure of a future once promised, where education was an investment linked to future employment, propels people's desire to find a scapegoat: the European 'others' who are portrayed as 'draining' society's resources by abusing the social security system, or worse. Moreover, the linkage between the middle strata and the lower strata has successfully been erased by the ideology of austerity. Consequently, the middle classes usually lack the awareness that the scaling down of welfare and rights is not necessarily momentary, but may rather be a process exposing ever more people to conditions of exploitation, discrimination and misery.

As we have seen in this book, the colonial divide inside Europe is an essential component of this ideology and its success: from the point of view of a white, European, middle-class position, downsizing of welfare, mounting structural discrimination, and the surge of anti-immigrant and racist movements is something that concerns the European Others, rather than themselves. Several studies (cf. Kraal *et al.*, 2009; Runnymede Trust, 2009; Open Society Foundations, 2014) indicate that Europe's working class is becoming less white, and in order to prevent the formation of trans-racial or multicultural working-class solidarity, right-wing and nationalist politics fuel racial division and conflict. In this sense, too, the development of a post-political Europe entails a society contaminated by risks, and an austere futurity looms large on the horizon: a constant peeling off of rights and entitlements that renders invisible the underlying conflict between labour and capital.

It appears, then, as if we are approaching an austere futurity in which it becomes clear that Europe, which once gave up its expansive imperialism and racial anthropology, has become a container of an austere anthropology that spells out the same message as the old one: 'Just let them die'. Instead of taking the leap out of the circle of repetition that excludes the colonial subject and the postcolonial citizen from rights – and this imperial exclusion was always the context, both for the philosophical arguments among the social-contract philosophers of the seventeenth and eighteenth century, and for its practical realization in the US-American and French revolutions – one may ask if we are moving towards a world order where this separation is becoming permanent – that is, towards an austere citizenship that is tied not to the human subject as a human being, but to the subject's imaginary identity and its ability to serve as a site of value extraction, or cheap labour. In the words of Guénif-Souilamas, this austere logic is one that reverses the narrative of emancipation by converting rights into privileges. It would be a movement that began in 1789, when members of the nobility renounced their 'liberties' (which at the time referred to the privileges of their estate) and turned them, at least in principle, into universal *liberty* for all, and that now, having come full circle, reconverts generalized liberty – as codified in equal citizenship – into liberties for the wealthy, that is, into privileges.

A wounded history/history of the wound

Here we should recall a point made by Nicolas Bancel and Pascal Blanchard as well as Gurminder Bhambra in their contributions. They disclose the symptomatic nature of recent statements by leading European politicians, who have expounded that the colonial past is nothing that present-day Europeans are responsible for.[3] The nihilism of the present seems to go in two temporal directions. Whereas many thinkers have pointed out history as inheritance (Marx, Benjamin, Arendt), the unhistorical nihilist position bears no responsibility for inherited past deeds, except when convenient. The atrocities made in Europe's name were made by other men and women, long since deceased, and there is thus no reason for their contemporary heirs to acknowledge, apologize and pay reparations for these deeds. This remarkable immunity also says something about the futurity that these politicians imagine: one for which they and their heirs will not be held accountable.

The general idea that the crimes committed in the colonial period have since long expired also implies that colonialism remains firmly in the past. But the recognition that coloniality as a power structure continues to exist also begs the understanding that this does not imply an unbroken continuum going straight from the fifteenth century to our present. As Gayatri Spivak states,

> [c]olonial discourse studies, when they concentrate only on the representation of the colonized or the matter of the colonies, can sometimes serve the production of current neo-colonial knowledge by placing colonialism/imperialism securely in the past, and/or by suggesting a continuous line from that past to our present.
>
> (Spivak, 1999: 1)

Coloniality is thus metamorphic, which implies that contemporary forms of neo-colonialism take different shapes, their techniques being embedded in a neoliberal reason of decentred power and modes of capitalist commodity chains that constitute a different problem-space than what pertained in nineteenth- and early twentieth-century colonialism. National decolonization and independence cannot be offered as responses to present conditions of coloniality, since the nature of the problem has altered (cf. Scott, 2004). As we have seen, too, austerity is today one of the dispositions of power that maintains inequalities established by 'the colonial divide'.

Colonial wounds are, as Walter Mignolo and René Vásques (Mignolo, 2009a; Mignolo and Vásques, 2013) have pointed out, 'historically true and still open in the everyday experience of most people on the planet'. The colonial wound is open insofar as Europe has yet to recognize and confront its colonial past on a general level. In Rebecca Comay's words: '[t]he occlusion of the traumatic past cuts off any relation to a radically (perhaps catastrophically) different future' (Comay, 2005). Without this confrontation with the past, the circle of colonialism – however metamorphic – will continue to repeat itself. The wound cuts through Europe (and the world) and this is what Mignolo refers to as 'the colonial divide' and Madina Tlostanova, following Mignolo, as 'the imperial-colonial divide' (Tlostanova, 2005).

The colonial divide can be studied as pure mathematics. It manifests itself among those who occupy the wrong side of the divide as lower life expectancy, lower income, precarious work life, inferior health, increased likelihood to be subjected to racial profiling, police harassment and lethal police violence, under-representation in cultural, political and educational institutions, and religious discrimination. For those on the other side, the descendants of the colonizers, it manifests itself as higher pay, higher employment rate, better health and access to health care, representation in most contexts, recognition of the self by all significant institutions, from cultural heritage to the political, and, above all, in the notion that these achievements are explained with reference to individualism and meritocracy.

The racial separation between colonizer and colonized, as one of the corner-stones within the coloniality of power (Quijano, 2000: 534), may be said to have resulted in a necropower where some humans are seen as disposable, and whose dead bodies are ungrievable (Mbembe, 2003; Butler, 2009; see also the discussion of 'dispensible lives' in Mignolo, 2009b, as well as the concept of 'bare life' in Agamben, 1998). As Guénif-Souilamas discusses in her text, this colonial divide is now being transferred to migrants and refugees in Europe. Let us illustrate the situation by a statement made by a 13-year-old girl, Sophia Adamp-our, on the chat line of Norway's public broadcasting network a few days after Anders Behring Breivik's terrorist assault on 22 July 2011, which killed 77 people, among them 69 young social democratic activists massacred by Breivik at a summer camp.

This is what Sophia Adampour wrote:

> Hi. I am 13 years old and Norwegian Muslim. I feel that I am to be blamed. He says that he killed everyone because I am here. Should I move out to protect Norwegian children in the future? This is what I feel. Regards, Sophia.
>
> (For discussion, see Strand, 2015: 181–6)

The statement caused commotion and confusion. On 4 August 2011, Sophia Adampour was interviewed in a talk show on national television. Asked what she was thinking when writing, she answered: 'I have learned, through my upbringing and the fact of being Norwegian and Muslim and Iranian that we should care for each other and protect each other no matter background or orientation … hmm … yes … and appearance' (quoted in Strand, 2015: 182).

We can see Sophia Adampour's statement as a cipher of Norwegian, European and global history in the making. She takes it upon herself to absolve Norway of the fascist crimes committed by its native son. A case of internalized racism, the victim resolves the problem of racist exclusion in Norway by excluding herself and moving out, thus fulfilling the racist programme. At the same time, however, Sophia speaks in the name of a coming community: 'Norwegian and Muslim and Iranian'. She thus consolidates the creolized subject position whose possibility she at the same time denies. Moreover, while she obviously represents the civic virtues – caring for others, protecting the children – endorsed by Western civilization, she also implies that there is no place for citizens like her in this civilization. Sophia Adampour thus at once inscribes and erases, at once includes and excludes, the multicultural subject of Europe and the West.

If we could decode the lesson of this statement, we would perhaps be able to see what, exactly, the object lesson of austere history is. Caught in a double bind, Sophia Adampour shows Norway's and Europe's future as split between irreconcilable alternatives, and she incarnates the origin of both, in the sense that her disappearance founds a history of Norway as white, Christian and proto-fascist, whereas her presence founds a global history of Norway as multicultural. The problem, of course, is that she also conveys the unsettling sense that both alternatives are impossible.

As mentioned, the imperial-colonial divide not only divides human beings but also implies a temporal rupture between a colonial past and a globalized present. As Lars Jensen and Elsa Peralta discuss in their chapter, the appreciation of the colonial past may even work as a lubricator for international affairs. This temporal and human divide works in such a way that coloniality is displaced to what is outside, alien and foreign – to what is not of concern – to the European, while at the same time historical agency remains tied to the central 'I' of the 'European', who thus can continue to place colonialism 'overseas'. This 'denial of coevalness' (Fabian, 1983) relieves contemporary Europeans from any sense of complicity. The resources, minerals, land and lives that were stolen and which financed European modernity are also part of the past. The debt, which was never recognized as a theft or a debt in the first place, is forever written off.

How, then, to avert the austere futurity that forces Sophia Adampour to take on the responsibility for her future executioners? There are counter movements – efforts to unsettle a settled past are being made despite austere regimes of historiography. They include not only the academic interventions mentioned earlier, but also initiatives from below.

One example is the Rhodes Must Fall campaign, which started off at Cape Town University in South Africa in March 2015. Students demanded the removal of a statue which commemorated Cecil John Rhodes, and pointed out the very linkage – white supremacy – between racial discrimination today and imperialism and colonialism in the past. Subsequently, the movement spread to other South African universities, as did the call for a decolonization of the university. This movement also made its way to Rhodes' native country, to the universities of Edinburgh and Oxford, including the call to decolonize the university. Part of this was also the question 'Why is my curriculum white?', which interrogated the perpetuation of a white, Western canon, despite the university being a multicultural space, tangent to what Robbie Shilliam discusses in his contribution to this volume.

In Cape Town, the Rhodes statue was finally removed. At Oxford, however, the Oriel College decided in January 2016 that neither the Rhodes statue in question, nor a commemorative plaque, would be removed, contrary to what it previously had stated. Major private donations to the college had been withdrawn, due to Rhodes Must Fall's demands, which gave the college cold feet (Srinivasan, 2016). As we see, the linkage between capital and coloniality is still vivid, and in austere times, interests of private donators weigh more heavily than those of any protesting student.

Yet, how shall Europe deal with the vast amount of memorials that from a national point of view commemorate 'Great Men' (and less so women), but who, given Europe's imperial and colonial past, often concurrently, risk praising the darker side of modernity: slave trade, colonialism, theft, apartheid, murder, torture and genocide. The historian David Olosuga suggests that instead of removing statues of Rhodes and his like, such memorials should be contextualized and branded 'with the truth about who these men really were' (Olosuga, 2016).

Europe stops short in the face of these colonial heritage institutions, memorials or statues: once aimed at displaying the greatness of the empires, today embarrassing evidences (and museum objects are sometimes referred to as precisely 'evidence') of this colonial past, leaving a double function of civilization as barbarism. Today we can register a variety of anxious responses to this 'crisis'. One response has been to remould former ethnographic museums into museums of 'world culture' (that is, the world outside Europe and 'the West'), where contextualization, which Olosuga asks for above, has been one of the strategies. In other cases – as Nicolas Bancel and Pascal Blanchard, and Esther Captain extricate in their respective contributions – management of the colonial heritage has resulted in colonial melancholia or nostalgia, and has counteracted any ambition of 'displaying' coloniality as living history.

Another response is of course to just shut down such institutions, as in the Dutch case explored by Captain. In such cases policies of austerity and budget cutbacks may serve as a welcome excuse to resolve the colonial question by doing away with whatever documentation and knowledge there exists on the subject, which then also has the 'benefit' of averting economic and political risks to which the Netherlands may be exposed because of the country's wounded attachments to coloniality. Still another response is the demand to decolonize or dis-collect and empty museums and archives.[4] Whereas such a response can be understood as a reparative move away from colonial complicity, it also runs the risk of delinking Europe from its imperial past. In some places, such as the Museum of World Culture in Gothenburg, the bulk of the collections are simply kept in storage, as though pending the historiographical decision that will determine the future role of the objects, something which 'creates a sense of a prevailing mausoleum in the storage room' (Muñoz, 2011).

The problem is that these museums – be they called ethnographic museums, museums of world culture, 'Far Eastern antiquities', 'Africa galleries' or the like – continues to place the rest of the world outside of Europe, whereas in fact the two are irreversibly connected. In this volume, Gurminder Bhambra offers an alternative to the austere historiography in her development of Sanjay Subrahmanyam's concept of 'connected histories' as 'connected sociology'. Subrahmanyam argues that we need a 'geographical redefinition' in order not to repeat a fixed idea of where the centre always was and where history always was written: in Europe (Subrahmanyam, 1997: 761). The idea of connectedness also becomes a means to dig into concurrent historical layers of connections, commonalities and affinities that we have been blind to because of a tendency, which seems inherent in methodological nationalism, to emphasize difference. His approach allows for the narration of the very porosity of history. Bhambra therefore argues that 'connected sociologies [...] recognizes a plurality of possible interpretations and selections of historical accounts, not as a "description", but as an opportunity for reconsidering what we previously thought we had known' (Bhambra in this volume, p. 30).

An alternative perspective is what Mignolo and Vásques (2013; see also Mignolo, 2009b) propose in terms of a shift from a Eurocentric *aesthetics* that emanates from colonial reason to what they call 'decolonial *aestheSis*', which stems 'from an embodied consciousness of the colonial wound and moves towards healing'. In this view, decoloniality counteracts by unveiling the wound of coloniality/modernity: it 'makes the wound visible, tangible; it voices the scream. And at the same time decolonial aesthesis moves towards the healing, the recognition, the dignity of those aesthetic practices that have been written out of the canon of modern aesthetics' (Mignolo and Vásques, 2013). In order for the wound to be healed, it needs to be exposed.

The notion of decolonial aesthesis invites us not only to turn to other ideals (or rather to reject ideals), practices and genealogies of thought, but also to decentre the centre. As Robbie Shilliam explains in his chapter, to read a canonized text in a canonized context will maintain status quo, but to read it against a marginalized context may begin to, as we mentioned above, shift the weight of our interpretations of history away from traditional hierarchies of power and meaning.

As Susan Buck-Morss has argued, this shift in practice, which exposes the wound that for so long has been suspended, can be summed up by attending to a sometimes overlooked meaning of Hegel's concept of *Aufhebung*, usually translated as 'sublation'. The term means 'to cancel' or 'negate' something, as well as to 'raise' something to a higher level, but Buck-Morss seizes its third meaning: it is an 'expression for "to keep, to save", as in saving a material trace, a memento of the past' (Buck-Morss, 2010: 72). A decolonization of Hegel, as well as his successors and interpreters, would thus enable us to see how uses of the past that 'cancel' coloniality and seek to 'raise' history to another level – as in the different examples of austere histories analysed in this volume – refuse to see how colonialism transformed Europe, and how it is therefore *preserved inside Europe*.

When Europe colonized the world, it simultaneously infected itself with its wound. This is what Aimé Césaire pointed out when he stated that colonization dehumanized both 'the indigene' and 'the civilized'. When the latter viewed and treated the former as 'the beast' (*la bête*), he himself became a beast. The past as an unhealed wound – although shared as a connected or universal history – remains divisive. Yet, it is in the very recognition of the wounding that the healing – as reparation, reconciliation and redemption – may start. Such an approach would open up another path into the future, releasing history and letting it revolt against those forces that in every instance wish to declare its end.

Notes

1 The Coloniality/Modernity/Decoloniality project has been developed by first and foremost Latin American scholars and thinkers, with the focus on the Spanish colonization of the Americas. It could, however, be argued that another starting point to Coloniality/Modernity would be the year of 1415, and the Portuguese seizure of Ceuta, which allows us to see that Africa was part and parcel of the Coloniality/Modernity project from its very beginning.

2 We use the term 'historical grammar' here as a metaphor for the way in which Eurocentric historiography has viewed and interpreted ideas and influences as causes and effects always coming from the North trickling down to the South, or, when coming from the South, as coming to full potential in the North.

3 To the examples given by Bancel and Blanchard, and Bhambra we add David Cameron's declaration when visiting India in 2013 that

> I think there is an enormous amount to be proud of in what the British Empire did and was responsible for. But of course there were bad events as well as good events. The bad events we should learn from and the good events we should celebrate. [...] In terms of our relationship with India is our past a help or a handicap? I would say, net-net, it is a help, because of the shared history, culture, and the things we share and the contributions that Indians talk about that we have made.
>
> (*Guardian*, 2013)

4 We are here discussing decolonizing initiatives from museum staff, and not legitimate repatriation claims which continuously are being declined by big institutions such as the British Museum, the Louvre, the Neues Museum in Berlin and Sweden's National Museums of World Culture.

Bibliography

Agamben, G. (1998) *Homo Sacer: Sovereign Power and Bare Life*. Stanford: Stanford University Press.

Arendt, H. (1958/1998) *The Human Condition*, 2nd edition. Chicago: University of Chicago Press.

Benjamin, W. (1937/1975) 'Eduard Fuchs: Collector and Historian'. Transl. Knut Tarnowski, *New German Critique*, 5 (Spring), pp. 27–58.

Buck-Morss, S. (2009) *Hegel, Haiti and Universal History*. Pittsburgh: Pittsburgh University Press.

Buck-Morss, S. (2010) 'The Second Time as Farce … Historical Pragmatics and the Untimely Present'. In: Douzinas, C. and Žižek, S. (eds), *The Idea of Communism*. London: Verso, pp. 67–80.

Butler, J. (2009) *Frames of War: When is Life Grievable*. London: Verso.

Comay, R. (2005) 'The Sickness of Tradition'. In: Benjamin, A. (ed.), *Walter Benjamin and History*. London: Continuum.

Comay, R. (2011) *Mourning Sickness: Hegel and the French Revolution*. Stanford, CA: Stanford University Press.

Dussel, E. (1993) 'Eurocentrism and Modernity (Introduction to the Frankfurt Lectures)'. *Boundary 2*, 20 (3), pp. 65–76.

Fabian, J. (1983) *Time and the Other: How Anthropology Makes its Object*. New York: Columbia University Press.

Guardian (2013) 'David Cameron defends lack of apology for British massacre at Amritsar'.

Available at: www.theguardian.com/politics/2013/feb/20/david-cameron-amritsar-massacre-india [accessed 16 March 2016].

Hegel, G.W.F. (1977/2004) *Phenomenology of Spirit*. Oxford: Oxford University Press.

Hofmeyr, I. (2004) *The Portable Bunyan: A Transnational History of The Pilgrim's Progress*. Princeton: Princeton University Press.

Kraal, K., Roosblad, J. and Wrench, J. (2009) *Equal Opportunities and Ethnic Inequality in European Labour Markets: Discrimination, Gender and Policies of Diversity*. Amsterdam: Amsterdam University Press. Available at http://imiscoe.org/docman-books/381-kraal-et-al-2009/file [accessed 20 March 2016].

Linebaugh, P. and Rediker, M. (2000) *The Many-Headed Hydra: Sailors, Slaves, Sommoners, and the Hidden History of the Revolutionary Atlantic*. Boston: Beacon Press.

Mbembe, A. (2003) 'Necropolitics'. *Public Culture*, 15 (1), pp. 11–40.

Mignolo, W. (2009a) 'Epistemic Disobedience, Independent Thought and De-Colonial Freedom'. *Theory, Culture & Society*, 26 (7–8), pp. 1–23.

Mignolo, W. (2009b) 'Dispensable and Bare Lives: Coloniality and the Hidden Political/Economic Agenda of Modernity'. *Human Architecture: Journal of the Sociology of Self-Knowledge*, 7 (2), Spring, pp. 69–88.

Mignolo, W. (2011) *The Darker Side of Western Modernity: Global Futures, Decolonial Options*. Durham: Duke University Press.

Mignolo, W. and Vásquez, R. (2013) 'Decolonial AestheSis: Colonial Wounds/Decolonial Healings', *Social Text*. Blogpost, 15 July. Available at: http://socialtextjournal.org/periscope_article/decolonial-aesthesis-colonial-woundsdecolonial-healings/ [accessed 25 February 2016].

Muñoz, A. (2011) *From Curiosa to World Culture: The History of the Latin American Collections at the Museum of World Culture in Sweden*. Doctoral dissertation in Archaeology. Gothenburg: University of Gothenburg.

Nuttall, S. (2009). *Entanglement: Literary and Cultural Reflections on Post Apartheid*. Johannesburg: Wits University Press.

Olosuga, D. (2016) 'Topple the Cecil Rhodes statue? Better to rebrand him a war criminal'. *Guardian*, 7 January. Available at: www.theguardian.com/commentisfree/2016/jan/07/cecil-rhodes-statue-war-criminal-rhodes-must-fall [accessed 5 July 2016].

Open Society Foundations (2014) *A Report on Six European Union Cities: Europe's White Working Class Communities*. Available at: www.opensocietyfoundations.org/sites/default/files/white-working-class-overview-20140616.pdf [accessed 20 March 2016].

Quijano, A. (2000) 'Coloniality of Power, Eurocentrism, and Latin America'. *Nepantla: Views from South*, 1 (3), pp. 533–80.

Runnymede Trust (2009) *Who Cares About the White Working Class?* Available at: www.runnymedetrust.org/uploads/publications/pdfs/WhoCaresAboutTheWhiteWorkingClass-2009.pdf [accessed 20 March 2016].

Scott, D. (2004) *Conscripts of Modernity. The Tragedy of Colonial Enlightenment*. Durham: Duke University Press.

Scott, D. (2014) *Omens of Adversity: Tragedy, Time, Justice, Memory*. Durham: Duke University Press.

Shareef, A.A.M. (2005) *The Islamic Slave Revolts of Bahia, Brazil: A Continuity of the 19th Century Jihaad Movements of Western Sudan*. Paper. Pittsburg: Institute of Islamic-African Studies International.

Shilliam, R. (2015) *The Black Pacific: Anticolonial Struggles and Oceanic Connections*. London: Bloomsbury Academic Press.

Spivak, G.C. (1999) *A Critique of Postcolonial Reason: Toward a History of the Vanishing Present*. Cambridge, MA: Harvard University Press.

Spivak, G.C. (2004) 'Righting Wrongs'. *South Atlantic Quarterly*, 103 (2/3), Spring/Summer, pp. 523–81.

Srinivasan, A. (2016) 'Under Rhodes'. *London Review of Books*, 38 (7), March, p. 32.

Strand, T. (2015) 'Thinking Democracy and Education for the Present: The Case of Norway after July 22, 2011'. In: Jezierska, K. and Koczanowicz, L. (eds), *Democracy in Dialogue, Dialogue in Democracy: The Politics of Dialogue in Theory and Practice*. Farnham, Surrey: Ashgate, pp. 177–92.

Subrahmanyam, S. (1997) 'Connected Histories: Notes towards a Reconfiguration of Early Modern Eurasia'. *Modern Asian Studies*, 31 (3), pp. 735–62.

Tlostanova, M. (2005) *The Sublime of Globalization? Sketches on Transcultural Subjectivity and Aesthetics*. Moscow: URSS.

Index

2012 Ageing Report (EC) 139

Act of Union 1707 25
Adampour, Sophia 188
aesthesis 191
African-Americans, pathologization 94–5
African-Caribbean children, expectations of 95
African-Caribbean people: migration to UK 97; secondary education 93, 97–102
African-continental people: educational attainment 99; migration to UK 97; secondary education 93, 97–102, 103; social mobility 101–2
agency 76
Alexander, C. 23
Algerian war: commemoration 46–7; memory and remembrance 39; representations of 40
alienation, black students 106
alternative histories, possibilities for 182ff
Anderson, D. 26
Andersson, M. 152
anthropology, austere 186
anti-immigration measures 86–7
anti-Muslim hostility 154
anti-repentance 41–2
Arab boy 171–2
Arabs, racialization 168–9
Arton Capital 128
asiento de negros 62
asylum policy 137–8; *see also* migration policy
Aufhebung 191
austere anthropology 186
austere community 12
austere curricula: black students and deficit creation 97–103; chapter overview 10–11; context and overview 92–3;

decontextualization and compliance 105; deficit model 93–7; focus group 105–6; racialization 103–6; racialized exclusions 105; secondary education 93, 97–102, 103; summary and conclusions 106–7
austere governance, features of 8
austere historiography: as concept 3; what is at stake 14–15
austerity: acceptance of 185–6; disciplinary force 152; meaning of 1; racialization 92
austerity regime, compliance with 76
Avramopoulos, D. 138

Balkenende, J.-P. 67
Barcellini, S. 39
Barker, A. 144
Benjamin, W. 175, 184, 185
Biblioteca Alexandrina 66
birthright citizenship 118–19
black heritages 105
black identity 43
Black Power 94, 95
black students: decontextualization 105; experiences of exclusion 105–6; at universities 99–103; *see also* African-Caribbean people; African-continental people
blackness, pathologization of 103
blame 2–3, 188–9
Bloembergen, M. 71
Blyth, M. 1, 6, 7–8
Boliver, V. 100
border control 137–9, 140
borders 33, 76
Bouchareb, R. 40
Boulahcen, Hasna Ait 174–5
Bourdieu, P. 93

Braidotti, R. 60
Bramall, R. 7
branding, Treaty of Utrecht 63
Braudel, F. 28–9
Bărbulescu, R. 128
Brexit 135
Britain's Racist Election (Channel 4) 32
British Empire 23, 26, 31
British Nationality Act 1948 22
Brown v. *Board of Education* 94
Brubaker, R. 123; on citizenship 117–18
Buck-Morss, S. 184, 191
budgets, and migration policy 151–3
Buisson, P. 44
Burke, E. 24
Butler, J. 178–9

Calais 'jungle' 167
Cameron, D. 22, 192n3
Césaire, A. 191
Ceuta 137–8
chapter overviews: cases 8–11;
    conjunctures 12–13
Charlie Hebdo 175
Chirac, J. 47
circular migration 146–9
citizenship: aims of economic programmes
    125–6; and austerity measures 126;
    birthright 118–19; and circular
    migration 146–9; commodification 123,
    125–7, 130; context and overview 115;
    criticism of economic programmes 126;
    Dominica 124; double function 117–18;
    double standard 128–30; effects of
    economic crisis 124–5; as entail 119,
    123–8; feminist perspective 117; and
    French Revolution 117; functions of
    122; global perspectives 117–23; and
    inequality 119–22, 130;
    institutionalization 115, 116; as
    insurance 128; intergenerational transfer
    118–19; by investment 123–30, 131n4;
    as means of exclusion 117–23; as means
    of inclusion 115–17; nation-state
    perspectives 115–17; postcolonial 30–1,
    68–9, 122; poverty migration 128–30;
    premium 126–7; principle of allocation
    117–18; and racial classification 125;
    and residence planning 127; restrained
    equality 163; Saint Kitts and Nevis
    123–4; as social closure 117–18;
    summary and conclusions 130; threat
    scenario 129; world-systemic
    perspective 119–22

*Citizenship and Nationhood in France and
    Germany* (Brubaker) 117
civilizing mission 14–15, 43, 49
clash of civilizations 177–8
Coard, B. 95
collaborative resistance 76–7
collective memory: and crisis of identity
    68–70; French colonialism 50;
    multidirectional 3–4; survival of 38
Cologne assaults 173–4
colonial aphasia 41, 52, 67
colonial crimes, expiration 187
colonial debt 189
colonial divide 186, 187–9
colonial history: and genealogy 53;
    positioning writings 182–3; scholarship
    182–3; visibility of 52
colonial memories 14; conflicting
    socializations 41–3; as divisive 40;
    museum projects 48–50; and social
    exclusion 5–15
colonial modernity 82
colonial past: debate 46–7; issues of
    39–40; manifestation of 176, 178; media
    representations 52–3; representations of
    70–1; responsibility for 186–7
colonial space 75
colonialism: civilizing mission 43; denial
    and acceptance 33; Denmark 75–6,
    82–5; England and Scotland 25; erasure
    of Dutch archive 66; legitimation of 84;
    nostalgia for 45–8; Portugal 75–6, 83–5;
    positive values 49–50; recognition of
    183; reminders of 69–70; and restrained
    equality 164; speaking of 67–8; Sweden
    11
coloniality: modernity as 183; of power
    123, 188; presence of 183
colonization: heirs to French 38; as
    infection 191; by Netherlands 59–60
Comay, R. 184, 187
commemoration: Algerian war 46–7;
    critical 47–8; Empire builders 47;
    functions of 41; nostalgia 45–6; post-
    colonial period 47; of Vichy 41; of
    victims 54n8; of wars 38–40
commemorative culture, of empire 85
commodification, citizenship 123, 125–7,
    130
compensation, slave-owners 28
complacency, about slavery 27–8
comprehensive approach to migration 140
Comtean positivism 51
connected histories 22, 190–1

connected sociologies 30, 190–1
conservatism, universities 103–4
constitutional revision, Portugal 83
continental developmentalism 82
Coquery-Vidrovitch, C. 41–2
cosmopolitanism, in history 14
Coubel, L. 43
counterstrategies, global financial crisis 76
criminalization, of migration 128
cultural capital 93–4, 97, 98
cultural values, transfer of 94
Culture and Imperialism (Said) 4
culture of commemoration 38–9
Cyprus, citizenship 125, 126

Danish Cartoons 175
de Maizière. T. 146
debt 189; Greece 76
decolonial aesthesis 191
decolonial perspective 29–30
decolonization, Denmark and Portugal 84
deconstructivism 51
deficit model 10, 93–7; critical scholarship
    96–7; deficit creation 97–103;
    emergence in UK 95; good and bad
    immigrants 99; and race 94
dehumanization 191
Demie, F. 103
democracy: incomplete 161; unequal 165
democratic climate change 162–3
democratization, and race 104
demographic deficit 139–42; European
    Union 135, 136; refugee dividend
    149–50; refugees as demographic boost
    142–6
denial, of past 32
Denmark: as colonial power 75–6;
    colonialism 82–5; Gini coefficient 78;
    global financial crisis 77–8; migration
    83, 86–7; post-World War II 82
Denmark and Portugal study: anti-
    immigration measures 86–7; chapter
    overview 10; context and overview
    74–6; Danish colonialism 75–6;
    decolonization 84; economic crisis –
    Denmark 77–8; economic crisis –
    Portugal 78–81; effects of economic
    crisis 85–6; entry into EC 84–5; Expo
    '98 85; global restructuring 85–6;
    Portuguese colonialism 75–6;
    reimagining global nation 81–6;
    situating current crisis 76–7; summary
    and conclusions 87–8; tourism 85;
    transformation 82

Der Spiegel 129
diaspora, vs. immigrants 98
discipline, of austerity 152
discrimination, and remembrance 53
disinvestment, black students 106
disposition of power 8
diversity: cultural institutions 67;
    Netherlands 69
division, of history 68
domestic orientalism 74
Dominica, citizenship 124
double standard, citizenship 128–30
Draper, N. 28
Drayton, R. 26
Drieënhuizen, C. 70
Dutch Council of Churches, apology for
    slavery 63
Dutch East India Company 63, 67
Dutch–Indonesia relations, proposed study
    of 70
Dutch royal family, role and position 63–4
Dutch West Indies Company 59
Dzankic, J 131n4

economic austerity 6–8
economic crisis, funding for institutions 66
economic growth, and refugee-related
    spending 153
economic liberalization, European Union
    140–1
economic perspective, on austerity 2
education 92–3; about colonial past 42–3;
    aspiration and socio-economic
    background 99; attainment gaps 98;
    black community responses 96;
    compliance 105; critical scholarship
    96–7; decontextualization 105; deficit
    model 10, 93–7; exclusions 97;
    experiences of exclusion 105–6; and
    inequality 92; lack of cultural awareness
    97; London effect 98–9;
    multiculturalism in 92–3, 96; national
    values 53; politicization 104; racialized
    expectations 95; segregated 94;
    structural inequalities 98; structural
    transformations 103; *see also* austere
    curricula
elitism, universities 103–4
Elkins, C. 26
Elliott-Cooper, A. 25
emigration, Portugal 87
empire: commemorative culture 85;
    continuity of 30–1; narratives of 27, 38;
    significance of 30

Empire builders, commemoration 47
Empire (Paxman) 26–8
empires, construction of 26
Empires without Imperialism (Morefield)
    27
employment prospects, racialized
    differences 102
entail: of citizenship 123–8; citizenship as
    119
epochs, recognition and labelling 183
Equalities Act 2010 103
Erdogan, T. 144
ethnic discrimination, responsibility for
    2–3
ethnic homogeneity 163
EU Action Plan on Return 145–6
EU Seasonal Workers Directive (Dir.
    2014/36/EU) 148
eugenics 95
EUNAVFOR MED 143
Euramerica 179
eurocentrism 183
Europe: acquisition of mineral resources
    29; power asymmetry 76; refugee crisis
    33; relation with rest of world 28–9;
    self-recognition 11; self-representation
    182
European Community, Danish and
    Portuguese entry 84–5
European Economic and Social Committee
    142
European Economic Community, basis of
    32–3
European modernities 75
European Union: asylum policy 137–8;
    attitude to migration 128–30; border
    control 137–9, 140; borders 33; colonial
    past 32–3; contradictions of migration
    136; crises 135; demographic deficit
    135, 136, 139–42; economic
    liberalization 140–1; external labour
    migration (ELM) 139–40, 142–3,
    146–8; free movement 135; illegal
    immigration 141; migration crises 135;
    response to global financial crisis 80;
    visa-free travel 127
European Union military operation in the
    Southern Central Mediterranean 143
Europeanness 74–5
exclusion 2–3; through citizenship
    117–23
Expo '98 85
external labour migration (ELM) 139–40,
    142–3, 146–8

Fabian, J. 189
Falaize, B. 43
Faulques, R. 44
feminist perspective, on citizenship 117
Ferguson, N. 25
financial sector, and political power 7
fiscal conservatism 6–8
fiscal irresponsibility 154–5
Folch, A. 40
foreign relations, Netherlands 59
Foucault, M. 8, 162
France study: attitudes of right wing 42;
    black identity 43; chapter overview 9;
    Chirac period 47; colonial memories
    39–40; commemoration of victims 54n8;
    competition within right wing 43–4;
    context and overview 38–40; critical
    commemoration and remembrance 47–8;
    debate of colonial past 46–7;
    discrimination 53; education about
    colonial past 42–3; functions of
    commemoration 41; Maison de l'histoire
    de France 51–2; Marseilles museum
    project 49–50; media and writers 44;
    media representations 52–3; memorials
    48–50; memories and remembrance
    38–40; memory and remembrance 38–9;
    monuments 48–50; museum projects
    48–50; national pride 51–2; nostalgia
    45–8; October 1961 massacre 43–5;
    perceptions of immigration 50;
    perspectives represented 42; pilgrimage
    46; polarized memories 52–3; positivism
    51; postcolonial commemoration 47;
    rehabilitation of past 44–5; repentance
    and anti-repentance 41–2; repentant
    intellectuals 43; socializations of
    colonial memories 41–3; visibility of
    colonial history 52; xenophobia 42; *see
    also* restrained equality
Frederick, W. 70
free movement 135
freedom of speech 175, 177
French empire, heirs to 38
French History Museum 51–2
French Revolution, and citizenship 117
Freudian perspective, on austerity 1–2
future: expectations 184; material
    conditions for 185
futures 184–6

Gabriel, S. 152
gender: and inequality 122; *see also*
    restrained equality

genealogy, and colonial history 53
General Certificate of Secondary
  Education (GCSE) qualifications 98
genocide 29, 70
Germany: budget 151–2, 153;
  multiculturalism 21–2; need for
  immigrants 146; new solidarity project
  152; refugee dividend 149–50; shifting
  migration policy 150–2, 154
Gini coefficient: Denmark 78; international
  comparison 119–21
Global Approach to Migration and
  Mobility (GAMM) 147, 148
global financial crisis: contagion 79;
  counterstrategies 76; Denmark 77–8;
  effects on citizenship 124–5; EU
  response 80; narratives 77–8; and
  notions of austerity 74; origins 77,
  78–80; Portugal 78–81; reimagining
  global nation 81–6; situating 76–7
global nation, reimagining 81–6
global restructuring 85–6
global social mobility 121, 125
global stratification 123
Gove, M. 22
governmentality, racialized 162
Greece: citizenship 125; debt 76
Greenland 82–3, 84, 86
Griotteray, A. 44
guilt 188–9

Hall, C. 28
Hall, S. 171
Hansen, P. 32–3
Hasenbalg, C. 125
Hassel, A. 154
healing, as erasure 184
Hegel, G. W. F. 184, 191
hegemonic history 183, 184
Henley&Partners 127–8
heritages, black/white 105
heritagization 41
heteronormativity 171–2
higher education *see* austere curricula;
  tertiary education
Higher Education Funding Council for
  England (HEFCE): expectations 103–4;
  report 101
historical consciousness 3–4
historiography: hegemonic 183, 184;
  relationship with austerity 5–6; role of
  identity 5
historiography of austerity, defining 5
history: cosmopolitanism in 14; division of

68; dominant perspectives 4–5; as
  inheritance 187; nationalism in 14;
  plurality 30; positivism 51;
  representation of 4; review of UK
  national curriculum 22–3; teaching of
  40; victims of 39; weaving analogy 184;
  from winners' perspective 29; wounded
  186–91
Holmwood, J. 92, 97
homogeneity, cultural 21
How Europe Underdeveloped Africa
  (Rodney) 28
human rights 33–4n3; *see also* rights
Hungary: border control 138; citizenship
  124–5

Iceland, financial crisis 77
identity: assigned 166; black 43; and
  collective memory 68–70;
  commodification 82; as disciplinary
  1–2; Europeanness 74–5; in
  historiography 5
ideological power 7
ideology, of austerity 6–8
illegal immigration, responses to 141
immigrants, vs. diaspora 98
immigration: perceived effects 24–5, 32;
  perceptions of 50; restriction of 69
imperial nostalgia 10
imperial-colonial divide 187–9
imperialism 25; Anglo-American
  scholarship 27, 28; pride in 66–7
indentured labour 28
Indigènes de la République 41
inequality: and citizenship 119–22, 130;
  Denmark 78; and education 92; factors
  in 122; and global social mobility 121;
  racialized 92
inequality equilibria 120
inheritance: of citizenship 118–19; history
  as 187
Institute of Present Day History (Institut
  d'histoire du temps présent, IHTP) 39
institutional habitus 104
integration, fear of 94–5
International Monetary Fund (IMF) 153–4
investment, for citizenship 123–30, 131n4
Islam: attitudes towards 169;
  representations of 69

Johansson, M. 146
John, G. 96
Johnson, L. 94
Jones, G. 67

Jonsson, S. 32–3
Joseph Rowntree Foundation 99
Juncker, J.-C. 144
jus pecuniae 125
jus sanguinis 118, 125
jus soli 118, 125

Kanther, M. 137
Keynesian economics 153
Korzeniewicz, R.P., on citizenship
   119–22
Koser, K. 150, 151
Kurdish refugees 137

labour market integration 153–4
labour migration 139–42, 143; austere
   rights regime 149; management of
   146–7; seasonal workers 148
Lacan, J. 2
Lavisse, E. 51
Le Pen, J.-M. 41
Lefeuvre, D. 49
Legacies of British Slave Ownership
   project 28
legacy of racism 66–7
Legêne, S. 65, 68
legitimation, of colonialism 84
Lellouche, P. 129
Lemoine, H. 51–2
Limpach, R. 70
Lisbon Strategy 139
Löfven, S. 146
London effect 98–9
Los Angeles Times 150
Lugan, B. 44

McNeill, W. 29
Madrick, J. 7
Maison de l'histoire de France 51–2
Malmström, C. 142–3, 149
Malta, citizenship 126, 127–8
Manceron, G. 41–2
Marche des Beurs movement 43
market rationality 79
Marseilles, J. 40
Marseilles museum project 49–50
Marshall, H. 23
Marshall, T.H., on citizenship 116
Mbembe, A. 179
media and writers, France 44
mediation: austerity–economy and culture
   7; historiography–austerity 6
melancholia 92; *see also* nostalgia
Melilla 137–8

memorials, contextualization and branding
   190
memories: colonial and postcolonial 14;
   official 47; polarized 52–3
memory and remembrance, obliteration of
   185
memory war 40
Merkel, A. 21–2, 150, 153
metamorphism 187
middle class, development of 185
Mignolo, W. 123, 187, 191
migrant camps 167
migrants: access to benefits 24; speaking
   of experiences 67–8
migration: contradictory attitudes 136;
   criminalization 128; defining by wealth/
   class 123, 128–30; Denmark 83, 86–7;
   global social mobility 121; illegal
   immigration 141; political/media focus
   135; Portugal 86–7; postcolonial 92, 97;
   threat scenario 129
Migration Advisory Committee (UK) 141
migration policy: austere rights regime
   149; and austerity 151–5; border control
   137–9; budgetary responses 151–3;
   circular migration 146–9; compatibility
   of policies 147–8; comprehensive
   approach 140; context and overview
   135–6; and demographic crisis 139–42;
   EU Action Plan on Return 145–6;
   external labour migration (ELM)
   139–40, 142–3, 146–8; labour market
   integration 153–4; maximalist labour
   migration 139–42; militarization 143;
   minimalist refugee migration 136–9;
   need for immigrants 146; North Africa
   focus 147; policy shifts 141–2, 150–2,
   154; popular engagement 151; public
   spending and investment 154; refugee
   crisis as opportunity 154; refugee
   dividend 149, 152–3; refugee-related
   spending 153; refugees as demographic
   boost 142–6; returns policy 145–6; role
   of business 149–50; role of Turkey
   144–5; safe countries 144–5; security
   focus 147–8; summary and conclusions
   155; unwelcoming 177–8; zero
   migration policy 140
Million+ Group 100
Mills, C.W. 162
mineral resources, European acquisition of
   29
missionaries 27
modernities 75; colonial 82

modernity, as coloniality 183
modernity/coloniality 123
Modest, W. 65
Mogherini, F. 143
Moldova, migration and citizenship 129
Montagnon, P. 44
Montenegro, citizenship 126
monuments 39–40; nostalgia 45–6;
    perspective 42
moral economy 176
moral panics 173–4
morality play analogy 1
Moran, T.P., on citizenship 119–22
Morefield, J. 27
Moynihan report 94
Muelle, R. 44
multiculturalism: challenge to traditional
    canon 104; disavowal of 21–5, 92; in
    education 92–3, 96; secondary education
    103; and understanding of contemporary
    state 32
multidirectionality, collective memory 3–4
museum practices, and colonial memory
    38
museum projects, perspective 42
museums: colonial memories 48–50;
    Marseilles project 49–50; problems and
    solutions 190–1
Muslims: racialization 168–9;
    sexualization 169

narratives of empire 27, 38
national identity, Netherlands 68
National Institute for the Study of Dutch
    Slavery and its Legacy (NiNSee) 64, 65
national narrative 38, 50, 51, 177
national space 75
national values, teaching of 53
nationalism 42, 51–2, 163; and deficit
    model 95; in history 14
nationality, Portugal 89n8
neoliberal perspective, on austerity 2
neoliberalism 82; counterstrategies 76; as
    end of history 185
Netherlands: colonization 59; diversity 69;
    foreign relations 59; immigration policy
    69; political consensus 69
Netherlands–Indonesia war 69–70
Netherlands study: chapter overview 9;
    collective memory and crisis of identity
    68–70; commemoration of slavery 63–4;
    context and overview 59–60; diversity
    67; division of history 68; Dutch–
    Indonesia relations 70; effect of loss of

colonies 68; erasure of colonial archive
    66; forgetting 66–8; funding for
    institutions 64, 65, 66; institution
    closures and cuts 65–6; legacy of racism
    66–7; national identity 68; postcolonial
    citizenship 68–9; postcolonial
    institutions 63–8; pride in imperialism
    66–7; reminders of colonialism 69–70;
    representations of colonial past 70–1;
    role and position of royal family 63–4;
    Royal Tropical Institute, Amsterdam
    65–6; sociopolitical context 64;
    speaking of colonialism 67–8; summary
    and conclusions 70–1; Treaty of Utrecht
    60–3
new solidarity project 152
Nietzsche, F. 3
nihilism 187
Nimako, K. 68
nineteenth century, representation of 183
No Child Left Behind 96–7
Northern Europe, conceptualization 74–5
nostalgia 40; for colonial Algeria 45–8;
    expression of 45–6; imperial 10; *see
    also* melancholia

Oakeshott, M. 104, 105
Occidentalism, perspective on citizenship
    121
October 1961 massacre (France) 43–5
Offenstadt, N. 42
Oostindie, G. 68
Operation Sophia 143
orientalism 175, 178; domestic 74
orientalization, Northern Europe 74
others: ambivalent space 82; fear/hatred of
    69; scapegoating 185–6
Ould-Aoudia, J.-P. 45
Our Island Story (Marshall) 23
Outside the Law (Bouchareb) 40
Oxfam 130

Parsons, T., on citizenship 116–17
partiality, 184
Pateman, C. 162
pathologization: African-Americans 94–5;
    of blackness 103
Pax Britannica 25–6
Paxman, J. 25, 26–8
Pearcey, J, 24
Pellisier, P. 44
Pettman, J.J. 117
'*Pieds-noirs*, a French Wound' 40
PIGS/PIIGS 74

Piketty, T. 153
pilgrimage 46
pluralities, of futures 184–5
Podemos 76
polarization, of memories 52–3
police harassment and violence 167–8
Policy Plan on Legal Migration (EC) 139,
    142
politicization, of education 104
politics of fear 178–9
Portugal: anti-austerity protest 80–1; as
    colonial power 75–6; colonialism 83–5;
    constitutional revision 83; emigration
    87; fragile position in Europe 83–4;
    global financial crisis 78–81;
    legitimation of colonialism 84;
    migration 86–7; nationality 89n8; *see
    also* Denmark and Portugal study
positivism 51
postcolonial citizenship 122
postcolonial institutions, Netherlands study
    63–8
postcolonial memories 14
postcolonial perspective 29–30
postcolonial theory 4
poverty migration 128–30
poverty, responsibility for 2–3
power: coloniality of 188; disposition of 8;
    ideological 7; political and financial 7
power asymmetry, Europe 76
precarization 2
premium, citizenship 126–7
proletariat, forgetting 185
protest, Portugal 80–1
psychoanalytic perspective 1–2
public policies, shift in 163–4
public spending and investment 154
purity 184; ethnic and cultural 21

Que se Lixe a Troika (To Hell with the
    Troika) 80–1
Quijano, A. 123, 188

race: articulation of 168–9; and deficit
    model 94; and democratization 104; and
    employment prospects 102
Race Equality Charter 92–3
racial austerity 154
racial contract 162
racial profiling 128
racial separation, colonizers/colonized
    188
racialization: Arabs and Muslims 168–9;
    austere curricula 103–6; history of 92;

working class 186; *see also* restrained
    equality
racism: internalization 188–9; legacy of
    66–7; virtuous 168, 170–2
radicalization 53
re-orientalization 175, 178–9
recognition, competition for 43
refugee crisis 33, 76, 135; as opportunity
    154
refugee dividend 149, 152–3
refugee Keynesianism 155
refugee-related spending 153
refugees 128–9, 130, 153–4; as
    demographic boost 142–6; minimalist
    migration 136–9; *see also* migration
    policy
relativism 51
remembrance: critical 47–8; and
    discrimination 53
repentance 41–2
Representative Council of Black
    Associations (CRAN) 41, 43, 53
research, compartmentalization 135–6
resistance, collaborative 76–7
restrained equality: analytical perspectives
    178; assigned identities 166; chapter
    overview 13; citizenship 163; context
    and overview 161; effects of 164;
    effects of colonialism 164; effects of
    regulation 164–5; freedom of speech
    175, 177; Hasna Ait Boulahcen 174–5;
    heteronormativity 171–2; hidden agenda
    162–4; homophobia 171–2;
    islamophobia 170; modes 164–5; moral
    panics 173–4; orientalism 175; policies
    164–5; public discourse 166;
    racialization of Arabs and Muslims
    168–9; re-orientalization 175, 178–9;
    repressive policies 163; rights as
    privileges 165–6, 177; role of police
    167–8; sexism 170–1; and sexuality
    170–2; source of effectiveness 164; state
    of terror 163, 166, 176–9; structural
    division 162–5; summary and
    conclusions 179; techniques 163;
    terrorism 174–6; value of lives 179;
    virtuous racism 170–2; welfare
    universalism 165; women's experiences
    168; *see also* France study
returns pilot policy, UK 23
returns policy 145–6
revisionism 14
Rhodes Must Fall campaign 189–90
right wing, France 42, 43–4

rights 33–4n3; exclusion from 186; loss of
  186; as privileges 165–6, 177, 186;
  winning 185
Rijksmuseum (Netherlands) 64–5, 70–1
Rodney, W. 28
Romania, citizenship 129
Ross, K. 82
Rothberg, M. 3
royal family, Netherlands 63–4
Royal Tropical Institute, Amsterdam 65–6
Ruhs, M. 141
Russell Group 100
Rutte, M. 64

safe countries 144–5
Said, E. 4, 175
Saint Kitts and Nevis, citizenship 123–4,
  126–7
Salafism 53
Sarkozy, N. 22, 40, 44, 45–6, 48, 51
scapegoating 21, 23–4, 185–6
Schäuble, W. 150, 151
Schengen zone 129
Schmitt, M. 44
scholarship, colonial history 182–3
schools, review of UK national curriculum
  22–3
Scott, D. 182
Scruton, R. 24–5
search-and-rescue 167
Searle, J. 104
seasonal workers 148
sexism 170–1
sexual contract 162
sexuality 170–2
Seymour, R. 1, 8
Shachar, A. 123, 130n2; on citizenship
  118–20, 121
Shane, J. 66
Shilliam, R. 8
Shoah 38–9
Sinclair-Webb, E. 144–5
slave-owners, compensation 28
slavery: Britain 27–8; commemoration
  63–4; Dutch Council of Churches
  apology 63; Europe 29; and global
  inequality 120; Treaty of Utrecht 62–3
Smethwick 1964 election 32
social class, and citizenship 123
social exclusion 2–3; and colonial
  memories 5–15
social mobility 101–2; global 121, 125
socio-economic background, and
  educational aspiration 99

Southern Europe, characterization of 76
space: ambivalent 82; national and colonial
  75
Spahn, J. 150
Spain: border control 137–8; mobilization
  76
Spivak, G. 173, 183, 187
state-multiculturalism 22
state of terror 163, 166; and politics of
  austerity 176–9; *see also* terrorism
status quo: challenges to 183–4;
  challenging 191
stereotypes 42
stigmatization 42
Stoler, A.L. 41, 67
stop-and-search 167
Stora, B. 41–2, 44–5, 52
Strand, S. 103
stratification, global 123
sublation 191
Subrahmanyam, S. 30, 190
supplementary schools project 96
surveillance 162, 163, 166, 168
Swann Report 95
Sweden: budget 152, 153; need for
  immigrants 146; refugee dividend
  149–50; representation and image 11;
  shifting migration policy 150–1, 154

Tahrir Square 173
Temple, R. 31
temporal dimensions, non-convergence
  182
temporal rupture 189
terrorism: gender, racism and religion
  174–6; responses to 166; *see also* state
  of terror
tertiary education: attainment differences
  100–1; employment prospects 102;
  multiculturalism 92–3; proportion of
  black students 99–100; student routes
  through 100; *see also* austere curricula
'The Colonial Legacy of the Treaty of
  Utrecht' 60, 61
The Economist 149
'The General Statistics of the British
  Empire' (Temple) 31
'The Work of Art in the Age of Mechanical
  Reproduction' (Benjamin) 175
them and us distinction 32
threat scenario, migration 129
Toulon, remembrance 45–6
*Traces of Slavery in Utrecht, A Walking
  Guide* 62

traditional canon 104
Treaty of Utrecht 60–3; city branding 63; slavery 62–3
Treaty of Utrecht Foundation 60, 61
Turkey, and EU migration policy 144–5
Turner, B., on citizenship 116–17
Tusk, D. 137

UK Independence Party (UKIP) 32; increasing support 23
UK national curriculum, review of 22–3
UN High-level Dialogue on International Migration and Development 147–8
unemployment, responsibility for 2–3
union, England and Scotland 25
United Kingdom: African-Caribbean migration 97; African-continental migration 97; illegal immigration 141; returns pilot policy 23; *see also* austere curricula
United Kingdom study: chapter overview 9–10; collective expression 25; context and overview 21; continuity of empire 30–1; denial of past 32; disavowal of multiculturalism 21–5; effects of empire 25–8; *Empire* (Paxman) 26–8; indentured labour 28; politics of austerity 21; postcolonial citizenship 30–1; slavery 27–8; understanding of contemporary state 32
United States 94–5
universities: black students 99–103; creation of disadvantage 102; elitism and conservatism 103–4; institutional habitus 104; Million+ Group 100; prestige 100; prestige and attainment 101; purpose of study 104; Russell Group 100; *see also* austere curricula; tertiary education

Valletta Summit on Migration 147–8

Van Vree, F. 71
Vásques, R. 187, 191
Venner, D. 44
Verenigde Oost-Indische Compagnie (VOC) *see* Dutch East India Company
Veyne, P. 3
Vichy, commemoration of 41
victims: commemoration of 54n8; of history 39
virtuous racism 168, 170–2
visa-free travel 126–7
Visa Restriction Index 127, 129

Wallerstein, I. 29
war of memories 38
War of Spanish Succession 60
war on poverty (US) 94
Weber, M., on citizenship 116
Weiner, M. 67
welfare: dismantling of 168; policy shifts 163–4; scaling down 186
welfare state, expansion 185
welfare universalism 165
Werbner, P. 117
West Indische Company *see* Dutch West Indies Company
whispering 67–8
white heritages 105
Wilders, G. 64
Wolf, M. 136–7
working class, racialization 186
World War II, memory and remembrance 38–9
wounded history 186–91

xenophobia 42

Yuval-Davis, N. 117

zero migration policy 140
Zetsche, D. 149